A Cognitive Theory of the Firm

A Cognitive Theory of the Firm

Learning, Governance and Dynamic Capabilities

Bart Nooteboom

Professor of Innovation Policy, Tilburg University, The Netherlands. The Chair is sponsored by the municipality of Tilburg

Edward Elgar

Cheltenham, UK • Northampton, MA, USA

Published by
Edward Elgar Publishing Limited
The Lypiatts
15 Lansdown Road
Cheltenham
Glos GL50 2JA
UK

Edward Elgar Publishing, Inc.
William Pratt House
9 Dewey Court
Northampton
Massachusetts 01060
USA

Paperback edition 2010

A catalogue record for this book
is available from the British Library

Library of Congress Control Number: 2008943836

ISBN 978 1 84844 210 8 (cased)
ISBN 978 1 84980 169 0 (paperback)

Printed and bound in Great Britain by
Marston Book Services Limited, Didcot

Contents

Figures

Tables

Preface

In this book I develop and apply a social cognitive theory of firms and organizations more generally and of organization between organizations, with a focus on learning and innovation. Cognition here is a wide notion, going beyond rational inference, know-what and know-how, to include perception, interpretation, value judgements, morality, emotions and feelings. This wide notion of cognition is associated with a denial of Cartesian separation of body and mind (Merleau-Ponty, 1964; Damasio, 1995) and goes back to the work of Spinoza (Damasio, 2003). It is consistent with modern social psychology, which demonstrates how judgements and actions are driven by feelings and impulse, in a variety of decision heuristics (Bazerman, 1998; Kahneman and Tversky, 1979), often with post hoc rationalizations (Damasio, 2003) that distort what happened (such as 'cognitive dissonance'). Decision heuristics may be seen as procedurally rational in the sense that they are adaptive, contributing to survival in the course of the evolution of man, under conditions that judgements and decisions (for example of danger, flight, opportunity, attack) had to be made swiftly and under uncertainty, while substantively they often do not conform to canons of rationality (Barkow et al., 1992; Nooteboom, 2002). In the theory used in this book cognition is social in that it is constructed mostly in interaction between people (Mead, 1934).

Economists have been wary to enter into psychology but such a move is inevitable in order to avoid an ongoing blindness to realities of motivation and behaviour. Institutional economists have been wary to go into sociology but institutions form an inherently sociological category. Innovation entails learning; and learning is psychological and social. This book is, and in my view needs to be, interdisciplinary, connecting ideas from specific branches of economics, management and organization, cognitive science, social psychology and sociology. Underlying this endeavour is the conviction, increasingly supported by evidence of progress over many years, that insights from cognitive science provide a basis for a novel, integrative behavioural science. As a result, the roots of this book go wide and deep.

In economics the main connections of this book are with the work of Penrose (1959) and Schumpeter (1942). As in Penrose's work, the focus is on learning rather than on efficient utilization of resources or appropriation of returns from them. This view can also be seen as going back to

Marshall, who saw the firm as a form of organization that manages and develops knowledge (Loasby, 2002; Foss, 2002; Richardson, 2002). Also as in Penrose, in this book the underlying view of cognition is a constructivist one, according to which people with different experience view the world differently. So far, the book is consistent with Penrose. However, it also adopts and further develops some of the criticism of her views, concerning the role of other human resources than managers in organizational learning, problems of conflicts of interest and governance within the firm, dynamic capabilities for developing new capabilities, and, above all, the alternative of collaboration between firms, for learning and innovation, in the combination of capabilities between rather than within the firm. In particular, it argues that, in contrast with Penrose, there are limits to firm size.

Penrose (1959) suggested that the sources of innovation lie in firms (see also Pitelis, 2002; Turvani, 2007). However, while Penrose's account of the growth of the firm includes managerial learning, in the discovery and utilization of as yet unutilized potential of existing resources, and suggests that this moves on to the development or adoption of new resources, it hardly shows how the latter is done. In other words, dynamic capabilities are assumed rather than analysed and explained. To use the terminology of exploitation and exploration (March, 1991), Penrose showed how firms learn new ways to exploit resources but hardly showed how exploration of new resources takes place and what the problems and limits of that are, within the firm. Goshal et al. (2002: 291–2) distinguished between Penrosian growth, in what the firm can do, and Schumpeterian growth in what would be possible to do.

According to Adam Smith, discovery is a process in both markets and firms. According to Hayek (1945) knowledge is dispersed, which suggests that the variety of views needed for exploration, on what might be possible to do, largely lies dispersed outside firms. According to Schumpeter (1942) firms are needed to shelter novel entrepreneurial vision from established practice and ideas, which cannot make sense of such vision, to give it a chance to develop (Ghoshal et al., 2002). Here, as in Penrose, from the beginning the crux of the firm lies not in efficient utilization but in innovation, and the theory of the firm is also a theory of entrepreneurship.

Building on these views, in a nutshell my view is as follows. Assuming that innovation arises from 'novel combinations', as Schumpeter (1909, 1942) proposed, two questions arise: where do the elements to be combined come from, and where does the combination occur? My answer will be as follows. The elements for novelty come from markets (knowledge indeed being dispersed, as Hayek claimed), firms serve to provide a niche for entrepreneurial vision (as Schumpeter proposed) and to carry it into realization, in ongoing novelty of combinations of potential services offered by resources (as Penrose proposed). Here, I am bringing together Hayek, Schumpeter and Penrose, one could say. They all share a notion of differential cognition, that is different people having different perceptions, views and understandings, and that is also a cornerstone in my approach.

I employ cognitive science to underpin and deepen the notion of social, constructivist and differentiated cognition that was used, explicitly or implicitly, by Penrose, Hayek and Schumpeter. In cognitive science I drew early inspiration from the work on the development of intelligence in children by Jean Piaget (1970, 1972, 1974) and Lev Vygotsky (1962) that, I believe, has later been vindicated by work in a line of cognitive science called 'embodied cognition', by Gerald Edelman (1987, 1992), Lakoff and Johnson (1999) and Damasio (2003). This work in 'embodied cognition' gives an underpinning on the basis of neural research of the experimental work of Piaget and Vygotsky on intelligence as 'internalized action', in an 'activity theory' of knowledge (Blackler, 1995) according to which cognitive categories, and their underlying neural structures, are constructed on the basis of action in the world. Because cognitive categories are constructed and embodied one cannot claim fully objective knowledge and in order to have a basis for correcting one's errors one needs interaction with others who have constructed their cognition differently, along different life paths. I also use insights from cognitive science to develop further understanding of how exploitation and exploration connect and build upon each other (March, 1991). Here, I make use of an earlier book on that subject (Nooteboom, 2000)

The constructivist view of cognition yields the notion of 'cognitive distance'. To the extent that people have constructed their cognition along different life paths, their perception, interpretation and evaluation of the world will differ. For learning and innovation this yields both a problem and an opportunity (Nooteboom, 1999a). The problem is that people understand each other more or less imperfectly, which hinders collaboration. The opportunity is that such difference of understanding is a source of learning and innovation.

The basic idea behind this book is the Schumpeterian view that a firm serves to establish and implement a particular cognitive focus, setting it apart from the variety of views outside the firm. The notion of organizational cognitive focus may be related to Penrose's view of the firm as coherent administrative unit that yields an area of 'administrative coordination and authoritative communication' (Penrose, 1995: xi). However, cognitive focus causes myopia, and while it enables the implementation and elaboration of a novel view, it also limits the innovative potential of the firm in the generation of radically novel views. Innovation requires a view of novelty plus the ability to implement it (Ghoshal et al., 2002). A view requires implementation but implementation requires a limitation of view. To repair this myopia firms need complementary cognition from relations with outside firms with a different cognitive focus (in 'external economy of cognitive scope', Nooteboom, 1992). In this way, next to learning, innovation and entrepreneurship, inter-firm collaboration also forms an integral part of my theory of the firm.

In sociology, the main connections of this book are with the work of Georg Simmel (1950) and with a more recent stream of work on innovation networks, in order to develop the external organization between organizations. These connections are needed to proceed with organization between organizations, in dyadic and triadic relationships. As demonstrated by Simmel, a fundamental step here is that from the dyad to the triad. Constellations beyond that can be largely reconstructed as combinations of dyads and triads. The analysis of constellations of organizations leads on to a flourishing literature in the geography of innovation, which adds considerations of location and agglomeration, following on but also expanding Marshallian external economies of location. However, in this book that connection will only be developed to a limited degree.

An important issue, in internal relationships within firms as well as external relations between them, is that considerations of competence (understanding, capabilities) and governance (dealing with relational risks) need to be combined (Nooteboom, 2004a). While much of economics, for example Transaction Cost Economics, focuses on the hazards of collaboration, to the neglect of learning and innovation, in much of the innovation literature there is a reverse neglect of relational risk, in favour of issues of knowledge and competence. Paradoxes and ambiguities concerning effects of the structure and strength of ties in networks can only be resolved by taking a combined look at competence and governance. For example, dense, strong ties may be bad for the variety and flexibility needed for new knowledge and Schumpeterian novel combinations (Granovetter, 1973; Burt, 1992), but good for reputation mechanisms, bonding and trust that aid governance (Coleman, 1988). In geography, I suspect, and this has been noted in the relevant literature, that geographical proximity is needed not so much for reasons of competence (mutual understanding, knowledge sharing) as for the opportunity of chance meetings, in a 'churning' of encounters, and for governance (gossip and reputation mechanisms). Within firms also, in the study of 'communities of practice' or 'learning groups', one needs to combine competence and governance perspectives (Bogenrieder and Nooteboom, 2004). Governance and competence also connect with each other. For example, in collaboration with specialized professionals it is difficult to monitor their performance, which hinders contractual governance.

In line with the distinction between competence and governance, cognitive distance has a dimension of competence, in technical ability and understanding, and a dimension of governance, in normative, moral views of man, in collaboration and competition between people.

I will argue that a division of labour arises between different levels of organization. Within the firm we find communities of practice, with people at short cognitive distance in both competence and governance, a firm or organization where people, and communities, may be at considerable but limited cognitive distance in competence and small distance in governance, communities of professionals across organizations, with limited cognitive distance in competence but possibly large distance in governance, alliances between firms where distance is substantial but limited in both competence and governance, and the wider market where distance ranges large in both competence and governance. Together on the system level of people, firms and markets, they produce high levels of both exploitation and exploration.

In the end, I will agree with Penrose that the rate of growth of the firm, by undertaking novel activities, is limited by the fact that expansion of the range of activities requires an expansion of coordinative capabilities, for which resources must be set aside to introduce new people (but not just managers) into the firm (and, I would say, its organizational focus), and the fact that the speed at which incoming people can absorb such focus, and be absorbed in it, is limited. However, counter to Penrose I will add that there are also limits to the *size* of a firm, in that there is a limit to which one can usefully widen cognitive focus, increasing cognitive distance. At some point this will detract too much even from Penrosian 'administrative coordination and authoritative communication'. At some point it will detract too much from capabilities of exploitation, and it becomes more attractive to seek further expansion and exploration in external collaboration with other people or organizations, at larger cognitive distance. Next to arguments concerning cognitive coordination, and partly connected to them, there are subsidiary arguments concerning obstacles and limits to diversification in terms of speed and flexibility.

In another strand of analysis, this book connects with evolutionary theory (Nelson and Winter, 1982; McKelvey, 1982). In the study of innovation, the evolutionary perspective has the enormous benefit of showing how novelty can arise other than by ex ante design and planning. This has important implications against instincts towards central, top-down design and planning in public innovation policy and private management of innovation. Also, evolutionary economics promises to combine and perhaps integrate Austrian and institutional economics (Dulbecco and Dutraive, 2007), and it may help in my endeavour to better understand how organizational processes connect with market processes and institutional change. However, my stance on the use of evolutionary theory is ambivalent. On the one hand I think evolutionary theory is and remains very useful when it is interpreted in the loose sense of combining the three basic principles of variety generation, selection and transmission, which may be further specified in a variety of ways that may deviate radically from their specification in biology. On the other hand, it seems to me that such specification needs to be done on the basis of theory of cognition, language, social psychology and sociology, and I am not sure whether the result can be expected to be usefully seen as part of a generalized Darwinism, as is claimed by Hodgson (2002b) and Hodgson and Knudsen (2006). I will argue that in economies co-evolution between firms and markets and institutions is such that the strength of selection forces is sometimes questionable. The selection environment of markets and institutions may be shaped to favour existing firms and technologies to such an extent that entry of competence destroying innovations is blocked. Firms may shape their environment before they can be selected by it. I will also argue that both selection and transmission also generate variety. In exploitation, which is associated with selection, one generates insights for exploration, associated with variety generation (Nooteboom, 2000). In communication, associated with transmission, people transform the knowledge that they absorb to the extent that one may no longer meaningfully speak of 'replication'. If the constituent processes of evolution become thoroughly mixed, what remains of evolutionary theory? However, some may see this line of analysis as a sideline, and readers not interested in such excursion can skip that part of the book (Chapter 6).

1. Purpose, scope, concepts and positioning

INTRODUCTION

In this book I develop and apply a social cognitive theory of firms and organizations, and of organization between organizations, with a focus on learning and innovation. Cognition here is a wide notion, going beyond rational inference, know-what and know-how, to include perception, interpretation, value judgements, morality, emotions and feelings. This introduction starts with the central research question of this book, a first sketch of an answer, and more detailed research questions. Second, to position the book in the literature, I discuss similarities and differences with respect to the most closely related, existing views of innovation and the firm, in particular Schumpeter's views on resource creation, Penrose's views on the growth of the firm, Williamson's views on transaction costs, and evolutionary views from Nelson and Winter, W. McKelvey and Aldrich. Also, pointers are given to literature on cognitive science used in this book. Third, this chapter gives methodological and programmatic points of departure, and reasons to include a cognitive theory and a theory of meaning in the theory of the firm. Fourth, it offers definitions or characterizations of basic terms. Finally, I specify the structure of the book and give some guidance to readers.

RESEARCH QUESTIONS

This section states the central question of this book, gives a first sketch of an answer, and specifies more detailed research questions.

Key Question and a First Sketch of an Answer

The central, overarching question of this book is: what are the sources of innovation? Beyond the customary economic analysis of efficient utilization of resources, and appropriability of their returns, it focuses on the creation of resources. While this may seem new from the perspective of most economic theory, which has focused on efficient or profitable use of existing resources, some scholars have shown that the question of resource creation goes back as far as Adam Smith, for whom division of labour and new resource creation went together. Best (2002: 179) quoted Smith as connecting division of labour with 'new improvements of art'. This leads to the question: what are the roles in innovation of firms/organizations, markets and intermediary structures of alliances and networks of organizations, how are those roles related, and how are they played?

Penrose (1959) seemed to suggest that the sources of innovation lie in firms (Pitelis, 2002). However, while Penrose's account of the growth of the firm includes managerial learning in the discovery and utilization of as yet unutilized potential of existing organizational resources, in novel combinations between them, and suggests that this moves on to the development or adoption of new resources, it hardly shows how the latter is done. In other words, she assumed rather than analysed dynamic capabilities. To use the terminology of exploitation and exploration (March, 1991), Penrose showed how firms learn new ways to exploit resources, but hardly showed how exploration of new resources takes place, and what the problems and limits of that are, within the firm. Ghoshal et al. (2002: 291–2) distinguished between Penrosian growth, in what the firm can do, and Schumpeterian growth in what would be possible to do.

According to Adam Smith, discovery is a process in both markets and firms. According to Hayek (1945), knowledge is dispersed, which suggests that the variety of views needed for exploration, on what might be possible to do, largely lies dispersed outside firms. According to Schumpeter (1942), firms are needed to shelter novel entrepreneurial vision from established practice and ideas, which cannot make sense of such vision, to give it a chance to develop (Ghoshal et al., 2002). Here, from the beginning the crux of the firm lies not in efficient utilization but in innovation, and the theory of the firm is also a theory of entrepreneurship.

Building on these views, in a nutshell my view is as follows. Assuming that innovation arises from 'novel combinations', as Schumpeter (1909, 1943) proposed, two questions arise: where do the elements to be combined come from, and where does the combination occur? My answer will be as follows. The elements for novelty come from markets (knowledge indeed being dispersed, as Hayek claimed), firms serve to provide a niche for entrepreneurial vision (as Schumpeter proposed) and to carry it into realization, in ongoing novelty of combinations of potential services offered by resources (as Penrose seemed to be saying). Here, I am bringing together Hayek, Schumpeter and Penrose, one could say. This book is dedicated to an elaboration of this basic intuition. Hayek, Schumpeter and Penrose all share a notion of differential cognition, that is different people having different perceptions, views, and understandings, and that is also a corner-stone in my theory.

The basic idea behind my theory is the Schumpeterian view that a firm serves to establish and implement a particular cognitive focus, setting it apart from the variety of views outside the firm. This view can also be seen as going back to Marshall, who saw the firm as a form of organization that manages and develops knowledge (Loasby, 2002; Foss, 2002; Richardson, 2002). However, cognitive focus causes myopia and while it enables the implementation of a novel view it also limits the innovative potential of the firm in novel views. Innovation requires a view of novelty plus the ability to implement it (Ghoshal et al., 2002). A view requires implementation but implementation requires a limitation of view. To repair for this myopia, firms need complementary cognition from relations with outside firms with a different cognitive focus (Nooteboom, 1992). In this way, next to learn-ing, innovation and entrepreneurship, inter-firm collaboration also forms an integral part of my theory of the firm.

Exploitation, Exploration and Cognitive Distance

A recurring theme in this book is the relation between exploitation and exploration (March, 1991). To survive in the short term, firms and larger economic systems must efficiently exploit existing resources, including knowledge, which requires a certain clarity and stability of goals, stan-dards, meanings, roles, tasks and skills. To survive in the long term they must also engage in exploration, which entails ambiguity of meanings, and break-up of existing standards, roles, tasks and skills. The combination of exploitation and exploration is a paradoxical and arguably the most important challenge for both firms and economies. In those terms, roughly speaking the market generates exploration, firms generate exploitation, and inter-organizational alliances and networks connect the two.

However, exploration and exploitation may be combined, to a greater or lesser extent, within organizations. Organizations that are able to do that have recently received the fashionable label of 'ambidexterous' organiz-ations (Duncan, 1976; Gibson and Birkinshaw, 2004; He and Wong, 2004). The question then is how a firm can establish an organizational cognitive scope that accommodates both. This will be discussed in Chapter 3. However, I will argue that at some point exploration gets constrained no matter how wide organizational scope is allowed to be, and outside contacts are needed to tap into sources of wider diversity.

An elaboration, and partial formalization, of the argument will be based on the notion of 'cognitive distance'. Here, cognition is a wide notion, including not only rational inference but also perceptions, interpretations, value judgements, emotions and feelings, and the different elements of cognition interact. People construct their cognitive structures from experience. Since they do this along different life trajectories, they differ in their cognition to the extent that those trajectories are different. This implements Hayekian dispersion of knowledge.

Cognitive distance yields both a problem and an opportunity. The problem is that the more people perceive, interpret and evaluate the world differently, and have different goals, values and norms of behaviour, the more difficult it is for them to collaborate and combine their cognition. The opportunity is that larger distance yields a greater potential for more radical novelty. As indicated, a key challenge, for organizations as well as larger economic systems, is to combine or connect exploration and exploitation. This entails a trade-off between problems and opportunities of cognitive distance, seeking an optimal distance that is large enough to yield novelty but not so large as to preclude understanding and collaboration. For exploitation, ability to understand and collaborate weighs more heavily, yielding a smaller optimal cognitive distance, and for exploration novelty value weighs more heavily, yielding a larger optimal distance. Organizations offer the first, markets the latter. These propositions will be presented more formally, using a little mathematics, in Chapter 4.

The problems and opportunities of cognitive distance lead to the notion of an organization as a 'focusing device' (Nooteboom, 1999a). The role of organizations is to yield a cognitive focus, by cultural means, by which people with different capabilities sufficiently understand each other, and are sufficiently willing and motivated to collaborate, in order to utilize the potential of novel combinations between them. In other words, focus serves to sufficiently limit cognitive distance for the sake of exploitation. The main art of organization is to coordinate cognition as little as possible, insofar as needed for exploitation, thus leaving as much scope as possible for variety of cognition, for the sake of exploration. However, organizational focus yields a problem of organizational myopia, which results, by definition, from the limitation of cognitive distance. To compensate for this, organizations should tap into outside sources of cognition, at larger cognitive distance, to employ a wider scope of exploration (Nooteboom, 1992). There lies the main economic function of inter-organizational alliances and networks. This view is similar, I think, to Richardson's (1972) view that the boundary of the firm is determined by its capabilities, and that firms serve where capabilities are complementary and similar, inter-firm alliances serve where they are complementary and dissimilar, and markets serve where they are both weakly complementary and dissimilar (Pitelis, 2002: 137). What is gained in this book, I claim, is a greater depth of analysis of the nature and the limits of the firm, which includes inter-firm collaboration as an integral part of the analysis.

Further Research Questions

Above, I indicated the main goal and central research question of this book. Here, I give an elaboration in a number of more detailed questions. Nowadays, a theory of organization should answer a whole range of questions that derive from what other theories of the firm have put on the research agenda and that have become part of ordinary discourse in the field. Those other perspectives are briefly discussed later in this chapter, but here I specify the questions derived from them.

From the perspective of economics, after transaction cost economics any theory of the firm should be able to explain 'why organizations exist', what determines their boundaries, why organizations collaborate with each other, and how such collaboration is managed. What advantages or needs are there to integrate activities within an organization rather than disperse them across maximally disintegrated units with the minimal size of one person? From the perspective of social network analysis, the question is what effects of different forms of 'embeddedness' are on conditions and results of inter-organizational interaction, in particular the effects of the structure and strength of ties in networks.

After Penrose (1959), and the competence/capability view inspired by it, any theory of the firm should be able to explain how, on the basis of what firm-specific, difficult to imitate capabilities, firms can achieve more or less lasting competitive advantage, what, if any, the constraints on firm size are, what, if any, the constraints on the rate of growth are, and by what dynamic capabilities, if any, organizations can change their capabilities to survive, and generate changes of technology, markets, institutions and organization.

From the perspective of the literature on management and organization, any theory of organization should explain what problems of coordination there are, and corresponding capabilities and methods to solve them.

To escape from both an overly rational managerial view and an external determinism of technology, markets and institutions without agents, any theory of the firm should explain how internal causes of agency interact with external causes in the form of conditions of technology, markets and institutions. Evolutionary theory makes a strong bid for achieving this. From an evolutionary perspective questions then are what causes the stability or inertia of the firm, why differences between industries are greater than within them, to what extent dynamic capabilities are informed by demands from selection and to what extent organizations can mould their selection environment.

The questions are summarized in Table 1.1

A cognitive theory of the firm

Table 1.1   Twenty research questions

Source	Question	Chapter with answer
Transaction cost economics	1 Why do organizations exist?	3
	2 What is the (dis)advantage of firms relative to markets?	3
	10 What determines the boundaries of organizations?	4
	11 Why do organizations collaborate?	4
	12 How is inter-organizational collaboration governed?	4
Competence/ capability view	7 What is the basis for organization-specific capabilities?	3
	9 What are dynamic capabilities?	3, 4, 5
	3 What, if any, are limits to the size of a firm?	3
	4 What, if any, are the limits to the growth of a firm?	3
Management/ organization lit	5 What problems of coordination are there?	3
	6 What are capabilities to solve them?	3
	15 How can we avoid both excessive managerial rationalism and external determinism?	6
Social network analysis	13 What are the effects of network features on the conditions and results of collaboration between organizations?	4
	14 How to explain network dynamics?	5
Evolutionary theory	8 What causes the stability of firms?	3
	16 Why are inter-industry differences larger than intra-industry ones?	6
	17 To what extent are dynamic capabilities informed by demands from selection?	6
	18 To what extent is there 'inheritance' of acquired characteristics?	6
	19 To what extent can firms mould their selection environment?	6
	20 To what extent is transmission a source of variety generation?	6

Note: The first column indicates the streams of literature where questions originate. Questions are numbered in the sequence in which they are answered in subsequent chapters, and the matching chapters are indicated in the last column.

POSITIONING IN THE LITERATURE

To position this book in the literature, in this paragraph I discuss similarities and differences with respect to the most closely related, existing views of innovation and the firm, in particular Schumpeter's views on resource creation, Penrose's views on the growth of the firm, Williamson's views on transaction costs, and the evolutionary views from Nelson and Winter, W. McKelvey and Aldrich. Also, pointers are given to literature on cognitive science used in this book. A key feature of all these views of the firm is that unlike neo-classical economics they are interested not just in the notion of a firm as a locus of production, but also how inside the black box the firm functions as an organization.

Schumpeter

This book is, above all, Schumpeterian in its focus on resource creation and innovation by novel combinations, in creative destruction, and, as already indicated above, in its view of the firm as a niche where entrepreneurial vision, which deviates from established ideas and practices, and cannot be made sense of from their perspective, can be developed and implemented. For this, the entrepreneur needs to have sufficient charisma to convince others in his firm to support his ideas and help developing them. Here, that is seen as the start of organizational cognitive focus, and of organizational culture as a means to implement and maintain the focus.

I deviate from Schumpeter, and from most current innovation literature, on several points. Above all, while Schumpeter did not yield a theory of invention, and focused on the implementation of invention in innovation, I believe that a theory of invention is both needed and possible. It will not do to simply say that invention is a matter of entrepreneurial vision or of novel combinations or 'recombination' as a magical *deus ex machina*, without further explanation of how entrepreneurial vision arises and where novel combinations come from. In particular, it needs to be shown how new novelty arises from experience with the implementation of earlier innovation. Related to that, while one can conceptually distinguish innovation from diffusion, as processes the two are connected. In other words: exploration must somehow arise from exploitation. In the diffusion of an innovation, and adaptations to it under novel conditions, its limits and insights in novel opportunities appear. A proposal of how this might work was given in Nooteboom (2000), and will be applied and further developed in this book. Also, in my view innovation is not limited to exceptional, heroic individuals, but is exercised, in small and big ways, by many. This was recognized by Adam Smith (1998 [1776]: 17): 'A great part of the machines made use of . . . were originally the inventions of common workmen, who, each of them being employed in some very simple operation, naturally turned their thoughts towards finding out easier and readier methods of performing it' (quoted in Best, 2002: 180).

Penrose

Penrose (1959) proposed that firms achieve competitive advantage on the basis of organization-specific resources. It is not the resources themselves that yield results but the services that they may render. As they employ the firm's resources, managers discover new ways of employing them, in novel combinations, in response to entrepreneurial views of opportunities, and this provides a basis for ongoing growth of the firm. Such entrepreneurial views are cognitive constructions that are unlike objective reflections of reality, vary between people, and are therefore idiosyncratic. This view goes back to Boulding (1956), among others. The present book similarly adopts a cognitive constructivist view, yielding variety of cognition between people, to be discussed in Chapter 2.

According to Penrose, a firm is a coherent administrative unit that provides 'administrative coordination and authoritative communication' (Penrose, 1959: xi, 20), and its boundaries are determined by the limits of those. Her analysis suggests that in the long run the size of the firm is not constrained. Firm size is not constrained by limits to economies of scale, or diseconomies of scale, related to products or the size of their markets, since firms can expand by adding new products to their portfolio. Nor are there diseconomies of scale in management. Firm resources are never completely utilized, and yield scope for further extension of activities and capabilities. Penrose proposed that the rate of growth of the firm is constrained by the scope of managerial resources, in particular the ability of existing management to select and introduce additional management and the rate at which such incoming management can adapt to existing plans, procedures and so on. She noted that diversification is limited by the need to maintain necessary integration with the rest of the firm, and avoid bureaucracy (op cit.: 208), and that thus there is a crucial trade-off between speed of expansion and maintenance of control (op cit.: 189), in a 'fundamental ratio of managerial resources available for expansion'.

However, apart from that, Penrose neglected other problems involved in continued expansion of resources and capabilities, internally or by merger or acquisition, the need to maintain focus, and alternative opportunities of growing by collaboration with other firms rather than by expansion, as has been widely recognized in the literature (Pitelis, 2002). Corresponding with this, Penrose had too rosy a view of the capabilities of large firms, and neglected the potential of smaller firms. While Penrose's account fitted well with the development of capitalist firms in her day, since then there is much evidence of de-conglomeration, downsizing, divestment and sharpening of focus. Kay (2002) documents how the Hercules company, which was a central source of inspiration for Penrose, in its later development ran into failed diversification and had to divest and to shift its core. Cantwell (2002) showed the need for coherence in the technological and productive activities of the firm to continue to innovate. Lazonick (2002) showed how after the wave of conglomeration in the 1960s and early 1970s, from the 1980s large corporations reduced their range of activities, and how in the 'new economy' firms focused on concentrated skill bases. Partly, downsizing was motivated by the drive to increase shareholder value, as a basis for inflating managerial reward and to reserve share capital for share options needed to retain valuable personnel. This illustrates how other considerations, beyond competence but related to governance, can affect the boundaries of the firm. Patel and Pavitt (2000) showed, on the basis of technological profiles constructed from patent data, that while firms indeed incorporate a considerable scope of technological areas, as predicted by Penrosian theory, the profiles of firms are remarkably stable, indicating limited changes of composition outside a given focus of techno-logical areas. Thus, the empirical evidence indicates that while there may indeed be a wide scope for combining complementary capabilities, scope, and hence the size of the firm, is subject to limits.

Therefore, in contrast with Penrose I will argue that from the perspective of organization as a focusing device, and from a perspective of dynamic capability there are limits to firm size. As a firm grows by adding new activities, at some point it will have to add new capabilities, and as it continues to do so it will dilute its focus too much, slow down its rate of innovation and reduce its flexibility for novel configurations of capabili-ties, compared with opportunities for engaging in more variable and more exploratory patterns of collaboration with other organizations, in alliances and networks. In other words, as firms expand into less related diversifi-cation they run into lower speed, lower flexibility and lower variety for innovation.

A second well-known point of criticism of Penrose that I share concerns the exclusive role that she accorded to management, in the identification of opportunities and in the learning of new uses of resources (Pitelis, 2002). There is a similarity here to the Schumpeterian view, indicated earlier, of the entrepreneurial hero standing far above common folk. Since the time when Penrose wrote her book, here also considerable change has occurred, in growing scepticism as to how managers would be able to identify new opportunities better than staff that actually operate technology and interact with customers and suppliers. Now, we are more inclined to accord innovative potential to human resources more generally. I propose that there is a corresponding shift in the task of management. The central task no longer lies in identifying opportunities and guiding novel combinations, but, I propose here, on a meta-level of managing cognitive focus in order to enable people to understand each other and collaborate with each other, in their identification and implementation of opportunities, and to set cognitive focus in answer to the question how to combine exploitation and exploration, within or between organizations. In other words, managerial resources are seen as lying primarily in guiding and coordinating cognition in the firm.

I accept Penrose's view concerning the limit to the growth rate of the firm, with the difference that I focus on human resources more widely, discounting managerial ability to know and foresee all, so that the constraint becomes that of incorporating new staff more generally. The question is what, more precisely, it is that takes time for incoming staff to adapt to. Penrose (op cit.: 206) proposed that the growth of total supply of management services is faster than growth of the firm, up to a point, and then possibly declines. Why would that be? The view given in the present book is similar to that of Penrose, but more specific, in that the firm, and organizations more widely, are seen as limited by the ability to coordinate cognition in the firm, and new entrants to the firm, whether managers or other staff, need to adapt to what I call the cognitive focus of the firm.

A third well-known point of criticism of Penrose that I share is the neglect of internal conflict of interests and views, and corresponding problems of authority, monitoring, control, incentives and motives. In other words, a theory of the firm should include not only issues of competence but also issues of governance. In my theory, that is included in organizational focus, which has a competence side, for mutual understanding, and a governance side, for ability and willingness to collaborate.

A more detailed inventory of similarities and differences between Penrose's 1959 view and the view of this book is given in Appendix 1.1.

Limits to size and growth of the firm and the notion and role of organizational cognitive focus are discussed in Chapter 3, which forms the core of the present book.

Resources, Capabilities and Learning

With her view of organization-specific resources, Penrose inspired a stream of 'resource', 'competence' or 'capability' based theories of the firm, in the management and organization literature. In the literature, that view is claimed to stand in contrast with the 'market positioning view' attributed to Porter (1980, 1985), derived from industrial organization economics, according to which organizational capabilities are easily imitated and thus do not constitute a basis for durable competitive advantage.

However, it has been claimed, for example by Foss (2002) and Ghoshal et al. (2002), that most of the resource/competence/capability literature focuses not on the creation of new resources but on the utilization of resources once they are created, in particular on appropriability by some 'isolating mechanisms' from competitors, and thereby is closer to traditional industrial organization economics and Porterian views than they make out, while 'Penrose stresses entrepreneurship and learning in a world character-ized by change and uncertainty' (Foss, 2002: 156). Also, that literature did not implement Penrose's view of cognitive differentiation between people. Hence, since the present books focuses on resource creation, innovation and learning, and cognitive differentiation, I will not include most of the literature based on the Resource or Competence based View. However, I do include the 'dynamic capability' view that developed later (Teece et al., 2000; Dosi et al., 2000), and that did focus on learning and innovation. In particular, I include a branch of the capability view that is called the 'knowledge based' theory of the firm, which emphasizes capabilities in the form of knowledge (Kogut and Zander, 1992; Quinn, 1992; Nooteboom, 1992). The idea that nowadays knowledge constitutes the most crucial asset, and hence the ability to develop and employ knowledge is the most crucial organizational capability, forms a central part of this book.

Teece et al. (2000: 339) proposed that 'Dynamic capabilities . . . reflect an organization's ability to achieve new and innovative forms of competi-tive advantage despite path dependencies and core rigidities in the firm's organizational and technical processes'. So far, the literature has offered limited insight into how that is done, and this forms the focus of the present book. More precisely, the problem is how to combine exploitation and exploration. The combination of the two is a paradoxical and arguably the most important task of management. Here, use is made of Nooteboom's (2000) proposal of a path along which exploitation can yield exploration. Dynamic capabilities are discussed in Chapters 3, 4 and 5.

Transaction Cost Economics

Transaction cost economics (TCE) (Williamson, 1975, 1985) proposed that given bounded rationality organization serves to manage risks of opportunism by means of hierarchical monitoring and control. The analy-sis presented in this book includes this issue of governance, in the sense of management of relational risk. However, one key difference compared with TCE is that next to *dealing with* opportunism with instruments of control, here allowance is made for alignment of goals, values and motives that may *reduce* opportunism, substituting loyalty and intrinsic motivation, at least in part, for coercion and material incentives. In other words, in contrast with Williamson (1993), the present view allows for trust that goes beyond calculative self-interest, even though trust does have its limits and should not be and in fact seldom is blind or unconditional (Nooteboom, 2002). This is related to the idea of Hannan and Freeman (1977) of 'normative order' as part of 'organizational form'. For governance, organizational focus includes rules and norms, and underlying values of conduct.

One argument for this approach is that increasingly it has been recognized that for a variety of reasons ex-ante incentive design is problematic. Due to uncertainty concerning contingencies of collaboration, and limited opportunities for monitoring, ex ante measures of governance are seldom complete, and need to be supplemented with ex-post adaptation. Such uncertainties proliferate under present conditions of professional work and, especially, under the conditions of innovation that form the focus of this book. Professional work requires considerable autonomy for its execution and is hard for managers to monitor and evaluate, let alone measure. Rapid innovation increases uncertainty and makes formal governance, especially governance by contract, difficult to specify, which increases the importance of collaboration on the basis of trust. If specification of detailed contracts, with the purpose of controlling opportunism, is nevertheless undertaken, it threatens to form a straitjacket that constrains the scope for innovation. Furthermore, the attempt to use contracts to constrain opportunism tends to evoke mistrust that is retaliated by mistrust, while in view of uncertainty there is a need to use trust more than contract. Norms and values of conduct that form part of organizational focus serve as a basis for ex post adaptation.

A second difference with TCE is that in addition to potential problems of opportunistic exploitation of switching costs, emphasized by TCE, I recognize relational risk, in collaboration between firms, in the form of spillover risk, that is risk of loss of appropriability of returns from innovation. In contrast with the literature from Industrial Organization Economics and most of the Resource/Competence based theory of the firm, appropriability also is analysed from a cognitive perspective, in an assessment of spillover risk as a function of absorptive capacity, cognitive distance, tacitness of knowledge and speed of knowledge change (Nooteboom, 1999a).

A third and most fundamental difference with TCE is that here the focus is on (radical) innovation, which was neglected in TCE. Williamson (1999: 1103) admitted that TCE 'makes only limited contact with the subject of learning'. However, in spite of fundamental criticism I do retain some important insights from TCE, such as the notion of specific assets. Indeed, from the present perspective of cognition and learning, the building of mutual absorptive capacity and trust yield new forms of specific assets. The building of mutual understanding and trust is highly relation-specific. Here, I focus not so much on the implications of specific assets for the threat of opportunism ('hold-up'), though that can still be part of the story, but on the implication that such investments are not made unless there is a prospect for a relationship that is sufficiently intensive or lasting to recoup the investment. In other words, the main implication of specific investments is the need for a sufficient stability or duration of relationships, also in innovation, in view of specific investments in mutual understanding and trust building especially in innovation. That is an important point, since it argues against the intuition, and most policy views, that especially innovation requires maximum flexibility of relationships. I argue for optimal, not maximal flexibility, with sufficient stability to encourage the specific investments needed for innovation by collaboration, but not so large as to create undue rigidities in the ongoing formation of Schumpeterian novel combinations (Nooteboom, 1999b).

In the analysis of organization between organizations, in Chapter 4, use is also made of several of the notions and instruments of governance proposed by Williamson (1985), such as legal contracting, mutual dependence, shared ownership of specific assets and the use of hostages (mostly in the form of competitively sensitive information). While I argue that detailed contracts aimed at controlling opportunism can decrease trust and increase opportunism, the implication is not that there is no place for contracts. Limited contracts may be needed as a basis for building trust. Detailed contracts may be needed for technical reasons of coordination rather than for controlling opportunism. Nevertheless, more trust allows for less detailed and less constraining contracts. Both contracts and trust have limitations, and the one begins where the other ends. In sum, contracts and trust are both complements and substitutes (Klein Woolthuis et al., 2005).

Evolutionary Theory

Evolutionary theories of the firm (Nelson and Winter, 1982; McKelvey, 1982; Baum and Singh, 1994; Aldrich, 1999; Hodgson and Knudsen, 2004), analyse the dynamics of firms and industries in markets on the basis of the evolutionary explanatory principles of variety generation, selection and replication. While the content of these processes in economics and organization deviate widely from that of biology, one can maintain the principles in generalized form, abstracted from all specifically biological content, in 'Universal Darwinism' (Hodgson, 2002a). The result is perhaps best called a method or perspective rather than a theory, since biological theoretical content has to be replaced by economic and behavioural theoretical content.

The evolutionary perspective has a number of attractions. It accounts for development of new forms (of life, technology, products, organization) under limited foresight. In economics and management it keeps us from the error of an unrealistically rational, magical view of development as the achievement of somehow prescient, or even clairvoyant, managers, entrepreneurs and scientists, as well as from the opposite error of institutional or technological determinism (McKelvey, 1982). It forces us to recognize causes of change both within organizations ('autogenic') and outside them ('allogenic'). While characteristics of entrepreneurs and organizations have a causal effect on survival and growth of firms, causality can also go the other way, with characteristics being the result of processes of selection and retention (Aldrich, 1999: 336). In other words for the same issue, it helps to deal with what in sociology is called the problem of agency and structure. It forces us to recognize both the role of actors, with their individual preferences and endowments, in the processes of variety generation and transmission, and the enabling and constraining conditions for action, in structures of markets and institutions, in the process of selection. It makes allowance for the radical uncertainty of innovation (Shackle, 1961), and for evident and ubiquitous error and failure in human endeavour. It forces us to accept diversity as an essential element of development.

In a universal Darwinism, emptied of specifically biological content, the evolutionary processes need to be specified in terms of learning and innovation (variety generation), competition in markets and institutional environments (selection) and imitation, growth, teaching, and training (replication). Competition in markets and the constraining and enabling effects of institutions are straightforwardly seen as yielding a process of differential survival and retention of products and practices of firms. There is plausibility in seeing entrepreneurship and invention as sources of variety generation, and personnel turnover, training, personnel transfer, imitation, consultancy and growth as the replication of proven success.

Here variety generation in the form of learning is fundamentally a matter of cognition, and replication is fundamentally a matter of communication, so that the use of a cognitive theory is elementary for an evolutionary theory of organizations and economies.

In view of the programmatic importance of evolutionary theory, I dedicate a separate chapter (Chapter 6) to a discussion of issues and questions in evolutionary theory of organizations, and how they may be dealt with on the basis of the present cognitive theory. For the analysis I adopt two further notions from evolutionary theory. The first is the distinction between replicators and interactors (Campbell, 1974; McKelvey, 1982;

Hull, 1988) or *vehicles* (Dawkins, 1983) and the second is the notion of *populations.* Interactors/vehicles (in biology: organisms) interact with their selection environment, and are members of populations of similar but differentiated interactors (in biology: species). To function as an interactor, an entity must have a reasonably cohesive and stable set of components. This is the ecological side of evolution (Baum and Singh, 1994). Interactors carry replicators (in biology: genes) that generate, in interaction within the interactor as well as with its environment (in biology: gene expression in ontogenetic development), characteristics of interactors that affect their survival and replication. Note that it is not the replicators themselves that determine survival but the characteristics that they produce. Replicators from surviving interactors are replicated and re-combined, mostly within populations of interactors that partake of a common pool of replicators. This is the genealogical side of evolution. Organizations, in particular, are seen as interactors, in their environments of markets and institutions, as members of industries seen as populations, and their competencies (McKelvey, 1982) are seen as the corresponding replicators, with industries sharing a common pool of such competencies.

From a cognitive perspective, what are the 'replicators' carried by organizations as 'interactors', what determines the requisite coherence and stability of organizations as interactors, how does replication take place, and, above all, what are the sources of variation, and how do they relate to selection and replication, and how 'blind' are they?

Hannan and Freeman (1977) specified 'organizational form' as consisting, next to the 'normative order' already mentioned, of 'formal structure' and 'patterns of activity'. While I accept the normative order, which will play an important role in my conception of organizational focus, and I accept that at any moment an organization has formal structure and a pattern of activities, I claim that organizations can maintain their identity while changing formal structure and patterns of activity, and that, counter to Hannan and Freeman (1984), they may escape from organizational 'inertia'. I accept that on the whole the stability of organizations is an empirical phenomenon, and I recognize that, as many have pointed out, for evolution to work organizations should have a reasonably stable, cohesive identity (see for example Hodgson and Knudsen, 2004). However, this can be conceived other than by means of a fixed set of capabilities or activities, namely in terms of a stable cognitive focus.

Part of McKelvey's (1982: 115) definition of organizations is that they are 'myopically purposeful (boundary maintaining) activity systems'. In his view, 'myopic purposefulness' entails boundary maintenance. I accept that organizations are activity systems, and that due to bounded rationality they are 'myopically' purposeful, but I do not accept that this means, as McKelvey (ibid.) specified, that, in line with the evolutionary perspective, variety generation is 'mostly blind in terms of what will work in the long term in an uncertain, changing environment'. To what extent 'variety generation', that is invention, is blind is something to be investigated, not assumed simply because that is what the evolutionary perspective prescribes. McKelvey (op cit.: 170) saw organizational identity as formed by a set of 'dominant competencies' associated with 'primary tasks'. I sympathize with that, but organizational competence needs to be further unravelled. If it is tied to 'primary tasks', a problem arises concerning the identity of organizations with multiple primary tasks, such as conglomerates, as McKelvey recognized (op cit.: 211). According to Penrose, a firm can develop novel tasks on the basis of novel 'services' from resources.

Aldrich (1999: 2) defined organizations as 'Goal-directed, boundary maintaining, and socially constructed systems of human activity'. I accept all of this except the stable boundaries, if they refer to boundaries of activities. As indicated earlier, I claim that organizations can retain their organizational identity (not to be confused with legal identity, see Hodgson, 2002b), in spite of boundaries that are fuzzy, in the sense that activities are shared with other organizations, and variable, in the sense that activities are outsourced or integrated, and new activities can be developed on the basis of existing capabilities or resources, as Penrose indicated.

Yet, I share the idea that organizations maintain boundaries, in some sense, and I will argue that the boundary is determined not on the basis of any given portfolio of activities or tangible resources but on the basis of my notion of cognitive focus. This is discussed in Chapter 3.

Cognitive Theory

In this book, in Chapter 2, I reject the computational view of cognition that still appears to constitute the mainstream in cognitive science, in favour of a constructivist, 'embodied cognition' view, for which use will be made of the work of a variety of scholars. Since economists are part of the target audience for this book, reference will be made to the economist Friedrich von Hayek (1952: 'The sensory order'). His reflections on cognition are to some extent similar to those developed in more detail by the developmental psychologists Jean Piaget (1970, 1, 1974) and Lev Vygotsky (1962), as discussed in Chapter 2. Hayek's idea of levels of cognition seems similar to Gregory Bateson's different orders or levels of learning in his *Steps to an Ecology of Mind* (2000). This re-appeared in the literature on organizational learning, in Argyris and Schön's (1978) notion of 'single and double loop learning', and seems close to March's (1991) distinction between exploitation and exploration.

In Chapter 2, use is also made of more recent work in cognitive science, in a stream of thought that has become known as 'embodied cognition' (Lakoff and Johnson, 1999), based, among other things on an evolutionary theory of mental construction or 'neural Darwinism' (Edelman, 1987, 1992). The importance of this research is that it gives a neural underpinning of the constructivist ideas based on experimental behavioural studies by Piaget and Vygotsky. One of the features of embodied cognition is that it rejects Cartesian dualism of body and mind (Damasio, 1995) and recognizes that rationality is intertwined with feelings and emotions (Damasio, 2003). In terms of epistemology it is important in showing how mental representations may still be related, in 'embodied realism' (Lakoff and Johnson, 1999), with sensory impacts from actions in the world, without falling into the canonical, symbolic, abstract and static kind of mental representations assumed by computational theory. This helps to develop a constructivist perspective without falling into the radical relativism of some postmodern constructivist thought (Nooteboom, 2000).

Mostly, cognition-based studies in the literature on management and organization are likewise based, explicitly or implicitly, on a constructivist, interactionist view of cognition (for surveys, see Hedberg, 1981; Cohen and Sproull, 1998; Meindl et al., 1998). This view also appears in the 'symbolic interactionism' of G.H. Mead (1934), in sociology, and has later been called the 'experiential' view (Kolb, 1984) and the 'activity based' view (Blackler, 1995) of knowledge. In the organization literature, this view has been introduced, in particular, by Weick (1979, 1995), who reconstructed organization as a 'sense-making system'. That comes close to the view of organization as a 'focusing device' further developed and employed in this book. The notion of cognition as constructed from experience is also evident in Penrose's view that in firms from the use of resources management discovers new potential uses. For an edited volume of relevant classic papers on knowledge in general and knowledge in organizations in particular, see Nooteboom (2007).

Other Theoretical Tools

In the further development of the book, elements from other theories will be adopted as the need arises, and will be criticized when the relevance arises. For example, from the management and organization literatures use will be made of surveys of the literature, such as given by Scott (1992), general concepts concerning, among other things, the different types of interdependence of activities in the firm, and between firms, proposed by Thompson (1967), of the different kinds of coordination proposed by Mintzberg (1983). More in particular, use will be made of the distinction between single- and double-loop learning proposed by Argyris and Schön (1978), the notion of communities of practice (COP) proposed by Lave and Wenger (1991) and Brown and Duguid (1991). This connection is helped by the fact that those ideas and this book share an activity based view of cognition.

In the analysis of alliances and networks between firms, in Chapter 4, use will be made of the network literature from sociology such as Granovetter (1973), Coleman (1988), Burt (1992), Uzzi (1997), Krackhardt (1999) and underlying, earlier work from Simmel (1950).

From economics, and particularly industrial organization economics, I maintain and apply the usual toolbox of elementary notions such as opportunity costs, economies of scale, scope, experience, and time, network externalities, externalities more in general, fixed and variable costs, sunk costs, entry barriers, appropriability and spillover, free-ridership, adverse selection and moral hazard, transaction costs, specific investments, etc. In the analysis of dynamic capabilities I will build on the innovation literature.

RESEARCH PROGRAMME

Having set up the scaffold of my central argument, having indicated my research questions, and having positioned the book in the literature, I proceed to build up the elements that I need to support and develop my argument and to answer the questions posed for this book. This paragraph specifies the programme for this book. What are the methodological and programmatic points of departure? Why a cognitive theory? Why a theory of meaning? Why both firms and organizations, and what is the difference? Why include inter-organizational relationships?

Realism of Assumptions

One fundamental point of departure is methodological, concerning the famous, or infamous, debate on the 'realism of assumptions'. Readers not interested in this point can skip this section with little loss. The literature on this is enormous, and I will only briefly state my position for readers familiar with the issue, without much reference to that literature. For a more extensive discussion of my position I refer to Nooteboom (1986, 2000).

On the one hand we should accept that theory is always to some extent an abstraction from perceived reality and can and should never be realistic in the sense that it fully reflects reality. We cannot look at everything and from all possible perspectives at the same time, and some focus is needed.

Indeed, that also forms one argument for an organizational focus, in this book. We have to make simplifying assumptions. Also, we inevitably analyse phenomena from a certain perceptual and interpretive basis and from some explanatory perspective, with hard to question 'background assumptions', and with certain intentions of debate, application and the pursuit of interests. For that we make heuristic assumptions that are often tacit and difficult to make explicit. Abstraction and heuristics typically join in mathematical models, which reduce realism of detail for the sake of greater analytical power, for the sake of deducing implications that would otherwise have been difficult to identify.

On the other hand, the assumptions made about nature or behaviour should be realistic in the sense that they do not contradict what we know concerning the relevant features of the analysis, given its purpose, level of abstraction, and intended use of conclusions.

One reason for this stance is that in behavioural science empirical grip of falsification is weak. While necessary, agreement of implications of axiomatic assumptions with facts is not sufficient, since other assumptions may explain the phenomena equally well, facts may be biased by the theory in question, and *ceteris paribus* assumptions often preclude falsification. This view is well known from the relevant literature, and widely accepted. A second reason is that plausibility of assumptions, which I define as coherence with what we know concerning the phenomena the assumptions are about, increases coherence and efficiency of our body of knowledge as a whole (Nooteboom, 1986). In particular, then, cognitive science, economics and sociology can learn from each other and derive support of plausibility.

In my view, explanation is neither a logical or mathematical deduction from axioms plus side assumptions nor reduction to some basic, rock bottom, fundamental causality on the level of fundamental physics. In my view explanation is a configuration of influences between causally relevant variables (Craver, 2007). Causality here is anything that 'can make a difference'. On the level of organizations and people in it, one can use the Aristotelian notion of a 'final cause' (motivation, incentives) that in physics would be nonsensical. This allows for multiple levels of explanation and corresponding causality. In a theory of organization we may study the configuration of communities of practice, and on a deeper level we may study the interaction of people within communities, and on a yet deeper level we may study brain processes in individuals, and further down the biochemistry involved in synaptic connections between neurons. This view also allows for interdisciplinarity without the need for interdisciplinary integration in the sense of reducing one discipline to another. In studying the interaction between communities of practice we may use insights from sociology, for example in the effects of network structure, and from economics; in effects of scale or scope, and from cognitive science; in determinants of absorptive capacity, or in issues of interpretation, meaning and language use.

Let me give an example. In general, I would hesitate to make the assumption, common in mainstream economics, of rational choice by economic agents, because I am interested, in particular, in issues of organization, innovation and learning, in which bounded rationality and radical uncertainty belong to the core of the phenomena studied. In some studies, it may be legitimate to assume rational profit maximization even if it contradicts perceived reality, if the purpose is to set a benchmark against which more realistic analysis is compared. It may also be legitimate, up to a point, to adopt profit maximization as a heuristic assumption, on the evolutionary argument that market selection is so rigorous that only the most efficient can survive, if one can plausibly make that argument. Then outcomes may be 'as if' people made optimal choices. However, if rational decision making is avowedly against relevant perceived reality, one cannot derive recommendations for policy from it. In other words, if the argument is evolutionary, policy recommendations should also be evolutionary, for example in terms of how one might affect the selection environment of markets and institutions, not in terms of rational agents that know what to choose.

Abstraction and realism can be combined by alternating between them. To detect implications of assumptions, and to check the logic of an argument, one may use an abstract mathematical model, and next one may re-embed the results in the complexity of a more realistic account. Blaise Pascal, in his *Pensées* (2005 [1670]) proposed the distinction between '*esprit de géometrie*' and '*esprit de finesse*', which he describes as follows. The geometric spirit is 'difficult at first, in the movement of abstraction, where one turns one's regard away from complex reality, and then it becomes easy, for the analytical grip it affords', while the *esprit de finesse* is 'easy at first, in looking at the world as it presents itself, and then is difficult, not to reason erroneously with all such complexity'. He claims that both are needed, and they complement each other.

Thus, in this book, I will present a rich account of organization as a focusing device, as well as a more abstract, formalized version, in terms of optimal cognitive distance, from which I will return to the complications of reality.

Interdisciplinary Research

Related to my preference for realistic behavioural assumptions, another basic point of departure for this book is the intention to conduct interdisciplinary research, connecting elements from cognitive science, economics, sociology and social psychology. I have been dedicated to that for a number of years because I believe that it is needed for an adequate understanding of organizations and markets, that it is now feasible, and that the time is right for it.

For behavioural assumptions in economics we can learn, and make our assumptions more realistic, by making use of, in particular, social psychology. In our study of collaboration we can learn crucial lessons from sociology. For issues of mutual understanding and communication we need cognitive science.

To many, such interdisciplinary endeavour appears as an invitation to confusion, chaos and eclectic lack of coherence. And isn't it against my own argument for focus, developed in this book? My answer is consistent: we need focus to make novel combinations. And we can develop such focus. My claim is that we can arrive at an integrated framework that yields coherence and clarity. The basis for that framework lies in cognitive science. Hence, the discussion of theory of cognition, in Chapter 2, is relevant on two levels: for the cognitive theory of the firm in this book, and for interdisciplinary connections between economics and sociology that form part of my wider purpose.

Competence and Governance

Another basic programmatic point, also maintained over a number of years, is the attempt to combine a perspective of competence (ability, capability) with a perspective of governance, i.e. management of relational risk (Coriat and Dosi, 1998; Williamson, 1999; Nooteboom, 2004a). Transaction cost economics has focused on governance, in particular the management of risk from opportunism, to the neglect of competence and innovation. Most of the literature on technology and innovation, as well as much of the competence/capability literature, has neglected the problem of relational risks. The problem of governance has been recognized, for example by Nelson and Winter's (1982) recognition of organizational routines also serving to establish a 'truce'. However, there has been little elaboration of different kinds of relational risk and different instruments to govern them (Nooteboom, 1999a).

By focusing only on either competence or governance, to the neglect of the other, one arrives at a skewed, biased, incomplete treatment that can have adverse effects on understanding and policy. Too much preoccupation with opportunism neglects the possibilities of trust that are relevant, in particular, under the uncertainties of innovation that hinder governance by contract and incentives (Nooteboom, 2002). On the other hand, neglect of relational risk can lead to naïve, ill-conceived forms of collaboration that can do much damage.

Let me give an example from the debate concerning Transaction Cost Economics. From a perspective of governance, that is the control of relational risk, greater uncertainty yields a greater incentive to integrate activities within a firm since greater uncertainty yields more limits on the specification of contracts, so that we may have to revert to hierarchical control, with better opportunities for monitoring and for conflict resolution under the umbrella and authority ('managerial fiat') of an employment relationship. On the other hand, from a perspective of competence, under greater uncertainty, with greater turbulence of markets and technology, and a faster rate of innovation, firms need outside relations more, not less, in order to collaborate to repair organizational myopia in complementary outside cognition (Nooteboom, 1992). Is either view false? Not necessarily. They are discussing different things, and we should develop models that include both, in order to arrive at meaningful tests (Nooteboom, 2004a). Empirical evidence of more, not less, outside collaboration under greater turbulence of technological change is given by Colombo and Garrone (1998).

Let me give a further illustration in the area of network analysis. Concerning the effects of structure and strength of ties in networks, a pure competence view yields conclusions that contradict conclusions from a pure governance view. For example, according to Burt (1992) a sparse, non-redundant network, with bridges across gaps in connections ('structural holes'), enhances variety needed for innovation. According to Coleman (1988) a dense network, with redundant ties, helps to create commitment, collaboration and trust. They are both right, but Burt is talking about the competence side and Coleman about the governance side (Gilsing and Nooteboom, 2005). Apparent contradictions disappear when we combine competence and governance.

In this book, the combination of competence and governance arises in several places. First, cognitive distance may refer to distance in technical knowledge and skills (competence) and in values and norms of behaviour (governance). Related to that, organizational focus has a competence side, in mutual understanding (absorptive capacity), as a basis for collaboration, and a governance side, in alignment of incentives and motives for collaboration. Similarly, in trust we find a distinction between trust in competence and trust in intentions. One can trust someone's competence to conform to agreements or expectations, and on his intentions and commitment to do so to the best of his competence. Those are different dimensions of trust, with different sources, and different remedies when disappointment arises (Nooteboom, 2002).

Why Cognitive Theory?

Why a cognitive theory of the firm? Doesn't that make things too complicated? Doesn't it dilute disciplines, fuzzy focus, compromise coherence and hinder clarity? Most specifically, and most importantly, a cognitive theory of the firm is needed to lend more substance and analysis to current vague and unconnected, ad hoc notions in the literature, such as entrepreneurial vision, absorptive capacity, and variety and dispersion of knowledge.

More broadly, this book pays attention especially to innovation, and innovation entails invention, which entails change of knowledge, so that for a proper understanding the need for a theory of knowledge is evident and straightforward. However, even if innovation were not given special attention, production entails technology, coordination of complementary activities, marketing, sales, and sourcing of inputs, which all entail knowledge. Issues of cognition, widely interpreted, arise not only on the competence side of organizations, in individual technical skills and collective abilities of technical coordination, but also on the governance side of alignment of goals, motives, incentives and the prevention and resolution of conflict.

On the competence side, knowledge as a resource appears everywhere in firms, and has acquired increased salience as professionalization of labour and the production and use of science in a variety of areas, such as biotechnology, new materials, nanotechnology, robotics, computing and communication, and the widespread use of new technology, in particular information- and communication-technology, has increased, in the 'knowledge economy'. Nowadays, the notion of 'knowledge intensive industries' hardly serves to discriminate between industries. All industries are knowledge intensive, for example in that they need to keep up with developments of information- and communication technology (ICT).

That also applies in industries that used to be seen as 'low tech', such as retailing or other consumer services. In retailing the use of bar-coded goods is essential for pricing and payment of goods in a store, stock management, logistics and marketing information. Any theory of the firm entails an explicit or implicit theory of knowledge, and in economics that theory has remained implicit too much.

On the governance side, issues of cognition arise in the way people target goals, make value judgements, balance diverse interests of on the one hand survival and self-interest and on the other hand the need to belong and achieve social legitimation, and attribute competencies and motives to people by inference from their actions. This is reflected most clearly in analyses of the intellectual and emotional foundations of trust and processes of build-up and breakdown of trust (Nooteboom, 2002; Nooteboom and Six, 2003; Six, 2005).

Most, if not all, organizations are caught up in a struggle to keep up with an increasing pace of change, in technologies, markets and institutions, and hence need to continue to learn and to develop and maintain 'dynamic capabilities' (Teece et al., 1997). Teece et al., (2000: 339) proposed that 'Dynamic capabilities . . . reflect an organization's ability to achieve new and innovative forms of competitive advantage despite path dependencies and core rigidities in the firm's organizational and technical processes'. So far, the literature has offered limited insight in how that is done, and this forms a central issue of the present book, taken up in Chapter 5. In line with the policy to combine competence and governance, dynamic capabilities will reflect both intellectual and relational abilities.

However, in basing a theory of the firm on a theory of knowledge there is a price to be paid. The field of cognition is a wide one, with a variety of schools of thought, so that one has to familiarize oneself with the options and make a reasoned choice. I think that price must be paid. Chapter 2 makes an argument for adopting a branch of cognitive theory that has come to be called the perspective of 'embodied cognition', which is part of a wider view of cognition as being a constructive activity, on the basis of interaction between people, who necessarily vary in their cognition. That latter view now is the majority view, in sociology and in management studies, and part of the purpose of this book is to try and convince economists that they should follow suit.

The constructivist, interactionist view of knowledge used here has wide ranging implications for economics and management, as is demonstrated in this book. The implications concern the theory of the firm, the sources of innovation, and inter-firm relationships, in alliances and networks. Key concepts here are the notion of cognitive distance between people, the consequent need for an organization to act as a focusing device, the consequent myopia of firms and cognitive distance between firms, the consequent need for firms to engage in inter-organizational relationships, and the implications for the structure and strength of ties in firm networks. These implications form the main thrust of this book.

Beyond that, the constructivist, interactionist view of knowledge has methodological implications. In philosophy, it is closely related to American pragmatism (since Peirce, 1957) and the 'organicism' of Whitehead (1929), according to which any element in the system is an outcome of relations with other entities, and in which individuals both constitute and are constituted by society (Hodgson, 1993: 11). This enables us to transcend the methodological individualism of economics as well as the methodological collectivism of (some) sociology, and thereby helps to make a novel combination of economics and sociology, in what may perhaps be seen as a newly emerging integrative behavioural science. Thus, the stakes are high, and in the long run the effort to absorb insights from cognitive science will, hopefully, be rewarded.

Why Theory of Meaning?

As in theory of knowledge, in theory of language and meaning there are multiple schools of thought that need to be disentangled to arrive at a choice, and, as in the theory of knowledge, the question arises whether it is really necessary to make that effort.

In the most general terms, a theory of language is needed because in the interactionist perspective knowledge is supposed to arise from interaction between people, and it is by communication, in language use, that people interact with each other and thereby learn. In an evolutionary context, the evolutionary process of replication/retention is based on communication and hence on language and meaning. More specifically, the notion of an organizational cognitive focus, to be developed in this book, includes the establishment of shared meanings, in accordance with Weick's (1979, 1995) view of firms as 'systems of shared meaning', and engines of sensemaking.

To understand what we are talking about here we need a theory of meaning, sensemaking, and language. The theory of meaning selected here is consistent with the theory of embodied cognition selected earlier, in particular with the notion of situated action, which entails a view of meaning as context-dependent.

Firms and Organizations

While the theory of the firm is a familiar branch of economics, it is more appropriate to develop a theory of organization more widely, in which the firm is a special case, as is the practice in the management literature. As argued by Penrose (1959), seeing the firm as an organization, that is a constellation of productive resources whose use requires coordination, yields a very different notion from the traditional black box notion of the firm in economics, as a mere conceptual tool for the determination of price and volume of a given product. This book considers firms in the usual economic sense as units of production, in which inputs are transformed into outputs, or value is added in other ways, and it opens the black box of production, in considering firms as organizations. All firms are organizations but not all organizations are firms (consider, for example, hospitals, universities, the fire brigade, ministries, and so on.)

Here, organizations are defined as:

> Myopically goal-directed, socially constructed, more or less focused systems of coordinated activities or capabilities.

This definition adopts elements from definitions offered by McKelvey (1982) and Aldrich (1999), but also deviates from them. As argued by McKelvey, organizations are 'myopically goal directed' in that rationality is bounded, and knowledge and insight into requirements and opportunities of technology and markets and institutions in the organization's environment are limited. Further, goal directed systems of activity generally entail a certain 'focus' on core or distinctive competencies. The system of 'activities' includes actions, knowledge and technology, and 'capabilities' in which the three come together. The focus of the system may be oriented at a given set of 'activities', or at a set of generic 'capabilities' that provide the basis for a range of activities, or a combination of the two. I add the distinction between activities and capabilities in view of the insight offered by Penrose (1959) that a 'resource' yields a range of possible 'services'. I focus on 'resources' in the form of capabilities, and activities as the 'services' that they offer. The notion of a system refers to coherence and complementarity between activities or capabilities (Teece, 1986; Langlois and Robertson, 1995; Levinthal, 2000). It includes a variety of coordination mechanisms, which may or may not be hierarchical, leaving room for mutual adjustment and self-organization.

A certain stability of the system of activities is needed for an organization to function, compete, build absorptive capacity (Cohen and Levinthal, 1990), build and retain competencies, attract and train people, and to build internal and external relationships. However, the definition does not stipulate stability of an organization's boundary of activities. In line with Penrose's insight, with a stable system of capabilities one can have a variable range of activities.

Note that the definition given above does not require organizations to have multiple persons, and includes the single-person, owner/manager firm. That would also need to be the case, since it would be odd if a firm is not an organization until an owner/manager engaged a partner or employed another person, even if it were a part-timer for only, say, one hour a month, or if it stopped being an organization if it hived off some activity and its corresponding employee. Excluding single person firms would also entail that 50 per cent of all firms would be excluded from organizational analysis. Single owner/manager firms satisfy the definition of an organization in that they entail coordination of actions, knowledge and technology. Take a single-person butcher, shoe repair shop, or consultant. In different ways they need to coordinate the search and handling of material and informational inputs, technology, knowledge and skills to absorb and process them, search, knowledge and supply of customers, and institutional conditions (legal, financial, and so on).

A single person shoe repair shop that typically repairs shoes as well as other leather goods (purses), may manufacture simple leather goods, such as belts, may add the cutting of keys, and sell related goods, such as polish, laces, purses and belts. It requires the requisite skills and machinery. The craft activities should have a short cycle, allowing for frequent and sudden interruption to serve incoming customers and thereby utilize time in between customer arrivals that would otherwise be idle (Nooteboom, 1982). The choice and coordination of space, machinery, portfolio of activities, purchasing, finance, administration and requisite knowledge and skills requires organization.

Nowadays, in the Internet economy, in many cases one can have an idea for a product, outsource its artistic and technical design, outsource its production, probably in a low-wage country, search for and contact suppliers via the Internet, have materials shipped directly to the producer, outsource distribution of the product to customers, search for customers, contact them and maintain communication with them on product quality via the Internet, send their data to an outside agency for invoicing, and have the data sent to an outside accountant/tax consultant who also files tax returns. This entails much organization that can be done by a single person.

While traditionally production has been seen as the physical transformation of physical inputs into physical outputs, this applies too narrowly to manufacturing while the majority of employment now lies in a wide variety of services. Therefore, the notion of production has to be extended to other ways of adding value. While manufacturing yields a utility of form and function of some physical good, in services one can produce utilities of time and place in distribution and transport; utility of financial means and security in banking and insurance; utility of physical and mental well-being in health services; utility of entertainment and enjoyment in the hospitality and sports business; utility of knowledge and information in the media business, teaching and consultancy; utility of justice in legal services; and utilities of a wide variety of public services and amenities. Here inputs and outputs may be abstract, in the form of information or feelings, and transformation may concern reduction, abstraction, expansion, combination or shift of information, mental or psychic states, and so on (Nooteboom, 2007).

Organization Between Organizations

A theory of organization should include a theory of the 'boundaries of the firm', and a theory of inter-organizational collaboration and networks. It should be able to explain differences between organizations within industries and the, presumably larger, differences between industries, and the stability of such differences and of organizational identity. These issues are taken up in Chapters 3 and 6.

The definition of an organization given earlier allows for an organization to outsource activities without becoming a different organization. Organizations can hive off or integrate activities without thereby having to substantially alter their cognitive focus. Note, however, that while organizations may not have clear boundaries of activities, in sharing activities with other organizations, and may have shifting boundaries, in outsourcing and integrating activities, firms do and should have a clear legal identity, as pointed out by Hodgson (2002a). Unclear boundaries of legal ownership and liability would create institutional havoc. Note also the condition, familiar from the alliance literature, that when organizations outsource activities they must often still retain absorptive capacity with respect to those activities, to properly collaborate and coordinate with outside sources (Granstrand et al., 1997) in what Patel and Pavitt (2000) called 'background' next to 'core' competencies. In other words, some of the related competence remains part of organizational focus.

Organizational focus creates organizational myopia, and in addition to all the other motives for inter-firm alliances, familiar from the extensive alliance literature, this gives an additional, cognitive reason, to prevent myopia by means of complementary outside cognition from alliance partners (Nooteboom, 1999a), in what Nooteboom (1992) called 'external economy of cognitive scope'. Questions then arise concerning organization between organizations, taken up in Chapter 4. There, use will be made of the literature on alliances and inter-organizational relationships, including insights from the social network literature concerning networks effects on interorganizational innovation and organization, such as effects of network structure (such as density), an organization's position in a network (such as centrality, in some sense), and the content and strength of ties.

TERMINOLOGY

There is considerable confusion of terminology. Rather than going into a lengthy, and boring, discourse on differences between definitions in the literature, I will go straight to the specification of my definitions, and my main reasons for them. Definitions do not represent essences but conventions, and for that reason it makes sense to stick to existing conventions as much as possible. Thus my general policy is to use definitions that remain as close as possible to meaning in ordinary language. However, that is often ambiguous and imprecise and may be in need of greater clarity and precision. That does not rule out remaining ambiguity. Sometimes ambiguity is unavoidable and even fruitful, to allow for knowledge and meaning to develop further, rather than fixing it prematurely and arbitrarily. Innovation entails ambiguity.

Cognition, Learning and Invention

In this book, cognition is a wide concept, going far beyond cognition in the narrow sense of rational inference and knowledge. It includes proprioception (motor activity of touch and manipulation of objects), perception, sense making, interpretation, categorization, inference, declarative knowledge (of facts, logical and causal relations), procedural knowledge (skills), but also goals, preferences, priorities, and technical, institutional and personal standards, norms and values, including those concerned with governance and conflict resolution. In other words, as indicated earlier, it includes aspects of both competence and governance.

Following others, I reject Cartesian separation of body and mind, and consider cognition and feelings, and emotions, as closely linked, and mind as embedded in the body (Merleau-Ponty, 1942, 1964; Damasio, 1995, 2003; Nussbaum, 2001). Indeed, this is a key feature of the perspective of 'embodied cognition' that is used in this book, and is set out in Chapter 2. According to that view, knowledge is formed on the basis of mental categories, in the mind, that are constructed in interaction with one's physical and social world. In this wider view of cognition, there is a distinction but also connection between knowledge and skill, between know how and know that, and between procedural and canonical knowledge (Cohen and Bacdayan, 1996). The constructivist, interactionist theory of knowledge used in this book emphasizes the social dimension of cognition.

Cognition as mental activity by definition cannot apply to aggregates such as firms or organizations. However, such aggregates can be seen as engaging in the use and production of knowledge, and people in an organization can share views, interpretations, understandings, values and norms of behaviour, that are not shared outside the organization. More fundamentally, they share underlying basic categories concerning Man, the World, Knowledge, and the relations between Man and World and between Man and Man, in organizational culture, that govern the construction of views, interpretations and opinions (Smircich, 1983; Schein, 1985; Weick and Roberts, 1993; Weick, 1995; Cook and Yanow, 1996); referred to in this book as 'organizational cognitive focus'. It plays a crucial role in the theory of the firm developed in this book. In fact, the key feature of organization that is proposed, in contrast with other economic theories of the firm, but in line with views of organization in the management literature, is that it serves as a cognitive focusing device, that is as maintaining and developing such shared cognition. This is developed in Chapter 3.

Learning can be interpreted as the adoption, or better: reconstruction of existing knowledge from others, and it can mean the construction of new knowledge, in invention, on the basis of experience and interaction with others. Since adoption entails reconstruction, the difference between adoption of existing and construction of new knowledge may not be sharp. In this book the focus is on the production of new knowledge, since theory on that is least developed, in theory of organization as well as economics. As is familiar in the innovation literature, invention is not the same as innovation, which entails that the invention be carried into a technically and commercially viable product or practice. This book will connect with the innovation literature, but the focus will be on invention. As indicated earlier, a key issue, in Chapter 6, will be in what way there can be a dynamic capability to escape from organizational path-dependencies.

Change, Development, Evolution, Institution and Coordination

In this book, change is a very general term, close to the similarly general term 'dynamics'. It can refer to people, organizations, and industries, and entails growth, expansion, (trans)formation, evolution and learning. Development here means change of structure, composition, content, and can refer to knowledge, people, organizations, institutions or industries. Cognitive development entails development of perception, mental categories, understanding, meanings, values and associated feelings. Cognitive development may be needed to enable the absorption of knowledge from others, in the development of 'absorptive capacity'. It may also generate learning in the sense of the generation of new knowledge.

I reserve the term 'evolution' for development on the basis of evolutionary processes of variety generation, selection and replication/retention. Correspondingly, in this book co-evolution is not any parallel development, vaguely speaking, but more specifically evolution in which units of selection affect the selection conditions, for themselves and/or for other units of selection. For example, the innovation of self-service retailing was co-evolutionary in that it changed the selection conditions inside retailing by breaking down limits to shop size imposed by the service mode of retailing, and thus made life more difficult for small shops. It was also co-evolutionary in that it altered selection conditions in other, related industries, such as food, packaging and distribution (Nooteboom, 2005a).

On the basis of Hodgson (2006) I define institutions as pre-established, prevalent, explicit rules or more implicit norms, socially transmitted, and supported by habits, that structure, enable and constrain behaviour. Being rules or norms, institutions have normative content or import, and entail sanctions that may be material or immaterial, such as loss of legitimacy, or both at the same time. Institutions are pre-established, that is while they are constructed and re-constructed by actions, they also precede actions and form a basis for them. They are prevalent, that is they apply universally to members of some groups. They are socially transmitted, that is not genetically transmitted. They are supported by actions, that is the operation of institutions often entails, or even requires, that their following turns into habit, that is behavioral dispositions, which often become tacit. In this way, they tend to become taken for granted. In the incorporation of institutions into habit, idiosyncratic elements come in. For example, language is an institution, and there de Saussure (1979) distinguished between the intersubjective order of 'langue', which is the institutional part, and the idiosyncratic, creative, personal usage of 'parole'. It is impossible to make an exhaustive inventory of all possible institutions, regardless of context. What are relevant institutions very much depends on the context of action and aims of analysis. By the present definition of institutions, organizational cognitive focus for coordination, with a competence and a governance side, turns organizations into institutions.

In economics coordination may refer to allocation of given scarce resources to given goals, for which markets are supposed to be more efficient than planning. In this book, coordination refers to the combination of capabilities to utilize their potential of complementarity. That is a central task of organization.

Resources, Competencies and Capabilities

In this book, a resource is anything that may support economic activity. It includes things like water, air, energy, land, space, institutions, language, access to markets, and social position. It also includes assets, tangible and intangible, which are resources that may be built, designed, and owned, may spill over, and require investment. That includes knowledge, understanding, reputation, legitimation, trust and abilities. Abilities include competence and capability, and I am not sure about the difference between the two. They may include know-that, but certainly include know-how, and have a greater or lesser tacit component. According to ordinary language they may apply, I think, to both individuals and organizations, so I keep it that way. Perhaps the difference between competence and capability can be seen as follows. Capability is the ability to appropriately employ competence, depending on context, that is the ability for appropriate selection from a repertoire of possible actions. On an individual level, we speak of skills. On an organizational level I speak simply of organizational capabilities, which relate to coordination, combination and development of individual level competence and capability, within and outside the organization. What I call organizational cognitive focus is a central part of organizational capability.

March and Simon (1958: 140) proposed organizational capabilities in the form of performance programmes, including routines, rules and heuristics to reduce uncertainty and cope with complexity. Nelson and Winter (1982) used the term 'routines' for a very similar concept. I am hesitant about the term 'routine'. In accordance with Herbert Simon's (1983) notion of routinized behaviour, familiar behaviour is relegated to routinized conduct, in what Polanyi (1962) called 'subsidiary awareness', temporarily at least, so that scarce capacity for attention, in focal awareness, can be dedicated to unfamiliar situations. In view of limited mental resources for rational evaluation, this is rational, in the sense of adaptively efficient. Capabilities, by contrast, may be quite deliberate, residing in focal awareness. That was also the objection of Dosi et al. (2000: 4), who proposed that capabilities entail 'evident purpose and conscious choice'. I do not entirely agree with that. While capabilities may, in contrast with routines, be deliberate and conscious, they may also be routinized. This was, I think, allowed for in Simon's notion of performance programmes. In conclusion, I will employ the term 'organizational capabilities'.

If dynamic capabilities are defined as the ability to change ability, then they arise on as many levels as there are levels of ability (individual, organizational). An organizational capability may be the dynamic capability of altering people's capabilities, or of altering organizational capability in the coordination between existing individual capabilities. On any level, if capability entails the ability to select, as a function of context, from among a repertoire of possible actions, then a dynamic capability may entail a shift in the way choices from the repertoire are made or a shift of repertoire, or both. Then, shift of context would seem an important trigger of the change of capability. And dynamic capability would have to change when there is a shift from more or less familiar to entirely unfamiliar contexts. This role of the shift of context in the exercise and development of dynamic capability forms part of my proposal for a path where exploitation leads up to exploration, explored in Nooteboom (2000) and employed in Chapter 5.

STRUCTURE OF THE BOOK

Chapter 2 is dedicated to the underlying, 'embodied cognition' view of knowledge, also known as the 'activity theory' of knowledge, with its resulting notion of 'cognitive distance'. In Chapter 3 I derive the implications for the notion of the firm as a 'focusing device' to limit cognitive distance between people in organizations, for the sake of coherence and coordination. I analyse the dimensions of such focus, its origins, and its stability. I analyse the resulting role of an organization as a cognitive focusing device, and implications for limits to the size and growth of the firm. I also analyse the resulting differences between organizations, within and between industries, and their stability. In Chapter 4 I analyse the implications for the need for inter-organizational collaboration, particularly for innovation, in the utilization of 'external economy of cognitive scope', the incentive to select partners at 'optimal cognitive distance', issues and instruments for the governance of relational risk, and effects of network structure and position, and content and strength of ties. The ability to select partners, manage relations for learning, and select appropriate network positions is identified as one important organizational dynamic capability. In Chapter 5 I propose a second dynamic capability, to escape from organizational inertia and path-dependencies, along a path by which exploitation leads up to exploration. In Chapter 6 I discuss issues in evolutionary theory of organization, and analyse how cognitive theory deals with those issues. Chapters end with answers to the questions posed in the introduction. The book ends with a survey of the answers.

Chapter 2 can be skipped by readers not interested in the fundamentals of cognitive theory. Chapter 3 forms the core of the book. Chapter 4 is relevant, in particular, for readers interested in inter-organizational relations and networks. Chapter 5 is relevant, in particular, for readers interested in innovation, dynamic capabilities, organizational learning and network dynamics. Chapter 6 is relevant for readers interested in evolutionary theory.

APPENDIX 1.1 SIMILARITIES AND DIFFERENCES WITH PENROSE'S THEORY

Table 1a.1 Points of agreement with Penrose (1995 [1959]), with page references (1995 edition)

Basic view of the firm
- Growth, development of the firm as driver (p1, 7, 29)
- Theory of the firm needs to include an entrepreneurial perspective (32)
- Entrepreneurship entails seeing opportunities (imaginative effort, instinct for what will work (37)), willingness (strength of character, perseverance) and ability to use them (for example timing, persuasion, creating confidence (38)), committing effort and resources to speculative activity (33)
- The environment of the firm is not a given, in the same form for all, and its perception and creation are central (41)
- Firm resources are bundles of potential services (25), and it is the services that yield production (and a free resource can render services that are not free (78))
- Firm resources are largely firm-specific (24), and their services are heterogeneous across firms (199)
- There is a distinction between entrepreneurial and managerial resources (183)
- Firms have multiple activities, and growth takes place, in particular, by new activities, in diversification (70)

Incentives for diversification
- One incentive for diversification may lie in the need for a portfolio of products, in product line diversification (135)
- Another may lie in the evening out of fluctuations (138)
- Another may lie in the spread of risks in a portfolio (177)
- Next to internal expansion, firms may expand externally, by merger and acquisition

Limits to expansion
- Resources and the services they offer are to some extent an outcome of experience, and then cannot be purchased or hired in the form needed, and acquired services must be made to fit in the existing constellation of the firm (47)
- Managerial resources are taken up, in part, in guiding and training new management (47)
- Economies available only in expansion may disappear after expansion has been completed, and may then be made independent (101, 262)
- Threat of entry reduces take-over price of incumbents (167)
- The scope for diversification is restricted by the need to invest for the sake of competing in existing activities (134) and by the need to maintain necessary integration with the rest of the firm, and avoid bureaucracy (208)
- Thus there is a crucial trade-off between speed of expansion and maintenance of control (189), 'fundamental ratio of managerial resources available for expansion'
- New firms need disproportionate attention to current operations (205)

Table 1a.2   Points of difference with respect to Penrose

Penrose (with page references)	My cognitive theory of the firm
Basic view of the firm	
• Basic driver: growth and long run profits (29)	underlying that is will to expression, creation, power
• Firm as administrative organization (15, 24)	firm as focusing device
• Boundary of the firm as area of administrative coordination and authoritative communication (intro, 20)	boundary as trade-off between variety and cohesiveness
• Key resource is managerial	is cognitive and communicative
• Central issue: planning and administration	human resources, conditions for cognition, action, collaboration, motivation
• Structure is the creation of men who run the firm (31)	emergent from internal and external interaction
• Central challenge: combine administration of existing activities and expansion by diversification	connecting exploitation and exploration
• Large firms have absolute comparative advantage in all respects (225), no clear dis-economies of scale	diseconomies of scale in lack of focus and less variety and flexibility of configuration
Incentives for diversification	
• Increase of knowledge = increase of range of services from a resource (76)	also development of new capabilities
• Means of expansion: internal investment, merger/acquisition	also by external collaboration in alliances and networks
• Ratio needed for administrative work need not increase, due to increased division of labour and substitution of capital for labour (202)	possible relations with n people is $n(n-1)/2$, yields noise, requires bureaucratization, reduced flexibility
• Disadvantages of small firms (225, 238)	some compensating strengths, and repair of weaknesses in networks
Mergers and acquisitions	
• Apparently few problems in mergers and acquisitions; acquisition reduces managerial effort needed for expansion (209)	problems of integration due to difference in focus, reduced flexibility, reduced variety for innovation
• Acquisition easier the smaller relative size of acquired firm (210)	focus and value of small firm likely to be destroyed

2. Embodied cognition

INTRODUCTION

This chapter summarizes a theory of cognition, including a theory of meaning. That is a tricky endeavour, since concerning both knowledge and meaning there are a variety of theories and schools of thought that are more or less at odds with each other. Here a choice and selection is made from insights offered in the relevant literatures. This endeavour is inevitably essayistic. I claim that the selection I make is coherent and fruitful, and I provide some arguments for that claim but I cannot provide all the evidence, argument and counter-argument for all that I select. The theory selected is a constructivist, interactionist view of knowledge that has come to be known as the perspective of 'embodied cognition'. That view has roots in earlier developmental psychology (Piaget, Vygotsky) and in sociology (G.H. Mead), and more recently has received further more substantive evidence from neural science (Edelman). The theory entails the notion of cognitive distance between people that will serve as a cornerstone for the cognitive theory of the firm developed in Chapter 3. There, organization is viewed as a cognitive focusing device, limiting cognitive distance between people in an organization. This results in organizational myopia that necessitates compensation from external relations with other organizations at a larger cognitive distance. In that way, relationships between organizations become an integral part of the theory of the firm. Some of the text for this chapter is taken from Nooteboom (2000: Chapter 6) with additions from other sources, especially from an edited volume of published papers that was designed to provide the basis for insight in knowledge and learning in organizations (Nooteboom, 2006). The chapter is set up as follows. First comes a sketch of the traditional 'computational-representational' or 'information processing' view of cognition, and empirical and theoretical criticism of it. Then comes an exposition of an alternative, 'situated action', 'activity based' view of cognition, with its roots in developmental psychology, its more recent support in neural Darwinism, and its development in 'embodied cognition'. This is followed by a discussion of a related theory of meaning. Related to 'situated action' cognition, it explores and employs the notion of 'context dependent' meaning. Finally, a survey is given of the implications for the theory of the firm, to be developed further in later chapters.

THE TRADITIONAL VIEW

This first section summarizes the traditional 'Representational-computational view' of cognition, and discusses criticism of it.

The Computational View

The perspective of embodied cognition stands in opposition to the 'Representational-Computational' view of mind (RCVM) or 'Information processing' view that has been the dominant view in cognitive science. That view assumes that knowledge is constituted by symbolic mental representations and that cognitive activity consists of the manipulation of (the symbols in) these representations, called computations (Shanon 1988: 70). According to Shanon (1993), the representations according to RCVM are:

1. symbolic in the technical sense that in the use of signs there is a separation of a medium and the content conveyed in it;
2. abstract: the medium is immaterial; its material realization (physiology) is of no relevance;
3. canonical: there is a given, predetermined code which is complete, exhaustive and determinate;
4. structured/decomposable: well-defined atomic constituents yield well-formed composites; and
5. static: mind is the totality of its representations, structure and process are well demarcated.

In these features, particularly points 1 and 2, one recognizes Cartesian intuitions of a separation of body (material realization in physiology) and mind (abstraction, content). Another basic intuition behind this established view is that behaviour is based on beliefs, desires and goals, and representations are postulated as entities that specify them (Shanon, 1993: 9). There is also an ancient intuition of atomism and decomposition: variety and change are reconstructed as variable, combinatorial operations on fixed, given elements. In formal grammar it yields the 'standard principle of logic, . . . hardly ever discussed there, and almost always adhered to' (Janssen, 1997: 419), that the meaning of a compound expression is a function (provided by rules of syntax) of the meanings of its parts. It was adopted by Frege, in his later work (Frege, 1892; Geach and Black, 1977; Thiel, 1965; Janssen, 1997).

The motivation for this view is in a respectable scientific tradition to yield a parsimonious reconstruction, in terms of stable entities and procedures of composition of those entities into a variety of structures, to account for orderly and regular human behaviour across a large variety of contexts. It explains how people can understand sentences they never heard before. A subsidiary motivation is that by interposing the cognitive as an intermediate, abstract level between psychological phenomenology and physiology we can circumvent the need for a full reconstruction in terms of physiology, and we can thereby evade reductionism. However, there are empirical and theoretical objections to such a symbolic, semantic, representational view (Shanon, 1988; Hendriks-Jansen, 1996).

Empirical Criticism

If meanings of words were based on determinate representations, it should be easy to retrieve them and give explicit and complete definitions of concepts, as a computation on representations, but in empirical fact such complete definitions often cannot be obtained. A second empirical point is that people are able to re-categorize observed objects or phenomena, under a variation of context, which would mean that representations vary in an open-ended fashion, and then they are no longer determinate. Words generally have more than one meaning, and meanings vary across contexts. Closed, that is exhaustive and universal definitions that capture all possible contexts are often either infeasible or extremely cumbersome. For most definitions one can find a counter-example that defeats it.

For example: what is the definition of 'chair'? Should it have legs? No, some chairs have a solid base. Not all chairs have armrests or back rests. Neither has a stool, but we distinguish it from a chair. A child's buggy seat on a bike has a backrest, but is not called a chair. At least in some languages, a seat in a car is called a chair. A chair is used for sitting, but so is a horse. A cow is not a chair, but years ago I saw a newspaper item 'watch him sitting in his cow', with a picture of someone who used a stuffed cow for a chair. If it were customary for people living along a beach to collect flotsam to use for chairs, it would make sense, when walking along a beach, to point to a piece of flotsam and say 'look what an attractive chair'.

Another empirical point of fact, recognized by many (for example Putnam, 1975; Winograd, 1980), is that meanings are unbounded, and open-ended with respect to context. According to de Saussure (1968) the meaning of a word depends on the meanings of other words. Novel contexts do not only select from a given range of potential meanings, but also evoke novel meanings. Novelty is produced in contextual variation (Nooteboom, 2000). Summing up, representations cannot be exhaustive, or determinate, or single-valued or fixed. As Wittgenstein (1976) proposed in his 'Philosophical investigations', in his notion of 'meaning as use', words are like tools: their use is adapted to the context, in the way that a screwdriver might be used as a hammer.

Theoretical Criticism

One of the theoretical problems, recognized by Fodor (1975) even though he was a proponent of RCVM, is the following: if cognitive activity is executed by computation on mental representations, the initial state must also be specified in terms of those representations, so that all knowledge must be innate. That is preposterous, and certainly will not help to develop a theory of learning and innovation.

Another theoretical objection is that if one admits that meaning is somehow context-dependent, as most cognitive scientists do, also if they are adherents of RCVM, then according to RCVM context should be brought into the realm of representations and computations. Shanon (1993: 159) characterizes this as the opening of a 'disastrous Pandora's box'. To bring in all relevant contexts would defeat the purpose of reducing the multiplicity of cognitive and verbal behaviour to a limited set of elements that generate variety in the operations performed on them. Furthermore, we would get stuck in an infinite regress: how would we settle the context dependence of representations of contexts? Note that contexts in their turn are not objectively given, somehow, but subject to interpretation. As Shanon (1993: 160) put it: 'If the representational characterization of single words is problematic, that of everything that encompasses them is hopeless'.

Edelman (1987) also criticized prior information processing views of cognition: 'the chief difficulty . . . is their inability to remove the homunculus . . . who or what decides what is information' and he notes the challenge of explaining how we are 'capable of context-dependent pattern recognition in situations never before encountered' (Edelman, 1987: 43). He 'strongly challenge(s) any logic-based or "information-driven" explanation . . . the same object (is) classified differently at different times' (Edelman, 1987: 30). In the words of Hendriks-Jansen (1996: 261), Edelman, like all researchers in embodied cognition, resists the 'deep-seated belief in Western culture that the specification of form must precede its actual emergence'.

Summing up, compositionality is problematic due to context dependence plus the fact that contexts themselves are subject to interpretation and re-interpretation. Or, to put it differently: the meaning of the whole is not only determined by the meaning of the parts, but feeds back into shifts of meaning of the parts.

SITUATED ACTION

This section characterizes an alternative 'situated action' and 'constructivist', 'embodied cognition' view that forms the basis for this book.

Representation and Context

I don't see how we can account for learning and innovation on the basis of representations that satisfy any, let alone all, of the assumptions of RCVM: separation of medium and content; a predetermined, complete, exhaustive and determinate code; well-defined and static constituents of composites. However, this does not mean that we need to throw out the notion of mental representations altogether. If we do not internalize experience by means of representations, and relegate it only to the outside world, how would cognition relate to that world? How can we conceptualize rational thought other than as some kind of tinkering with mental models, that is representations that we make of the world?

Despite his radical criticism of RCVM, even Shanon (1993: 162) recognized this: 'On the one hand, context cannot be accounted for in terms of internal, mental representations . . . .; on the other hand, context cannot be accounted for in terms of external states of affairs out there in the world'. For a solution, he suggests (1993: 163) that 'Rather, context should be defined by means of a terminology that, by its very nature, is interactional. In other words, the basic terminology of context should be neither external nor internal, but rather one that pertains to the interface between the two and that brings them together'.

Shanon proposes a distinction between 'representational' and 'presentational' manifestations of a cognitive system. In the first, as proposed in RCVM, cognitive manifestations are 'composed of well-defined elements joined together in accordance with rules of well-formedness, the medium of their articulation may be of no relevance, and both their constituents and the dimensions upon which they are defined may be distinct and well differentiated' (Shanon, 1993: 285). In the 'presentational', cognitive manifestations, including verbal behaviour, thoughts, gestures and performance in general, lack such features. Thus, RCVM is accepted as part but only part of cognition, and not the most general, fundamental and foundational part of it. Cognitive development, Shanon proposes, generally moves from the presentational, where cognition is embedded and at one with context, is not composed of well-defined elements, content is blurred with medium, and is not amenable to clear-cut differentiation, to the representational. Categories are rarified, temporarily fixed abstractions from the rich, messy, shifting substrate of particulars. Ideas are not Platonic ultimate truths that lie behind the confusion of phenomena, but lies we tell ourselves to deal with complexity. I propose that all this is germane to the constructivist view, according to which cognition is actively created on the basis of action rather than being given in pre-determined structures. As Shanon summed it up: 'Conceptually, phenomenologically and developmentally, action is more basic than the manipulation of symbols' (1993: 291).

Similar criticism and conclusions were offered by Hendriks-Jansen (1996), who concluded that we should take a view of 'interactive emergence', and Rose (1992), who proposed the view of 'activity dependent self-organization'. This leads to the 'situated action' perspective. This perspective entails that rather than being fully available and complete prior to action and outside of context, mental structures ('representations') and meanings are formed by context-specific action.

One could say that up to a point the situated action view goes back to early associationist theories of cognition, proposed, in various forms, by Berkeley, Hume, William James and the later behaviourist school of thought (Dellarosa, 1988: 28; Jorna, 1990). However, a crucial difference with behaviourism (notably the work of Skinner and his followers) is that here there is explicit concern with internal representation and mental processing, even though those do not satisfy the axioms of the RCVM view.

Activity Based Cognition

In some important respects the 'situated action' view seems opposite to the RCVM view. The first proposes that action is not so much based on cognitive structure as the other way around: cognitive structure is based on action. However, the cognitive structuring that arises as a function of action provides the basis for further action. Thus both are true: action yields cognitive structuring, which provides a new basis for action. In history, ideas inform practices, which in enacting the ideas in specific contexts test and reproduce or shift them. Knowledge and meaning constitute repertoires from which we select combinations in specific contexts, which yield novel combinations that may shift repertoires of knowledge and meaning. Such shifts of knowledge and meaning occur in interaction with the physical world, in technological tinkering, and in social interaction, on the basis of discourse (see Habermas' 1982, 1984 notion of 'communicative action').

Situated action entails that knowledge and meaning are embedded in specific contexts of action, which trigger 'background knowledge', as part of absorptive capacity, in terms of which sense is made of what is going on. This notion of 'background' appears also in Searle (1992). Interpretation of texts or pictures is based, to some extent, on unspecified, and incompletely specifiable, assumptions triggered in situated action. When in a restaurant one asks for a steak, it is taken for granted that it will not be delivered at home and will not be stuffed into one's pockets or ears.

Background knowledge cannot be fully articulated, and always retains a 'tacit dimension' (Polanyi, 1962). This view is also adopted, in particular, in the literature on 'Communities of practice' (COP) (Brown and Duguid, 1991, 1996; Lave and Wenger, 1991; Wenger and Snyder, 2000). Canonical rules, that is complete, all-encompassing and codified rules for prescribing and executing work are an illusion since they can never cover the richness and variability of situated practice, which require improvisation and workarounds that have a large tacit component that cannot be included in codification of rules. The proof of this lies in the fact that 'work to rule' is a form of sabotage. Evidence for the claim that practice across contexts is not automatic and identically repetitive, and entails shifts, additions, and restructuring is given by Narduzzo et al. (2000) in their empirical study of network technicians in a cellular phone company.

The notion of tacit knowledge, derived from Polanyi (1962, 1969), has become something of a hype, but it has been misconstrued, for example in the literature on organizational learning. Nonaka and Takeuchi (1995), and later Cowan et al. (2000) and Zollo and Winter (2002), suggested that tacit knowledge is fully susceptible to explicitation into 'codified knowledge', subject only to the condition of 'finding the code' (Cowan et al., 2000). Polanyi explicitly ruled this out: 'While tacit knowledge can be possessed by itself, explicit knowledge must rely on being tacitly understood. . . . A wholly explicit knowledge is unthinkable' (Polanyi, 1969: 144). Typically 'the appearance of a thing at the centre of my attention (i.e. focus) depends on clues to which I am not directly attending (i.e. are in subsidiary awareness). In going from observation (or data) to interpretation (or theory), observations become subsidiary to the focus of interpretation in which the observations are integrated. This integration of the subsidiary and the focal constitutes tacit knowing' (Polanyi, 1969: 140). Typically, tools, including conceptual tools and language, become part of our subsidiary awareness while we direct the focus of attention to the task at hand. In other words, 'we interiorize these things and make ourselves dwell in them' (Polanyi, 1969: 148). This notion of 'indwelling' has been picked up in the literature on communities of practice in organizations (Lave and Wenger, 1991; Brown and Duguid, 1991). Note that this 'subsidiary awareness' corresponds with what was earlier called 'background knowledge'.

INTERNALIZED ACTION

This section provides an underpinning of the situated action, constructivist view from earlier work in developmental psychology.

Hayek, Piaget and Vygotsky

In his study of 'the sensory order', the economist Hayek (1976 [1952]) went into what he called the 'central problem' of 'the manner in which different stimuli affect our nervous system, or how they are classified by it' (Hayek, 1976: 9). While Hayek remains empiricist in the sense that he maintains that 'the whole sensory order can be conceived as having been built up by the experience of the race or the individual' (1976: 106), and flirts with the idea that mental structures are topologically equivalent, or isomorphous, with the 'system of sensory qualities' (p. 38), he deviates from it in recognizing that the notion of isomorphy is also 'somewhat inappropriate' (p. 40), and recognizes the 'cardinal error to think that individual stimuli and individual nervous impulses are invariably and uniquely related with individual sensory qualities' since they 'will depend on what other impulses are proceeding at the same time' (p. 41) and 'differences between these qualities must necessarily refer to the different effects which in different combinations they will exercise on succeeding events' (p. 44). In other words, sense and meaning are context dependent, and this is one of the basic themes in this book. Hayek also recognizes different levels of cognition 'for which the . . . lower levels constitute a part of environment'(p. 111). Different levels of cognition and learning also form a basic theme that recurs with subsequent authors. Hayek's recognition that 'one . . . event may appear both as an object of classification and as an act of classification' (p. 65) seems similar to Polanyi's (1962) distinction between focal and subsidiary awareness.

According to developmental psychologists Piaget (1970, 1972, 1974) and Vygotsky (1962) intelligence is internalized action, in 'construction proceeding from the lived to the reflective' (Piaget, 1972: 157). By interaction with the physical and social environment, the epistemological subject constructs mental entities that form the basis for virtual, internalized action and speech, which somehow form the basis for further action in the world. This internalized action is embodied in neural structures that can be seen as representations, in some sense, but not necessarily in the symbolic, canonical, decomposable, static sense of mainstream cognitive science.

In contrast with Piaget, Vygotsky (1962) recognized not only the objective, physical world as a platform for cognitive construction, but also the social world with its affective loading. While according to Piaget a child moves outward from his cognitive constructs to recognition of the social other, according to Vygotsky the social other is the source of the acquisition of knowledge and language. As quoted by Lotman (1990: 2), according to Vygotsky 'Every higher function is divided between two people, is a mutual psychological process'. Vygotsky proposed the notion of ZOPED: the 'Zone of Proximal Development'. This refers to the opportunity for educators to draw children out beyond their zone of current competence into a further stage of development. In language acquisition by children, a phenomenon on which Piaget and Vygotsky agreed was that at some point children engage in egocentric speech, oriented towards the self rather than social others, and that this subsequently declines. Piaget interpreted this as an outward movement from the self to the social other; a 'decentration' from the self. Vygotsky ascribed it to a continued movement into the self, in an ongoing process of formation and identification of the self and development of independent thought. The reason that egocentric speech declines is that overt speech is partly replaced by 'inner speech'. Before that stage, however, speech is preceded by and based on sensori-motor actions of looking, gesturing, pointing, aimed at satisfying a want. This view seems consonant with Shanon's (1993) view, discussed earlier, of cognitive development from the 'presentational', embedded in context, with intertwined content and form, towards the 'representational'.

The social dimension is not denied by the other authors discussed so far, and indeed most of them recognize it. It appears to be received wisdom to say that Piaget did not recognize the social roots of cognition and that according to him cognitive construction is internally generated (for example Spender, 1999: 427), but that is not accurate. Piaget went to great lengths to explain cognitive construction as generated by 'assimilation' of experience into existing cognitive structures, in a process that transforms those structures, in 'accommodation', so that construction is also 'outside-in'. And since much if not most of our experience is social, according to Piaget cognitive construction has social sources at least by implication. Here I elaborate on the social dimension.

The idea of the social constitution of the individual is important for its fundamental criticism of the methodological individualism that is part of the core of modern economic thought, and is needed to re-establish a connection between economics and sociology.

This re-embedding of the individual in his social context entails a movement against the tide of modern times. While in pre-modern times, prior to 1500, people were seen as 'in it together', the Reformation developed a view of individual moral responsibility (rather than sheltering under the sacraments of the Catholic church) and Descartes initiated the view of a self-sufficient rational individual, in an ongoing movement towards the 'disengaged individual' (Taylor, 1989). In economics, the social constitution of the individual was still present in the eighteenth century in Adam Smith's theory of moral sentiments, in his notion of 'sympathy', and in the early twentieth century in the work of American institutional economists such as Commons and Veblen, whose account is close to that of G. H. Mead. Mead elaborated on how 'The other is essential in the appearance of the self . . . It does not start from inside and go outside . . . The actual process begins at the periphery and goes to the center' (Mead, 1982: 156). This is reminiscent of Vygotsky's view of language being social before it develops into inner speech that enhances cognitive development. However, after Adam Smith mainstream economics followed the Enlightenment path towards the disengaged individual.

Berger and Luckmann (1966) elaborate on the social origins and conditions of knowledge and self. While they certainly recognize society as an objective, institutionalized reality, and indeed spend a 73-page chapter on it, they elaborate the building of subjectivity in a process by which reality is apprehended in individual consciousness. They distinguish between 'primary and secondary socialization', which goes back to the work of Simmel (1950 [1917]). In primary socialization of a child 'with language, and by means of it, various motivational and interpretational schemes are internalized as institutionally defined . . . as programs for everyday life . . . [which] differentiate one's identity from that of others' (Berger and Luckmann, 1966: 124). Note the connection with Vygotsky's idea concerning the internalization of language and subsequent cognitive construction. Secondary socialization results from 'division of labour and . . . social distribution of knowledge . . . [with an] internalization of sub-worlds . . . [with the] acquisition of role-specific knowledge . . . with role-specific vocabularies . . . [and] subjective identification with the role with its own system of legitimation' (op cit.: 127). Secondary socialization is easier to set aside as relevant only to the role-specific situation in question (op cit.: 131). This is highly relevant to the theory of organization, and of organizational learning that is the ultimate target of this book. It relates, in particular, to notions of organization as a 'sensemaking system' Weick (1979), a 'system of shared meanings' (Smircich, 1983), an 'interpretation system' (Choo, 1998), or a 'focusing device' (Nooteboom, 2000), which are discussed in Chapter 3.

Scaffolding

Both Shanon and Hendriks-Jansen use the notion of the 'scaffolding' as a support for meaning and understanding offered by the context. It is reminiscent of Vygotsky's notion of ZOPED. Literally, a scaffold is used in the building of an arch: stones are aligned along a arched wooden scaffold until they support each other and the scaffold can be removed. The paradigmatic case in cognitive development of children is the support provided to the infant by its mother. According to the account given by Hendriks-Jansen (1996), infants do not have an innate language capability as claimed by Chomsky.

> They have innate repertoires of activity sequences, such as facial 'expressions', eye movements and myopic focusing, kicking movements, randomly intermittent bursts of sucking when feeding, and random gropings. At the beginning these movements do not signify anything nor do they seek to achieve anything, and they certainly do not express any internal representations of anything. The mother, however, instinctively assigns meanings and intentions where there are none, and this sets a dynamic of interaction going in which meanings and intentions get assigned to action sequences selected from existing repertoires on the occasion of specific contexts of interaction. Thus the random pauses in sucking are falsely picked up by the mother as indications of a need to jiggle the baby back into feeding action. In fact it is not the jiggling but on the contrary the stopping of it that prods the baby to resume the action. The taking turns in stops and jiggles does not serve any purpose of feeding, as the mother falsely thinks, but a quite different purpose, for which evolution has 'highjacked' what was thrown up by previous evolution. It is 'used' to ready the child for the 'turn taking' that is basic for communication: in communication one speaks and then stops to let the other speak. Here, the child acts, stops, and triggers the mother to action, who jiggles and then stops and thereby triggers the baby to action. At first, the infant can focus vision only myopically, which serves to concentrate on the mother and her scaffolding, not to be swamped by impressions from afar. Later, the scope of focusing vision enlarges, and the infant randomly fixes its gaze on objects around it. The mother falsely interprets this as interest and hands the object to the infant, and thereby generates interest. The child is then prone to prod the mother's hand into picking up objects, first without and later with looking at the mother.

Groping and prodding develop into pointing, which forms the basis for reference that is the basis for meaning and language. While the child points and utters sounds, the mother responds with the correct words, and so language capability develops. In egocentric speech the child starts to provide his own scaffolding, which further contributes to the development of his own identity. Along these lines, meaning and intentionality do not form the basis for action but arise from it, with the aid of scaffolds from the context.

As indicated, according to Vygotsky overt speech is next internalized, to yield virtual speech, and cognitive constructs serve as a basis for virtual action: to explore potential actions mentally, by the construction of mental models, deduction, mental experiments. While cognition is not necessarily in terms of language, and can to some extent develop without it, its development is tremendously enhanced by language, in the development of internal speech.

The notion of scaffolding lends further depth to the debate, in the communities of practice literature, on the role of specific action contexts in specifying and elaborating the meaning of words and in generating new meanings, and on the way in which new entrants to a community, in order to understand, and to be understood and accepted, have to go through a period of 'legitimate peripheral participation' (Lave and Wenger, 1991). Often, behaviours or expressions that carry some socially accepted significance do not carry such significance from the start, corresponding to some internal states of mind, but pre-exist and are assigned significance and mental states later, on the basis of situated action. Scaffolding refers to the social environment lending significance to acts that thereby acquire that significance, which is internalized in the mind.

Levels and Stages in Cognitive Development

Hayek's idea of levels of cognition seems similar to the Gregory Bateson's different orders or levels of learning in his 'Steps to an ecology of mind' (2000). This re-appeared in the literature on organizational learning, in Argyris and Schön's (1978) notion of 'single and double loop learning', and seems close to March's (1991) distinction between exploitation and exploration. The notion that these levels of cognition, and exploitation and exploration, build on and transform each other on the basis of their use in action, already indicated by Hayek, is developed much further by Jean Piaget, in a stage theory of mental development. While Piaget was perhaps primarily a developmental psychologist, he was also, and perhaps at least as much, certainly in his own view, a developmental ('genetic') epistemologist, postulating general principles of development. The basic principle of development, which for children recurs cyclically in different stages of their development, is that by 'assimilating' experience into an existing cognitive structure, in a sequence of steps such structure is transformed ('accommodated') into a higher level of cognitive functioning, in subsequent stages of development. The steps in this sequence are as follows. First generalization, in which an existing mental scheme is applied in new contexts, where it is differentiated to match novel conditions. Next, the scheme undergoes 'reciprocation' with parallel schemes encountered in the novel context, yielding novel combinations, in a process of association, which lead on to novel mental structures, in accommodation. This stage theory of cognitive development was used by Kolb (1984) for a cycle model of cognition, and in a 'cycle of discovery' proposed by Nooteboom (2000). The latter was intended to develop insight, in organization theory, in the problem posed by March (1991) of how exploration and exploitation may arise from each other. In the extant literature on innovation novelty is claimed to raise from 'recombination', in analogy to recombination of genes in cross-over of parental chromosomes, but nothing is said about how in learning and innovation this recombination takes place.

Briefly, the logic of this cycle of discovery is as follows. New contexts of application, entered in generalization, are needed for learning in the sense of discovery. Such shift of context or application can be real, as in a new market for an existing product, or virtual, as in a computer simulation, or intellectual, as in the novel application of an existing theory. Generalization is needed for four reasons. First, it is needed to find an opening for deviance from established order. Second, to yield new insight into limits of applicability or validity of established ideas or practice. Third, to generate novel challenges to success and survival, which yield crises that provide a motive for change. Fourth, to yield novel material, found in the new context, for novel combinations. Change of context upsets the existing order of established practice, which previously had settled into a 'dominant design'. Mentally, this triggers awareness and critical scrutiny of tacit routines in background knowledge that had earlier been relegated to subsidiary awareness (Polanyi), to the extent that such opening to awareness is possible. In differentiation, to solve the crisis encountered in the novel context one first delves into existing repertoires, with memory of earlier ideas, practices, trials and experiments that did not survive at the time, but might work now. When differentiation does not suffice, and the crisis persists, we move on to reciprocation.

Mentally, reciprocation is association: novel ideas arise by connecting previously unconnected existing ideas. The novel context is required to encounter new ideas as the material for novel associations. In the process, old ideas acquire new meanings. The novel context provides the scaffold for such novel meanings of old ideas, in the generation of new ideas. In terms of economics and technology, reciprocation entails experimentation with hybrids: old and novel elements are forced together into old basic designs or architectures (Henderson and Clark, 1990). Examples of the role of such hybrids, in the history of technology, are given in Mokyr (1990) and Nooteboom (2000). Next, hybrids yield tensions, inefficiencies, and obstacles to the full utilization of the potential of novel elements that is increasingly crystallizing out. This yields a new crisis, generating the willingness to consider more drastic, fundamental change in basic design logic, and insights into where the obstacles lie. Experience with the hybrid and its problems may suggest where the main bottlenecks for realization of emerging potential lie, and in what directions new designs may be tried. If reciprocation is two- or many-sided, with an exchange of elements between two or more different practices, then different hybrids may be operating in parallel. This enables comparison of differential success of different design principles, which may yield indications for novel principles. This, then, may lead on to accommodation in the form of trials of novel architectures of old and novel elements. This puts strain on the elements, which may need to be modified to fit in the novel architecture. This may require antecedent innovations in components, including materials, instruments, and so on, or it may lead to a cascade of secondary innovations in components, to proceed with the architectural innovation.

This 'logic' is actually more like a heuristic. The process generally works well, but discovery does not necessarily follow this process. Associations (reciprocation) may arise without prior recall of old practices from memory (differentiation). Transitions between stages may be obstructed. In economic systems, entry barriers to markets may obstruct generalization. Novel challenges that lead to crises may be avoided or overcome by monopoly, oligopoly or incumbent power. Institutionalized practice may disallow deviation from established practice, in differentiation and reciprocation.

In Chapter 5, this heuristic will play an important role in one type of dynamic capability: the capability to harness this process of discovery. The analysis will give a more in-depth explanation of phenomena such as entrepreneurial spin-offs, 'external corporate venturing', and paths by which multinational firms innovate by internationalization. The analysis may improve our understanding of relations between headquarters and subsidiaries of such companies.

Learning by Interaction

Later, in Chapter 3, the notion of cognitive distance will be further developed, as both a problem for mutual understanding and an opportunity for learning. In Chapter 4 that notion will be used for a theory of organization between organizations. The notion of cognitive distance develops the notion, which emerged from evolutionary economics, and which was present in the ideas of Hayek of the market as a discovery process, that variety is a condition for innovation. Variety has three dimensions: the number of agents involved, differences between them, and the pattern of connections between them. Cognitive distance elaborates the second. But why, more precisely, would such difference yield learning in the sense of discovery? The cycle of discovery, just discussed, yields a further explanation.

In communicative interaction, at some cognitive distance, people are faced with the need to fit their ideas and practices into the mental frames of the other person. By the inventive use of metaphor and illustrations one can help each other to cross cognitive distance and trigger requisite shifts of thought. In terms of the cycle of discovery this positing of one's ideas into the minds of others entails generalization. Depending on cognitive distance, this yields misfits in understanding that require adjustment. People can help others to understand by 'putting it differently', thinking back to how they came to grips with the idea, what other ideas they tried, and what other ideas are related to it, in their experience. In terms of the cycle of discovery, this entails differentiation. As people do this reciprocally, they are stimulated to try and fit elements of the other's thought into their own thinking, in hybrids of thought and practice (reciprocation), which stimulate a novel integration of joint thinking and action (accommodation). Cognitive distance may be too small to yield any appreciable shift of cognition, and it may be too large for available absorptive capacity and ability in metaphorical explanation.

The two-sidedness or reciprocity of the process of learning by interaction yields immense leverage, compared with interaction with non-human nature, since in discourse the receiver can shift his stance and outlook to catch a meaning and the sender can adapt to such stance in pitching meaning, and revising metaphors and bringing in meanings from yet other contexts. On the receiver end the ability to do this depends on absorptive capacity, that is the scope of cognition one has developed, and on the sender side it depends on empathy, that is the ability to stand in someone else's cognitive shoes and understand how the other person thinks and feels, and on skills in the use of metaphor, and in drawing out understanding from the partner in communication (see Vygotsky's notion of ZOPED).

Note that this process obfuscates the traditional distinction, in the innovation literature, between the production and diffusion of innovation, and between the transmission and generation of knowledge, and between transmission and variety generation in evolution. In its transmission innovation is modified, in transmission knowledge is transformed, and in cultural evolution meanings ('memes') shift in their transmission.

NEURAL DARWINISM

This section provides a further substantiation of the situated action, constructivist view, on the basis of modern neural research, in particular 'neural Darwinism'.

Connectionism and Parallel Processing

As indicated, the situated action view contests the idea of semantic representations as a necessary and universal basis for all knowledge, but it allows for representations in some sense as the basis for at least some behaviour. For example, it might be consistent with connectionism: the view that cognition is based on neural nets, which can generate systematic regularity without the explicit specification of generative rules in underlying representations. Such nets are representations in some sense, generated, by some mechanism, from experience in the world (see Smolensky, 1988).

In parallel distributed processing (PDP) (see Rumelhart and McClelland, 1987) two radical steps are taken. One is no longer to accept the computer metaphor of sequential processing according to some algorithm, but to approach knowledge and learning in terms of parallel processes that interact with each other. The second is that knowledge is not stored in units, to be retrieved from there, but in patterns of activation in connections between units. We might still speak of mental representations in the form of traces in the brain in the form of activation potentials between neurons (Hurford, 2007). Knowledge is implicit in this pattern of actual and potential connections rather than in the units themselves (Rumelhart et al., 1987: 75). What is stored is the connection strengths between the units that allow the patterns to be recreated (McClelland et al., 1987: 9).

Edelman

Edelman avoids categorization by prior design of what makes sense (the homunculus), in the same way that Darwin avoided prior design (by a deity) of life forms: by evolutionary logic.

While Edelman's (1987) work is not always easy to grasp, even for insiders, perhaps the following summary is correct. Wittgenstein's notion of categorization by family resemblance is reflected in neuronal groups that partly overlap, in their 'arbours' of dendrites (neuronal inputs) and axons (neuronal outputs), thus giving a physical representation of 'members of the family' sharing some features but not others. These groups compete in the sense that selection among them is made by stimuli from the specific context, thus evoking 'members' that best fit the context. Successful selections are reinforced by adjustments in the synaptic thresholds that determine the patterns of neuronal 'firing' that define a group. In this way shifts in categorization and dominant exemplars can arise as experience shifts between contexts. As Edelman (1987: 317) noted: 'while certain general principles may underlie such categorization, its instantiations are always special purpose'.

This may give a perspective for resolving an old philosophical problem of how abstract, general, context-independent categories relate to context-specific particulars. According to Kant, 'schemata' are needed to connect pure categories to the empirical and practical, but it has remained obscure how that connection works. This issue is related, I think, to Shanon's distinction between context-specific 'presentation' and abstract 'representation'. We now know that we have separate memories for categories (semantic memory) and for individual events (episodic memory). Apart from its philosophical interest, the relation between abstract categories and specific instances and practice is of great practical importance. It connects with the problem noted before, in a discussion of 'communities of practice', of how canonical rules i.e. complete, all-encompassing and codified rules, fail to yield a complete, closed prescription of work in practice. The 'family' attached to a category has an open set of members, with some dying off and others being born, depending on their functioning in a variety of contexts.

These processes constitute what has been called mental 'association': new ideas arising from connections between pre-existing ideas. When distinct neural patterns are consistently activated simultaneously, they get connected in their firing, whereby firing in the one triggers firing in the other also in the absence of the conditions under which that happened before.

Edelman's (1987, 1992) 'neural Darwinism' seems to yield a viable perspective for understanding how situated action might work in terms of neural networks (or 'neuronal groups', as he calls them). Neuronal groups are selected and reinforced according to operative success. According to Edelman, memory, both short and long term, is not the 'retrieval' of some entity, but a process of re-categorization; of re-activating, and in the process possibly shifting, the process of selection among neuronal groups. This implies, in particular, that memory also is context-dependent, and that the process of recall may affect the template of future recall. The difference between connectionist models of PDP and neural selectionism is that the former aims to operate on some notional, abstract level between symbols and neural networks (Smolensky, 1988) whereas the latter operates directly on the level of neuronal groups. PDP retains symbols as some higher level, aggregate, emergent outcome of lower level processing.

The central point here is that a mechanism of selection among neuronal structures shows in what way performance may precede competence; how meanings may be constructed from discourse (sense making) and knowledge from action (intelligence as internalized action), while providing the basis for ongoing action. This account seems consistent with Johnson-Laird's (1983) account of mental models and Hendriks-Jansen's (1996) account of how children learn language. This approach indicates how mental structures might emerge from experience in a way that allows for openness and variability across contexts. It offers an evolutionary perspective rather than a perspective of rational design. The programmatic significance of evolutionary theory is that it forces us to explain development not as the result of conscious, goal-directed, top-down, rational design by decomposition of functions, but as selection from among a repertoire of activity sequences, on the occasion of the demands and opportunities of specific contexts.

Another feature of interest in Edelman's work is the notion of 'neural re-entry', where 'brain areas that emerge in evolution coordinate with each other to yield new functions' (Edelman, 1992: 85). This may give an explanation on the neural level of how Piaget's principle of reciprocation, indicated earlier, may work.

Just to make sure: neural Darwinism should not be confused with evolutionary psychology, which claims that psychological mechanisms are the outcome of the evolution of the human species, but refers to selection on the level of neurons as a function of experience.

Summing up, as a basis for situated action theory, and the interactionist, constructivist view of knowledge and meaning that it supports, I employ an evolutionary, connectionist theory of cognitive development. On the occasion of experience, selections and re-combinations are made from partly overlapping and competing patterns of neural connections (Rumelhart and McClelland, 1987; Edelman, 1987, 1992; Rose, 1992). According to these theories, performance, in interaction with and with support from the context, yields competence as much as competence yields the basis for performance. This underpins a principle of 'methodological interactionism'.

EMBODIED COGNITION

This section further elaborates the situated, constructivist view on the basis of processes of 'embodied cognition'.

Construction and Interaction

The principles of situated action, internalized action and neural Darwinism yield what has come to be known as the perspective of embodied cognition. Embodied cognition lends further support to an interactionist, constructivist theory of knowledge that is adopted, explicitly or implicitly, by most authors in the literature on organizational cognition and learning (for surveys, see Hedberg, 1981; Cohen and Sproull, 1996; Meindl et al., 1998). According to this view, people

1. construct their cognitive categories, or mental models, by which they perceive, interpret and evaluate phenomena;
2. in interaction with their physical and, especially, their social environment.

This view also appears in the 'symbolic interactionism' of G. H. Mead (1984), in sociology, and has later been called the 'experiential' view of knowledge (Kolb, 1984) and the 'activity' view (Blackler, 1995). In the organization literature, this view has been introduced, in particular, by Weick (1979, 1995), who reconstructed organization as a 'sense-making system'.

There is much evidence for the constructivist, activity based view from modern research of cognition, in addition to the work of Edelman that was discussed in the previous section. While the brain has some domain specificity, that is localization in the brain of cognitive functions, this domain specificity is plastic, that is not fixed prior to experience but is constructed from input. For example, blind people have been shown, with brain imaging techniques, to employ the visual cortex for object recognition based on proprioception. Another result that illustrates activity based cognition is that after people learn to use objects as tools, accompanied by activity, observed with brain imaging, in motor areas of the brain, the mere observation of the tools triggers brain activity not only in the visual cortex, but also in that motor area. It has been shown that people from different cultures focus on different parts of images, and observe change in patterns differently.

The mental frameworks that result from construction constitute 'absorptive capacity' (Cohen and Levinthal, 1990). People can turn information into knowledge only by assimilating it into those frameworks, and thereby they shape and mould it. Consequently, to the extent that people have developed their cognition in different environments or conditions, they interpret, understand and evaluate the world differently (Berger and Luckman, 1966). As a result, there is greater or lesser 'cognitive distance' between people (Nooteboom, 1992, 1999).

A constructivist perspective can slide, and has done so, into radical post-modern relativism. According to the latter, the 'social constructionist' notion of knowledge entails that since knowledge is constructed rather than objectively given, any knowledge is a matter of opinion, and any opinion is as good as any other. This would lead to a cop-out as soon as rival views become difficult to reconcile, and critical debate would quickly break down. Embodied realism saves us from such radical relativism in two ways. First, our cognitive construction builds on bodily functions developed in a shared evolution, and possibly also on instinctive psychological mechanisms inherited from evolution, as argued in evolutionary psychology (Barkow et al., 1992). In terms of Aristotelian causality,[1] in our cognitive construction there is some similarity of 'formal cause' (way in which we construct) between people. Second, by assumption we share the physical and to some extent also a social world on the basis of which we conduct cognitive construction. That constitutes a reality that is embodied (Lakoff and Johnson, 1999). In Aristotelian terms, there is some similarity of 'material cause' (the elements we construct cognition from). As a result of shared psychological mechanisms of cognitive construction and a shared world from which such construction takes place, there is a basic structural similarity of cognition between people. This provides a basis for debate. Indeed, precisely because one cannot 'climb down from one's mind' to assess whether one's knowledge is properly 'hooked on to the world', the variety of perception and understanding offered by other people is the only source one has for correcting one's errors. We need other people at some cognitive distance to correct our errors and learn.

Emotions in Cognition

Merleau-Ponty (1942, 1964) and before him Nietzsche (1885) and Spinoza (1996 [1677]) already emphasized, counter to Cartesian thought, that mind and body are intertwined, in that cognitive functions build on affects and underlying bodily functions. This view of 'embodied cognition' is made more tangible, in terms of neural structures and processes, in the work of Antonio Damasio, Gerald Edelman, and George Lakoff and Mark Johnson. While it is by no means logically or methodologically necessary to have a neural theory at the basis of a theory of cognition, it does help: insight into neural processes may resolve puzzles in epistemology, and an epistemology that is in flagrant contradiction with neural science is difficult to uphold.

Building on the philosophy of Spinoza, Damasio (2003) specified a hierarchy of cognition, where rationality is driven by feelings, which in turn have a substrate of physiology, in a 'signalling from body to brain'.

As a result, in the present book the term 'cognition' has a wide meaning, going beyond rational calculation. It denotes a broad range of mental activity, including proprioception, perception, sense making, categorization, inference, value judgements, and emotions.

In economics, a connection between rationality and emotions was recognized by Herbert Simon (1983). In view of limited mental resources for rational evaluation, it is rational, in the sense of economizing, to relegate familiar behaviour to routinized conduct, in what Polanyi (1962) called subsidiary awareness, so that scarce capacity for attention can be dedicated to unfamiliar situations, in focal awareness. However, a problem with routinized conduct is that it may continue in situations where it does not apply. A switch is then needed back into focal awareness, and this may require a jolt of emotion, on the occasion of unfamiliar and threatening events.

However, the role of feelings and emotions runs much deeper, beyond reasons of mental economy. In philosophy, Nussbaum (1990) explored the relation between emotions and knowledge. Emotions are informed by knowledge and they inform knowledge. However, they may provide both access and obstacles to knowledge. Emotions (fear, love, hatred, . . .) are directed towards specific objects or situations, and depend on our knowledge of them. When one is afraid of a dark shape in the twilight of a bedroom, one loses the fright when seeing that it is not a prowler but the shadow of a cupboard. Emotions may trigger awareness of insights and feelings that we have but were not aware of before. In other words, they may manifest tacit knowledge. By losing something of value one may become aware of how important it was. We may become aware of our love in the shock of losing a loved one. By being disappointed about a relationship we may gain insight into how that specific relationship works and about relationships in general. Emotion helps us to trust and to develop empathy for another, by which we not only gain insight into the other, but we may also achieve discovery by reciprocating knowledge between self and other. This is a crucial issue in an analysis of dynamic capabilities that will return, in this chapter and subsequent ones, in an analysis of learning by interaction. Emotion helps us to suspend disbelief, to move beyond the sceptical concerns of discursive thought, and thereby to gain access to novel sources of insight. Here, emotion does not replace discursive knowledge but complements it, by yielding new material for discursive knowledge to clarify. Part of this process is that while abstraction takes us away from the particular, to grasp the general or universal, emotion brings us back to a specific particular that upsets and shifts the general. Together, emotions and discursive thought enable us to bootstrap our knowledge.

One of the attractions of embodied cognition is that it provides continuity with social psychology, with its insights into heuristics of judgement and decision-making that combine emotions and rationality (Bazerman, 1998). For example, according to the 'availability heuristic' we give priority in attention to issues that are of overriding salience and are emotion-laden. We reflect on what emotions set on the agenda. According to the 'anchoring and adjustment' heuristic we are irrationally committed to established habits and judgements and we deviate less from them than rational evaluation of evidence would require. According to the 'escalation of commitment' heuristic we stick to decisions when they carried much sacrifice rather than because of their perspectives for the future. Against rationality, we do not apply the rational rule that 'bygones are bygones'. While these heuristics, and others, go against substantive rationality they may in evolution have been procedurally rational, and adaptive, to deal with radical uncertainty and the need to make fast decisions for fast actions.

Also according to social psychology (Kahneman and Tversky, 1979; Kahneman et al., 1982; Lindenberg, 2000, 2003; Tversky and Kahneman, 1983), we have multiple, sometimes mutually conflicting, mental frames, as complexes of mental schemas, in terms of which we interpret events, attribute competencies and intentions to people we interact with, and which guide our actions. One frame may be oriented at 'guarding one's interests' (what an economist attributes universally and unconditionally to people), another at 'acting appropriately' (what a sociologist tends to attribute to people, in the will to gain legitimacy and social acceptance; see Lindenberg). Our actions are interpreted, often not consciously, by others as signaling underlying mental frames (Lindenberg, 2000, 2003; Six, 2005). At any moment one frame may be 'salient' or in 'focal awareness' (Polanyi, 1962), but relational signals may trigger a switch to another frame, leaping from subsidiary awareness, by which our view of what happens and what needs to be done also switches. Thus we may vacillate between self-interest and acting appropriately.

This cognitive move in terms of multiple mental frames between which people shift as a function of what they attribute to other people on the basis of their relational signals, greatly helps to combine economic perspectives associated with the frame of guarding one's interests and sociological perspectives associated with the frame of acting appropriately. Both frames may be instinctive, having emerged from evolution, and together they make for puzzling, vaccillating and sometimes contradictory human behaviour. Their combination is crucial, for example, for a proper understanding of trust (Nooteboom, 2002; Nooteboom and Six, 2003; Six, 2005).

EMBODIED MEANING

Since interaction is important for theory of the firm, particularly for a cognitive theory, and interaction entails communication, an analysis of the meaning of expressions or concepts is important. Analysis of language is usually classified in four categories: phonetics (sounds), syntax (sentence structure), semantics (analysis of meaning) and pragmatics (actual language use). Perhaps we should add semiotics (analysis of signs). Phonetics and syntax will not be considered, and I focus first on semantics. Then I turn to pragmatics. The gist of the argument is that useful semantics, for the present purpose, entails pragmatics.

Sense and Reference

There are several ways of looking at meaning: what is meant or intended, what is understood, and what is proper usage or truth. Traditionally, semantics aims to deal with meaning in terms of truth conditions. Frege (1892) made a famous distinction between reference ('Bedeutung', 'extension', 'denotation'[2]) and sense ('Sinn', 'intension', 'connotation'[3]). Reference/denotation is that which a term refers to, such as an individual or a class of objects, or in case of a proposition its truth-value. Frege characterized sense as 'the way in which extension is given' ('Die Art des Gegebenseins'). The classic example is that 'evening star' and 'morning star' both denote Venus. I use the notion of sense not quite as intended by Frege but as 'how we establish reference'. This is reminiscent perhaps of Carnap's notion of meaning as method of verification, but here I refer to cognitive processes rather than logical argument or demonstration: how do we recognize particulars as belonging to a category, and how do we find out the truth of a proposition, if there is such a thing as truth?

One issue now is whether intension is a mental category, an idea, which yields 'psychologism', or constitutes some outside reality, which yields 'realism'. According to Frege it is separate from individual, subjective ideas: truth conditions are to be kept separate from the mental processes by which one may become conscious of them. If intension truthfully establishes extension, then it cannot be a subjective idea, because then all people would have perfect and identical knowledge. We would all be one in God. Thus to allow for human failure and preserve the idea that intension is in the mind, intension would no longer represent objective truth conditions but ways in which people determine class membership and seek truth, often erroneously. If intension represents personal knowledge, it is in fact a belief that can be false. If, on the other hand, we maintain that intension constitutes objective reality, we are back at the problem, indicated before, of how we can establish how our knowledge is hooked on to that reality, since we cannot descend from our minds. If it is external and objective, how do people grasp it and how does it guide their judgement? In sum, I turn to the psychology of meaning. That is probably a sin in the eyes of most linguists, but for my purpose I need it.

According to the old view, semantic knowledge is pre-packaged, prior to decisions on truth from world knowledge: semantics first, truth second. Modern research in cognition shows that semantics interacts with such decisions on truth. Meanings shift as a function of world knowledge. In other words, semantics (meaning) does not precede pragmatics (language use) but is intertwined with it.

A related issue is whether intension provides necessary and sufficient conditions for class membership and truth. An attractive ploy is to assume that there is some essence that constitutes such necessary and sufficient condition, and this is what the Fregean tradition in semantics has picked up. It brings us all the way back to Aristotle, who held that a concept has an immanent essence, which has no separate existence but can be grasped. According to the later philosopher Locke, such an essence can be arrived at by abstraction: by reducing characteristics of members of a class until we arrive at essential, common characteristics. Later, it was operationalized in the notion that there is a lexicon of all primitive terms, with appended to them 'selection restrictions' which limit its use to 'proper' use (Linsky, 1971).

Putnam (1975) proposed that there is a 'linguistic division of labour': specialists know the 'real' intension, such as the chemical formula and resulting properties of water (H_2O), and this ultimately establishes true class membership. Ordinary people can refer to it in case of doubt, but for day to day action employ a 'stereotype', such as water being clear, drinkable, boiling at 100 degrees Celsius, freezing at 0 degrees, and expanding when it freezes. This does not entail necessary and sufficient conditions, and is not always correct: when under pressure, water boils at a higher temperature than 100 degrees, and freezes at a lower temperature than 0 degrees.

> This may even be important in ordinary life. It makes skating possible, which is important for some. The high pressure of the thin iron of the skate melts the ice and yields a film of water on which one can glide. When it gets too cold this stops and you can no longer glide.

In fact, the stereotype can be false, and in conflict with what the specialist knows. An example Putnam uses is gold. The general idea of gold that prevails in the community includes yellowness, while in fact there is white gold.

This idea is interesting and useful, but the trouble with it is that new scientific discoveries may shift or even revolutionize the specialist's knowledge, and at any point in time we don't know whether this will happen or not, so that objectivity evaporates again.

Family Resemblance, Defaults and Prototypes

A familiar problem in pragmatics is that often categories escape necessary and sufficient conditions for denotation and correct usage of terms. Johnson-Laird (1983: 196) noted, reasonably, that we should keep in sight the differences that occur in the tightness (my term, not his) and character of intension. Technical terms often do satisfy necessary and sufficient conditions, as in mathematical or legal terms. In fact, those terms have been designed for it. Natural kind terms (water, gold, roses and the like) do satisfy something like Putnam's stereotypes plus specialist criteria we may refer to in case of doubt. By contrast, 'constructive' terms, such as chair, do not possess an underlying structure that determines membership; no appeal to experts.

Wittgenstein, in his later work the *Philosophical Investigations* (1976), achieved a revolution. According to him there are no necessary and sufficient conditions, and the criteria for judging a proposition to be true, or proper, or adequate, are pragmatic or conventional. Something is true if it achieves its operational purpose. In communication and joint action correct meaning is what aligns with common practice and satisfies established rules of the game. This is the notion of 'meaning as use', in which a concept is seen as an instrument. For an instrument we would not ask if it is true or what the necessary and sufficient conditions for proper use are a priori. Its adequacy appears in its specific use in a specific context. This is open-ended, and allows for unorthodox but nevertheless adequate use: we may in some conditions use a screwdriver for a hammer, with adequate results.[4] Austin (1955) and Searle (1969) further developed use theory of meaning, in the theory of 'speech acts'. Expressions may not be intended to inform but to affect, in 'illocution', in warnings, orders, threats, accusations, complaints, and so on.

Semanticists object to the notion of meaning as use as that use is affected by a host of cultural, social, psychological and other factors that have little to do with meaning (Katz, 1982). Any word can be used for illocution, in ironic use, invective, stereotyping, and the like, such as 'don't act like an old woman'. However, such radical context dependence of meaning is precisely what I am interested in. Any expression with propositional content might be used with illocutionary force (Hurford, 2007). Conversely, there may be purely illocutionary expression, without any denotational meaning. Hurford (2007: 174) hypothesized that in evolution language started with pure illocution (for example in warnings) and only later developed propositional content (for example to denote and specify the object of warning).

Johnson-Laird (1983: 189) employed Minsky's (1975) notion of 'default values' to elucidate how conventional criteria of meaning might work. Characteristics are assumed unless there is evidence to the contrary. They are assumed on the basis of established practice, that is on the basis of what it is possible to think, until contested by new practice, which shifts what we can think.

Wittgenstein offered the idea of 'typical cases' that represent a norm, and you deal with borderline cases by reference to the norm. Different occurrences, in different contexts, do not always share common features, let alone necessary and sufficient features, but sometimes at best only 'family resemblances'. Proximate members of a family may have shared characteristics, but distant members often do not. Members of a class form a chain, with common characteristics at each link, but no characteristic shared by all members of the class. X is in the same class as Y not because they have common characteristics but because they both share characteristics, but different ones, with a third member Z.

Others have subsequently proposed similar ideas. Well known is Rosch's (1977) idea of 'prototype', which represents an exemplar of a class that connects others in the class. Class membership is decided on the basis of resemblance to a salient case, or a typical case, which serves as a prototype. This allows for family resemblance: there may be no single trait shared by all members of the class. The prototype, being a salient case, depends on culture and natural conditions. For example, for the Dutch the prototype of a bird is a sparrow, and for the British it is a robin.

Note that the idea of a prototype goes back to the ancient notion of 'paradigm', discussed by Socrates, in the sense of an 'exemplar' to be emulated. This is useful in management. Co-ordination often takes place not by canonical rules, with their limitations, discussed before, but by setting exemplars for emulation, which leave room for interpretation depending on the context. Note that this brings us back to the Kantian question concerning 'schemata' that connect abstract categories to empirical particulars and practice, and may offer a possible solution for it.

Shank and Abelson (1977) attempted to give further content and structure to concepts, in terms of scripts, which cover a wide range of action-oriented concepts. A script is a structure of slots for component activities plus requirements about what can fill those slots. The example they use is the restaurant script, with component activities of entry, seating, ordering, eating, paying and leaving. The meaning of 'restaurant' shifted under invention of self-service restaurants, with a different ordering and different content of component activities. The overall script forms the 'background' against which component activities make sense or not. Waiting to be served does not work in a self-service restaurant.

This is particularly germane to organization theory, since scripts connect naturally with primary processes taking place in organizations. The notion of scripts was used in the organizational literature by Gioia and Poole (1984) and Nooteboom (2000). An attractive feature of scripts is that they may serve for a further specification of the concept of organizational capabilities and routines. Another feature is that is contributes to an understanding of the notion of a mental frame, mentioned earlier, and corresponding processes of attribution, and 'relational signalling'. As one observes an action, this may trigger in the mind the notion of a full script in which the action makes sense, upon which the entire script, with its customary intentions, is attributed to the observed agent. When someone sits down in a service restaurant this hopefully triggers a waiter to serve. Attribution of entire scripts facilitates fast inference under incomplete information, and as such contributes to survival under change and need for quick action. However, it also makes for prejudice.

Context Dependence

Earlier, it was noted that meaning depends on context. This is an important issue that merits deeper reflection. In recent developments in the logic of language, the notion has come up of 'discourse representation theory' (DRT). In the words of van Eijck and Kamp (1997: 181): 'Each new sentence S of a discourse is interpreted in the context provided by the sentences preceding it . . . The result of this interpretation is that the context is updated with the contribution made by S.' The contribution from this theory is that it yields a dynamic perspective on semantics: truth conditions are defined in terms of context change. This theory can even be formalized so as to preserve compositionality (Janssen, 1997). However, I propose that the dynamic of interpretation and context is more creatively destructive than is modelled in discourse representation theory: the interpretation of a novel sentence can re-arrange the perception of context and transform interpretations of past sentences. Evolutionary theory caused earthquakes of meaning shifts that reverberated throughout the linguistic system. Nevertheless, DRT offers the great benefit of a global/local distinction between context or scene and terms or expressions occurring within it (Hurford, 2007). The meaning of terms within a scene is dependent on, or relative to the context established by the scene. The scene provides the background to the meaning of what happens within it. According to Hurford (2007: 151) 'the perceptual distinction between global and local attention shows a kind of doublethink that is alien to standard logic'.

Hurford (2007: 99) argues that the identification of objects and assignment of features (predicates) to objects operate along different neural pathways. One pathway, known as the 'where stream' identifies the location of an object (identification), without giving further information about it. This runs from the retina through intermediate stations to the posterior parietal cortex (at the back of the top of the cortex). The (more detailed) information about what the object is (categorization) is delivered by a separate pathway, the 'what stream', which links up with semantic memory.

This stream runs from the retina to the lower temporal cortex (bottom of the cortex). Hurford (2007) connects this with the duality of global/local attention. Global attention (to a scene) is related to the 'where stream' and local attention is related to the 'what stream' (objects in the scene). Apparently when we observe a scene, we first scan the scene as a whole, as the background for what aspects of participating objects to look for and pay attention to, before shifting attention to them. The scene 'primes' attention to the objects. This may explain the hilarious experiment where people are asked to pay attention to people throwing balls to each other, and then fail to notice the gorilla walking across the scene. This analysis is interesting because it shows how context dependence of meaning may be embodied.

Truth by Coherence

Ferdinand de Saussure (1979) was perhaps the first to recognize that meanings of concepts do not stand-alone but are related to the meanings of other concepts. The signs of words ('signifiers') are arbitrary: a rose could be called by any other name, and in other languages than the English it is. The concept indicated by the word ('signified') has a meaning that is related to the meanings of other words: 'a word means what other words do not'. Meaning is not an autonomous entity but a systemic effect. A concept carries associations with other concepts, by which meaning becomes embedded in a field of connected meanings rather than a set of isolated meanings. In English we speak of the 'war of the roses', which to people not familiar with the rose as a symbol of British royalty might seem like the title of a new Disney film.

If we thus allow for differences between languages, and subcultures within languages, why not for individual people, and for different contexts for a given person? What keeps us from falling into radical, postmodern relativism? Here, I fall back again on embodied cognition, discussed above. Our cognition is realistic in the sense that our cognitive structures are constructed in interaction with reality. In the absorption of phenomena we construct our understanding of them. Thus the issue of realism as a connection between separate worlds of reality and cognition is fundamentally mistaken. Our cognition is not separate from reality but constructed from it, and in that sense it is realistic. This construction is shared between people, and is not arbitrary, because we conduct our cognitive constructions on the same biological basis, 'thrown up' by a shared evolution. A second reason why our cognition is to a large extent shared, and not arbitrary, is that we construct it from a shared physical environment, governed by universal laws of nature. In that nature we have to survive, and only those cognitive constructions will survive that yield adequate performance in the world. Note that this is consonant with the Wittgensteinian notion of 'meaning as use'.

As a result, while truth by correspondence with an objectively identifiable external reality is an illusion, we have some hold on truth by coherence of a focal part of cognition with other parts of cognition, in a seamless 'web of belief' (Quine and Ullian, 1970), and with the views of other people that have made alternative mental constructions, at some cognitive distance, as a result of mental construction along a different life path.

Metaphors and the Generation of Meaning

As discussed earlier, in embodied cognition meanings emerge interactively from use in action. Werner and Kaplan (1963) demonstrated 'that reference is an outgrowth of motor-gestural behaviour. Reaching evolves into pointing, and calling-for into denoting'. They note that 'it is in the course of being shared with other people that symbols gain the denotative function'.

Lakoff and Johnson (1999) proposed that the construction of mental categories is heavily based on proprioception (motor activities of touch and handling), in learning to survive in an environment of opportunities, threats, pursuit, flight, food, obstacles, shelter, instruments, and so on. They distinguish between *middle-range* categories, such as 'chair', which are on the level of objects we deal with, in primary experience, superordinate categories such as 'furniture', and subordinate categories such as 'baby chair'. The 'basic level' of meaning is the middle range, which is the highest level at which abstraction can be represented by a well-defined prototype in the form of an iconic image (some typical chair). According to Lakoff and Johnson, 'middle-range' concepts are most likely to be realistic. Realism of middle range concepts, relating to objects we deal with, is crucial for survival. If we did not adequately categorize things like threatening animals, people, stones, rivers, trees, tools, houses, cars, roads, and the like, our chances for survival would be dim. This applies much less to the lower and higher level concepts. We can survive if our characterization of the biological make-up of a sabre-toothed tiger is wrong, and if we attribute it to the wrong kind of species, but much less if we misjudge its speed and the danger of its fangs and claws. This suggests an evolutionary theory of meaning, but this will not be elaborated in this book.

Earlier, Lakoff and Johnson (1980) had argued that in the construction of meaning from actions in the world people employ metaphors. We grasp our actions in the physical world, in which we have learned to survive, to construct meanings of abstract categories, starting with 'primary metaphors' that build on proprioception and bodily survival. Thus, for example, good is 'up', because we stand up when alive and well, while we are prostrate when ill or dead. We are 'going ahead' with our work in analogy to advance in motion. Higher-level categories are built on these basic metaphors, to yield higher level metaphors. Thus we conceive of abstract notions in terms of containers, location, movement, and the like. For example, we conceive of life as a voyage, and meaning (reference) in terms of containers (extension). We are 'in' love or pain as we are in a house. We 'retreat from an idea' as we avoid confrontation with a prowling beast.

The analysis is important not only in showing how we cope in the world, but also in showing how metaphors can yield what Bachelard (1980) called 'epistemological obstacles'. I suspect that the primary metaphors, informed by experience with objects in the world, yield a misleading conceptualization of meanings, for example, as objects. Since objects retain their identity when shifted in space, we find it difficult not to think of words retaining their meaning when shifted from sentence to sentence. Underlying this is the 'museum metaphor' of meaning: words are labels of exhibits that constitute their meaning, and the 'pipeline metaphor of communication': with words meanings are shipped across a 'communication channel'. Meanings and communication are not like that, but we find it difficult to conceptualize them otherwise. In short, in abstract thought, we suffer from an 'object bias'.

While cognition is based on dealing with objects in the world, in embodied cognition, our cognition does remain a construction, and thereby it is not objective, and in that sense relativism is inevitable, even though it is not radical in a postmodern sense that any view is as good as any other. Especially judgements beyond the middle range are subject to error. Emotions and abstract notions are less easy to grasp directly than physical experience, and therefore we seek determination of the former in terms of the latter. There are systematic correlations between our emotions and our sensori-motor experiences, such as touching, grasping, pulling, pushing, lifting, dropping, breaking objects. These form the basis for metaphor. We experience ourselves as entities, containers, made of substances, and with sight and touch we experience boundaries. Time is understood as movement, causation in terms of manipulating objects, labour in terms of material resources, and argument may be perceived as battle (Lakoff and Johnson, 1980: 56–71). The notion of fuzzy boundaries of a concept may be instinctively scary because it triggers emotion-laden associations with a leaking roof that admits the rain and cold, or cracks in walls that might give access to the sabre-toothed tiger.

While basic metaphors tend to be shared across cultures, since they derive from survival in interaction with a shared natural environment, higher-level metaphors tend to vary. In present society social interaction has come to equal or even dominate interaction with the physical world as a basis for cognitive construction, and since in contrast with physical nature social environments vary, cognition may vary across cultures. Thus I come round to my earlier proposal that to the extent that people have developed in different physical and social environments they entertain different categories or forms of thought. In other words: different absorptive capacities. This will form the basis for my claim, in Chapters 3 and 4, that the fundamental purpose of firms is to create alignment in cognitive categories in order to achieve a common purpose. To Lakoff and Johnson I grant that variety of cognition operates on a substrate of more shared, object oriented cognitive constructions.

IMPLICATIONS

This final section gives a survey of the implications for the theory of the firm of embodied cognition and an evolutionary view of cognitive construction. One implication is the notion of cognitive distance, with the resulting notion of the firm as a cognitive focusing device, and further implications for collaboration for innovation between organizations. A second implication of the constructivist-interactionist theory of cognition concerns the philosophy and methodology of economics, in a principle of 'methodological interactionism'. A third implication is that the notion of 'embodied cognition' in the brain may serve as a model for collective cognitive construction in organizations, which yields a further elaboration of the notion of an organizational cognitive focus. Fourth, such collective cognition is further supported by the notion of truth by coherence rather than by correct reference. A fifth is the implication of context-dependence of meaning and the notion of 'scaffolding' for the embeddedness of cognition in contexts of action, in communities of practice. This entails that knowledge is often 'sticky' to context (von Hippel, 1999). A sixth is the implication of the role of prototypes in the theory of meaning for the function of 'role models' in organizations. A seventh is the use that can be made of the stage theory of cognitive development as a 'logic' for a dynamic capability of firms. These implications are developed in later chapters, but to offer an overview they are summarized below.

Cognitive Distance

If cognitive capability is constructed from situated action, people will perceive, interpret, understand and evaluate the world differently to the extent that they have constructed their cognition along different, weakly connected life paths. This yields the notion of 'cognitive distance'. That yields a problem for efficient coordination of actions needed to achieve a shared, organizational goal. As a result, organizations require an organizational 'cognitive focus', to sufficiently limit cognitive distance, for the sake of sufficient mutual understanding and ability to collaborate. This yields both a strength compared with markets, in favouring collaboration, and a weakness, in reducing cognitive variety. To compensate for this, firms need relations with other organizations, at larger cognitive distance. The theory of the firm will be fully developed in Chapter 3, and the derived theory of inter-organizational relationships will be developed in Chapter 4.

Methodological Interactionism

The analysis provides the basis for a principle of methodological interactionism that transcends both the methodological individualism that forms part of the 'hard core' (in the sense of Lakatos, 1970, 1978) of the 'research programme' of mainstream economics (Weintraub, 1988), and the methodological collectivism of (some) sociology, according to which individuals are programmed by their social environment. In my view, this yields a perspective for integrating economics, sociology and cognitive science in a new behavioural science. What this can yield, more specifically, in terms of the theory of the firm, including a theory of inter-organizational relationships, and theory of innovation in inter-organizational relationships, is shown in the remainder of this book.

The analysis also has implications for other debates on individualism versus collectivism (Realu, 2005). Communitarians (for example Etzioni, 1988) suggest that personal autonomy is best achieved within communities, which supply moral meaning, resist excessive selfishness and prevent alienation. On the other hand, psychologists have established that individualism can yield higher self-esteem, optimism, subjective well-being, and quality of life. Individuality, autonomy and self-sufficiency appear to be conducive to cooperation and solidarity. Based on data from House et al. (2004), Realu found in a cross-country analysis that interpersonal trust was negatively correlated with high levels of collectivism. If we see people as being constituted as individuals by interaction with others, this may become easier to understand. As reported in the trust literature, trust is favoured by both self-confidence (Deutsch, 1973) and mutual need (Nooteboom and Six, 2003). Self-confidence builds on individual autonomy and mutual need builds on differentiation between individuals. In a collective of undifferentiated individuals without autonomy, lack of self-confidence and lack of mutual need from differentiation inhibit trust.

Evolutionary Theory

The idea of cognitive construction by interaction also has implications for evolutionary theory. Evolution is driven by the processes of variety generation, selection and transmission. In cultural and economic evolution variety generation arises in invention or creation, selection is effected in competition, in markets, and in debates and processes of publication, in culture, and transmission is effected in imitation, economic growth, education, training, and communication. The analysis of cognition and meaning, given above, suggests that application and communication of ideas in selection and transmission at the same time yield variety, in an interpretative transformation of ideas when they are applied and communicated. In evolutionary terms that means that selection and transmission are also sources of variety, and the question arises what this does to the logic of evolution. This will be developed in Chapter 6.

Embodied Cognition, Coherence and Collective Cognition

In the literature on organizational cognition and learning, a well-known issue is in what sense one can speak of collective, organizational cognition other than as an aggregate of individual cognition (Cohen and Sproull, 1998; Meindl et al., 1998). According to embodied cognition, mental structures are developed on the basis of neuronal groupings, in a Darwinian process of tentative construction, often in parallel, in partly competing, and partly overlapping, groupings, which get selected, reinforced and differentiated according to success in action in the world. Such process of embodiment may serve as a model for how in organizations collective cognition arises from the construction of organizational structures of connected capabilities, corresponding practices and meanings, as an embodiment of organizational experience along its path of development in a variety of environments (Nooteboom, 1997). Thus, one may speak of organizational cognition as collective cognition, as a phenomenon arising from interacting organizational structures of activity, in a similar way as one can speak of individual cognition as a collective phenomenon from component neuronal processes (Minsky, 1975).

This notion of cognition as collective, in a web of connected processes, appears to be further supported by the notion of truth by coherence rather than by reference, particularly if one takes a pragmatist view of truth as adequacy in action. If something is true primarily when it coheres with other elements that are taken as part of our knowledge, then in organizations things are taken as true to the extent that they cohere with what is taken for granted in what is going on in the organization.

This is taken up in the elaboration of the notion of organizational cognitive focus, in Chapter 3. The idea of neural Darwinism is further taken up in the discussion of evolutionary theory, in Chapter 6.

Context Embeddedness

An implication of the notions of 'proximate zone of development' (Vygotsky) and 'scaffolding' (Shanon, Hendriks-Jansen) is that cognition is partly outside the mind, in the context of action, in machinery, instruments, conditions of work, interaction with people, in 'communities of practice' (Brown and Duguid, 1991, 1996; Lave and Wenger, 1991; Wenger and Snyder, 2000). This adds to the 'stickiness' of knowledge (von Hippel, 1999), that is the difficulty of transferring it to others, in other contexts of action.

Related to the 'situatedness' of cognition we noted the context dependence of meaning. Sense making of objects or agents (the local) depends on background assumptions triggered by an interpretation of the context (the global).

In sum, we can now identify the following sources of the stickiness of knowledge. First, there is the well-known problem of tacit knowledge. Well known is the problem that if knowledge cannot be codified it is less easily transferred, and such transfer requires interaction in joint practice. Less consistently applied is the notion of absorptive capacity. If the 'receiver' does not have the requisite absorptive capacity, they will not be able to absorb the expressions of the 'sender' even if they were fully codified. Hardly known is the effect of tacit knowledge on the receiver end. Tacit knowledge is taken for granted and is therefore difficult to subject to rational criticism. In other words: tacit knowledge can limit absorptive capacity. For rational criticism, tacit knowledge may first have to be made explicit, in an act of 'maieutics' (intellectual midwifery) (Nooteboom, 2000, 2003).

Now I add that knowledge and sense making are embedded in action contexts, and next to what is in the brain requires a connection with artefacts and conditions that form part of the context of action. In other words, cognition is partly external and local. This is further supported by the idea that meaning is context-dependent; that specific contexts of action may be needed to disambiguate meaning (pin down extension) and to trigger the associations and background assumptions that enable understanding (the intension or sense of meaning). This issue is taken up in a discussion of problems of collaboration between firms, in Chapter 4, and in a discussion of communities of practice, in Chapter 5.

Prototypes and Role Models

The notion of prototype, in the theory of meaning, indicates that since often one cannot specify necessary and sufficient conditions for correct reference, and canonical rules cannot fully proscribe practice, one needs a prototype or salient exemplar that guides reference by similarity or emulation of the prototype or exemplar. This is an important feature for organization, in the form of exemplary behaviour, in role models, for example of organizational 'heroes'. This is needed for two reasons. First, as indicated in the discussion of the role of prototypes in general, it is needed to guide behaviour without fixing or freezing it in necessary and sufficient conditions, and thereby leaving room for variety of interpretation and emulation, depending on conditions of specific action contexts. In other words, it leaves more room for variety needed for improvisation and innovation. As will be discussed in Chapter 3, organizational cognitive focus often consists of highly general, abstract categories, and this is needed to allow for a wide scope of capability and activity. However, such abstract principles are often not very appealing, and yield insufficient grip for translating them into specific action. Exemplars serve to provide an example to guide interpretation and application without freezing them into something that is too specific and rigid.

Cycle of Discovery

The levels of cognition (Bateson, Argyris and Schön) and stages of cognitive development (Piaget, Kolb) entail a 'logic of discovery' that can serve as a basis for the analysis of dynamic firm capabilities, as set out in Nooteboom (2000). This shows how exploration may build on exploitation (March, 1991); how applications of existing 'dominant designs' in novel contexts can yield the motive and then insight for differentiation, novel combinations and novel syntheses. This is developed in Chapter 5.

NOTES

1. While Aristotelian causality, with its efficient cause (agent), final cause (purpose), formal cause (method, technology), material cause ('stuff' used), conditional cause (surrounding conditions that affect production) and exemplary cause (model to be followed) is unfit for explaining nature, and in that field has been rightfully rejected, and ridiculed in the process, it is quite germane to explaining human action.

2. Strictly speaking, reference is what people do, denotation is what expressions (may) do, and extension is something that expressions have. People refer by using expressions that denote.
3. Connotations form part of sense making; are possible elements of sense.
4. Note that in accepting Wittgenstein's idea that meaning is pragmatic in its adjudication I do not necessarily accept that that is all there is to meaning. I do accept meanings and intensions as connected to processes in the mind.

3. Organizational focus

INTRODUCTION

This chapter forms the core of this book, with the main argument for the firm as a 'cognitive focusing device'. First comes a discussion of the need for focus, features of focus, and the resulting role of organizations. Second, the relation between organizational focus and culture. Third, for a more formal treatment the notions of cognitive distance and optimal cognitive distance. Fourth, an analysis of the origins and stability of focus and implications for limits to size and growth of the firm.

THE NEED FOR FOCUS

This section sets up the argument for 'organization as a cognitive focusing device'. It starts with a definition of organization and an overall characterization of organizational focus. It proceeds with an analysis of issues of governance, next to competence, and with features and properties of organizational focus. It ends with a specification of the role of organization, and an example.

A Definition of Organizations

The term 'organization' has been given a wide meaning, as the opposite of chaos, and as more or less synonymous with 'system', that is a set of elements that are connected to some extent and in some way. This would include stones, crystals, cells, plants, animals, people and universes (Boulding, 1961). Here, the focus is on organizations of people. As indicated in the introduction (Chapter 1), using elements from definitions from McKelvey (1982) and Aldrich (1999), I define organizations as follows:

> *Organizations are myopically goal-directed, socially constructed, more or less focused systems of coordinated activities or capabilities.*

The notion of organizational goals is problematic (Scott, 1992). There is a range of possible goals, such as survival, profit, social or political legitimation, competitive strength, political influence, creation, freedom or independence. Are such goals personal or collective? They can be either or both. Each of the goals indicated can be interpreted on a personal and on a collective level. Organizational and individual survival can both be goals and are not the same. People can succumb for the sake of organizational survival. People can be highly dependent on independent organizations. Goals are organizational when they are collective, that is when people pursue them and believe that others do so as well. How many people need to do so, and which, in the organization? At least some 'dominant coalition' (Cyert and March, 1963).

A similar puzzle concerning individual and collective arises concerning organizational cognition. As noted in Chapter 1, cognition as mental activity by definition cannot apply to aggregates such as firms or organizations. However, such aggregates can be seen as engaging in the use and production of knowledge, and people in an organization can share views, interpretations, understandings, values and norms of behaviour, which are not shared outside the organization. More fundamentally, they may share underlying basic categories concerning Man, the World, Knowledge, and the relations between Man and World and between Man and Man, in organizational culture, that govern the construction of views, interpretations and opinions (Smircich, 1983; Schein, 1985; Weick and Roberts, 1993; Weick, 1995; Cook and Yanow, 1996). In this book such shared views and categories are called *organizational cognitive focus.* The basic idea goes back further, for example to Boulding (1961: 57), who defined an organization as a 'structure of roles tied together by lines of communication, . . . (whose) existence . . . depends on the presence of a "public image" among those who participate in its roles'. It is also related to Penrose's (1959: 15/16) definition of the firm as 'an autonomous administrative planning unit, the activities of which are interrelated and are co-ordinated by policies which are framed in the light of their effect on the enterprise as a whole', the boundaries of which are determined by 'the area of administrative coordination'; and 'authoritative coordination' (op cit.: xi.)

The notion of organizational focus will help to answer these questions concerning the relation between the personal and the organizational. It is a feature of an organization that orients cognition (perception, interpretation, understanding), goals and actions of the people in the organization, and is in turn reconstructed or shifted by actions of those people. Guided and constrained by organizational focus, people in organizations may accept organizational goals, and contribute to their elaboration, maintenance, drift or shift, as an outcome of interaction between them, and between the organization and its environment. People are more than the organizational roles they play; they are also people 'qua persona' (Ring and van de Ven, 1994). Having different cognitive endowments and having interactions also outside the organization, the cognitive categories they construct will never become identical to those of other people in the organization. Cognitive distance is likely to decline, but not to zero. Personal goals are different from organizational ones, but they may be, and for viable organizational membership should be, aligned, in part, with organizational goals, as expressed in documents, slogans, exemplary and other symbolic behaviour.

Initially, at their founding, firms carry a strong imprint, in cognitive focus and organizational goals that it implies, from the founding entrepreneur(s). Subsequently, both goals and focus are subject to reconstruction and change as the outcome of interactions in the firm. This is indicated by the term 'socially constructed' in the definition of organizations. The 'more or less focused' nature of these systems refers to the condition that organizational focus can be more or less cohesive and inclusive. The features of organizational focus are elaborated later.

Goal direction of organizations is 'myopic' for several reasons. First, individual cognition is 'bounded' in that it is contingent upon mental categories that both enable and constrain cognition, and arise from experience along specific life trajectories, as set out in Chapter 2. In this 'activity based', 'embodied' cognition, insights, preferences and goals do guide action, but they are also constructed from it, and then follow rather than precede action (Weick, 1979). This makes cognition bounded not only in the sense that one has a limited capacity for rational evaluation, as Herbert Simon recognized long ago, but in the more fundamental sense that one's perspective is biased by experience and subject to unforeseeable development. In organizations, individual cognition is further guided and constrained by organizational focus. And finally, shifts of goals and focus of organizations are emergent, and hence unforeseeable, outcomes of complex interactions between people. In this process there arise discrepancies between official 'espoused' organizational goals, and actual goals 'in use' (Argyris and Schön, 1974). As a result, what appears to be a persistent entrepreneurial imprint may hide a shift of actual practice. People may not practise what they are expected to preach.

Goal achievement may have a larger or smaller accidental component, but is to a greater or lesser extent pursued intentionally by some coordination of actions, capabilities, means, outcomes or goals (Mintzberg, 1983), employing relevant know-how, under external commercial and institutional conditions. More briefly, there is coordination of a variety of causes, which may coherently be analysed, in a not too ad hoc fashion, by using Aristotle's multiple causality of efficient cause (here people), final causes (goals, outcomes), material causes (inputs, means) formal causes (technology, capabilities) and conditional causes (markets, institutions) (Nooteboom, 2000).[1] Those are combined in some pattern or other, and are to a greater or lesser extent dependent on each other, in different ways (Thompson, 1967). For example, on an organizational level profit is generally needed to achieve survival and independence. Means can be material (basic resources, energy, instruments, tools, machinery) or immaterial (finance). Technology available to the organization is a configuration of means and capabilities. Know-how includes individual-level and group-level capabilities, in skills and knowledge that may be technical, organizational and behavioural, and organization-level capabilities to configure and coordinate them (Penrose).

There is, in general, a multitude of ways to select and configure goals, actions, capabilities, outcomes, means, and conditions external to the firm. Coordination of specific activities is not necessarily a task of management, and may arise on other levels, by plan and design or more spontaneously. Coordination may be achieved by assigning capabilities to jobs, assigning people to jobs, defining the roles they have in the organization, and defining and governing relations between them. Here, Mintzberg (1983) proposed five forms of coordination: specification of outputs, processes, capabilities, direct supervision and mutual adjustment. Later, Mintzberg (1989: 221) added a 'missionary form', in coordination by ideology.

In these configurations of goals, actions, means, capabilities, outcomes and external conditions, choice is needed. Such choice is not necessarily rational in a calculative sense, and may be the outcome of heuristics, routines, or haphazard interaction, or in some evolutionary process. One cannot strive for everything at the same time. One cannot look in all directions at the same time, and if it were possible, one would probably see nothing. To guide processes of choice one needs some focus on goals, actors and actions, means and know-how, and on how to configure and coordinate them under what conditions. The ability for such guidance constitutes organizational capability. The central difference between firm and market is that in the former such focus is made and in the latter it is not, or to a much lesser extent (there still is a remaining, shared cognitive focus from shared culture and knowledge). Thus the market has the higher potentiality of variety of performance, and the firm has the higher actuality of performance.[2]

Organizational Focus

Focus means limitation of a range, of goals, activity, ownership, attention, meaning or capability. Organizational focus, then, can mean limitation of its range of activities, in terms of products, markets and technologies, of physical, cognitive or cultural assets, of individual or organizational capabilities, or a combination of all of those. Organizations may be constrained in their activities, assets or capabilities, by public regulations, budgets and the like. This applies, in particular, to public organizations, such as hospitals, universities, ministries, courts and so on. There, organizations are often rewarded for utilizing legitimate structures and processes, rather than for the quantity and quality of their products (Scott, 1992: 132). Firms generally have a wider scope for private initiative, are focused more on quantity and quality of products, and on profitability more than legitimacy.

From this perspective there are oddities in the drive towards privatization and commercialization of public organizations, that is towards turning them into firms. An essential part of commercial strategy is to differentiate products for selected market segments, which includes the option not to serve certain segments. This is done in order to differentiate oneself from competition, since competition on differentiated products is more profitable than competition only on price for a homogeneous, undifferentiated product. Then we privatize health care, say, but for reasons of social equitability enforce the indiscriminate service of all potential patients under identical conditions. We create firms while forbidding them to act like firms.

Many firms still define themselves in terms of specific activities, but as the pace of change of knowledge, technologies and markets increases, firms are learning to shift their focus from a given range of activities, products, production processes, physical assets, distribution channels and the like, to a focus of underlying capabilities that have the potential of generating and supporting a variety of products and production processes (Quinn, 1982, 1992). This yields greater flexibility to adapt to changing markets and technologies with changing product lines and production processes. That was also one of the essential points made by Penrose (1959). Capabilities (resources) can be applied to a variety of specific activities ('services').

Next, and beyond Penrose, there is increasing pressure to strengthen the focus of capabilities to those 'core capabilities' in which firms can maintain durable competitive advantage. While such focus limits the range of potential activities of the firm by itself, it yields a further increase of flexibility, in a wider scope of more variable configurations of the firm's capabilities with those of other firms. It also improves their distinction with respect to other firms, with the usual consideration, from industrial economics, that differentiation yields higher profitability than price competition with highly substitutable products. I will argue that such limitation of focus also increases speed of innovation, which is vital under increasing competition in all dimensions, of price, quality and innovation. I will argue that it also increases cognitive diversity, in collaboration between firms, as a source of innovation (Nooteboom, 1992). Furthermore, the external configuration of capabilities between firms is enabled by new technical opportunities, from information and communication technology, and emerging organizational capabilities, in the coordination of activities between firms. I will argue that all this yields limits not only to the growth of firms, as Penrose (1959) acknowledged, but also to the size of the firm. In her book, Penrose focused on the growth of the firm, and paid limited attention to limits to the size of firms, but the suggestion from her analysis was that there are no limits to size in the long run.

For any given focus of capabilities, in order to profit from complementarities between them cognitive coordination is needed on their interfaces, in the wide sense of cognition used in this book (see Chapter 2), to enable sufficient mutual understanding and ability to collaborate (competence), and willingness and commitment to do so (governance). Such alignment of cognition requires what I call 'organizational cognitive focus'. I propose that this constitutes a central organizational capability.

Note that in cognitive coordination not everyone has to have the same ideas on everything. In fact, it may even be that there is not a single idea shared by all. Diversity of ideas is good for innovation, and autonomy and room for initiative are often good for motivation. So, one should aim for minimum alignment of cognition needed to utilize opportunities from complementary capabilities. Variety of cognition should be limited only when needed for the feasibility and efficiency of collaboration.

On the competence side, focus is needed to enable people to understand each other and connect complementary knowledge, without unduly restricting variety and creativity. On the governance side, focus is needed to motivate people to collaborate and share and connect knowledge, without unduly restricting autonomy, ambition and competitive spirit. While some shared views on collaborative relations enhances the ease and efficiency of collaboration, it is seldom sufficient. Motivation to collaborate is also based on need, from mutual dependence. In sum, organizational focus is an institution, in that it constructs, enables and constrains actions within the organization.

Governance: Trust and Control

For collaboration, people should rely on each other, to some extent. Reliance and trust form a big subject that cannot be dealt with exhaustively in the present book, but they need to be summarized. For this I will use Nooteboom (2002). Rational and voluntary reliance is based on the inference of sufficient reliability. Following Nooteboom (2002), I make a distinction between reliance and trust, and, correspondingly, between reliability and trustworthiness. Reliability/reliance includes control, while trustworthiness/trust goes beyond control. Control may be based on hierarchy, contractual enforcement, or other incentives. Trust, beyond control, may be based on ethics, empathy, identification, personal ties or routinized conduct. Here, I agree with Williamson (1993) that trust has little meaning if it does not go beyond calculative self-interest. Contrary to Williamson (1993), however, I hold that such trust can exist, even in markets, although it does have its limits, depending on pressures of survival or competition.

Reliance may be defined as running a relational risk and accepting it in the expectation that the object of reliance 'will not cause great harm', for whatever reason, including reasons of self-interest from enforcement or incentives. Incentives include dependence on another's resources, in line with resource dependence theory (Pfeffer and Salancik, 1978). A has an incentive to refrain from doing B harm, or to surrender advantage to him, to the extent that A is more dependent on B than B is on A, that is A has fewer alternatives, or faces higher switching costs. Trust may be defined as accepting relational risk in the expectation that the trustee will not cause great harm, *even if he has both the opportunity and incentive to do so*. The sources of reliability are summarized in Table 3.1.

Not mentioned in Table 3.1 is the possibility of using trusted third parties for intermediation or arbitration (Simmel, 1950 [1917]; Shapiro, 1987; Nooteboom, 2002). The table shows sources of reliability in general, applying also outside organizations, and sources that are specific for organizations, and it shows sources of control and of trust going beyond

Table 3.1:   Sources of reliability

	Macro Universalistic Between organizations	Micro Particularistic, relation-specific Within organizations
Self-interest		
Opportunity control	Contracts, legal enforcement	Hierarchy, managerial 'fiat'
Incentive control	Reputation, dependence, hostages	Careers, bonus schemes
Altruism	Values, social norms of proper conduct, moral obligation, sense of duty, bonds of kinship	Empathy, routinization, benevolence, identification, affect, friendship, organizational culture

Source: Adapted from Nooteboom (2002).

control. Two kinds of control are distinguished. One lies in the constraint of 'opportunities for opportunism', constraining action space, supported by legal or hierarchical constraint and monitoring. Hierarchy is based on formal authority, invested in managers by higher authority (going up, in most firms, to the owners of the firm). Another form of control lies in incentive control, in the selection of options from available action space, which includes resource dependence and the maintenance of reputation. General sources of reliability, outside and inside organizations, are legal enforcement for opportunity control, and reputation, balance of dependence and hostages for incentive control. Hostages here often take the form of commercially sensitive information that may be surrendered to competitors in case of misconduct. For trust, beyond control, one has generalized ethics, with norms of legitimacy, underlying values of conduct, and common internalized goals and feelings of solidarity, as a feature of a social or religious community, family, clan (Ouchi, 1980), region, industry or country. These are often exemplified in myths or role models to be emulated. Apart from formal authority of hierarchy, ability to lead depends on whether leadership is endorsed by subordinates, on the basis of adherence to norms of legitimacy and other sources of trust.

Within organizations, and here lies their function, there is scope for hierarchical control, and, on the trust side, the building of further, more dedicated and specialized shared norms and values, empathy, identification and routinized conduct. Here lies the role of organizational cognitive focus. Empathy here means the ability to imagine oneself in the position of another, and understand to some extent how he thinks, without necessarily thinking the same. Identification means a sense of shared destiny and some common thought. Empathy is more related to crossing cognitive distance and identification more to reducing it. Empathy and, to a lesser extent, identification may arise between organizations but they tend to be the speciality of organizations.

Now, both between and within organizations trust and control are both substitutes and complements (Klein Woolthuis et al., 2005). Trust and control need each other as complements since both have their limits. Trust needs to be where control ends, and vice versa. However, they are substitutes in that more trust allows for less control. In the present context the conclusion is that organizations have the possibility and function to create cognitive focus as a basis for trust, with firm-specific ethics, values and norms of conduct, empathy and some degree of identification. However, that is seldom enough to establish cooperation, and in addition mutual dependence plays a role, as an incentive for collaboration. Hierarchy may still play a role for opportunity control, but for reasons indicated earlier, with the professionalization of labour the scope and grip of hierarchy is

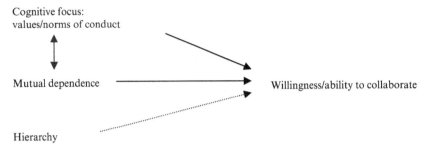

Figure 3.1   Governance

decreasing. The mix of sources of reliability varies between organizations. Some go more for moral alignment, as part of organizational cognitive focus, others more for mutual dependence, and others more for hierarchy. Generally some mix will occur, with different emphases. The combination of governance by dependence and by focus is illustrated in Figure 3.1. Hierarchy is also included, but with a dotted causal arrow to indicate its reduced salience. Note that there is also a bilateral causal arrow between values/norms of conduct, as a basis of trust, and mutual dependence. The effect of mutual dependence on trust is well-known from the literature on trust (see for example Nooteboom and Six, 2003). When people are strongly dependent, needing each other and having few alternatives, there is a strong pressure to 'get along and make it work'. Conversely, getting closer in trust on the basis of empathy and, perhaps, some identification, increases mutual dependence. One could also give this an interpretation in terms of specific investments: investing in shared values constitutes a specific investment, which increases dependence, and requires adequate duration of the relationship to recoup the investment.

Features of Focus

The question concerning boundaries of the firm is how far organizational focus goes or should go. Berger and Luckmann (1966) proposed that there is 'primary socialization' in childhood, which is most basic, and 'secondary socialization' in subsequent environments of training and work. Organizations yield secondary not primary socialization. Both inside and outside organizations, people have more goals, capabilities, roles and relations than those that are governed by organizational focus (DiMaggio, 1997). As noted before, Ring and van de Ven (1994) made a distinction between organizational roles people play and their behaviour 'qua persona'. This was presaged by the distinction Simmel (1950 [1917]) made between a person's function in an organization, which takes up only part of his personality, and his full personality. People bring into the organization perspectives derived from outside experience and cognitive construction, but they also bring back into their private lives the cognitive formation, or deformation, that they undergo within an organization. Outside perspectives yield a source of variety within the firm, which can cause innovation as well as coordination problems (March, 1991). Inside perspectives can be a source of both enrichment and stress in personal life. Psychological stress imposed by organizations is related to the Marxian notion of 'alienation' (Scott, 1992). Seeman (1959) recognized six forms of alienation: lack of control, incomprehensibility, socially unapproved means to achieve goals, violation of values and norms, intrinsically unrewarding activities, and sense of exclusion or rejection (Scott, 1992: 321). In other words, while focus is a tool of organizational efficiency, it is not necessarily humane or psychologically beneficial. So, an important question is how far organizational focus reaches in affecting people and their actions.

The content and extent of cognitive alignment may vary. In addition to the distinction between the competence and governance sides of focus, there are five dimensions for both. First, there is width, that is the range of different activities or areas of competence and governance to which focus applies. This depends on the range of capabilities that a firm encompasses. Second, there is reach, that is the number of aspects within each area covered by the focus. Does it cover all or only some key aspects of a given capability? A third dimension is tightness versus looseness, that is narrowness of tolerance levels of standards or rules imposed by focus, versus allowance for improvised, unforeseen meanings, actions, and so on.

Fourth, focus may have different content. In particular, on the governance side, there may be formal, that is depersonalized, norms of legitimacy, which regulate what managers and workers can do and can expect from each other. Such formal norms render relations more impersonal and thereby reduce tensions associated with the exercise of personal power, and they enlist workers' participation in the control of their colleagues (Scott, 1992: 306). The content of focus may also be more cultural, in the sense of offering guidance by more emotion-laden underlying values, expressed in symbolic entities, behaviours, events or processes. The two types of content are related, since norms of legitimacy may be expressed culturally, but can nevertheless be distinguished. One can have norms of legitimacy that are specified rigorously and formally, and one can have more informal, ambiguous, cultural features that do not express norms of legitimacy. The cultural side of focus will be discussed in more detail later.

Fifth, focus may relate to surface regulations concerning specific actions or to underlying more fundamental notions, in a deep structure of logic, principles, convictions or cognitive categories that form the basis for surface regulation. Simon (1976) already acknowledged that an organization controls not decisions but their premises. Nelson and Winter (1982) made a similar distinction, between routines and 'meta-routines' that guide the development of routines. As already indicated, Mintzberg (1989) allowed for 'missionary' organizations. Schein (1985) made a similar distinction in organizational culture. Below surface features such as specific rules, practices, symbols, myths, rituals, at the basis of organizational culture lie fundamental views and intuitions regarding the relation between the firm and its environment ('locus of control': is the firm master or victim of its environment), attitude to risk, the nature of knowledge (objective or constructed), the nature of man (loyal and trustworthy or self-interested and opportunistic), the position of man (individualistic or part of a community), and relations between people (rivalrous or collaborative), which inform content and process of strategy, organizational structure, and styles of decision-making and coordination. Schein also allowed for an intermediate level, connecting the fundamental cognitive categories with the surface level of specific structures and rules, in the form of general principles that express fundamental cognitive categories but are yet general and generic rather than specific to certain activities and contexts.

The difference between activities, surface regulation and deep structure is schematically illustrated in Figure 3.2. Here, for simplicity of exposition the intermediate level is left out. A given surface regulation enables a bundle of potential actions. An underlying cognitive category in deep level structure enables a bundle of surface level regulation. The establishment of coordination on the surface level (routines, if one wants to use that term) leaves freedom for a variety of underlying cognitive categories, but has to be set up ad hoc each time, and requires the solution of complications due to differences in underlying cognition. The establishment of coordination on the deep level yields more ex ante agreement for setting up surface regulation, and thus enhances speed of action, but it reduces variety of cognition on the deep level. It entails more indoctrination and thereby is more invasive, impinging on a deeper, more emotion-laden level and a wider range of the life world of people. Deep level coordination takes more time to develop, and hence also to change, and more time for people to socialize into when they join the organization. I will argue that organizations serve especially to coordinate on the deep level, with an advantage of easier and faster understanding and agreement and the disadvantage of less cognitive variety, while collaboration between organizations operates more on the surface level, with the advantage of greater variety on the deep level and the disadvantage of more limited or slower agreement.

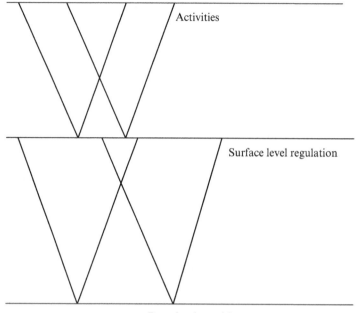

Activities

Surface level regulation

Deep level cognitive structure

Figure 3.2   Levels of coordination

Later, I will employ the notion of 'cognitive distance' (Nooteboom, 1992, 1999), and I will make a distinction between reducing and crossing cognitive distance. Reducing cognitive distance entails alignment on the deep level of cognition, so that people think more similarly. Crossing cognitive distance is making surface agreements while maintaining differences on the deep level, with people continuing to think differently. Reducing cognitive distance is equalization of capability, crossing it is connecting capabilities. When people who think differently continue interaction, starting from surface agreements, they may in time come to think more similarly, that is share underlying cognition, in a reduction of cognitive distance. Connecting capabilities may lead to sharing them. In sum, organizations need to limit cognitive distance to a greater or lesser extent by means of organizational cognitive focus. Focus is stronger, imposing more limits on cognitive variety, to the extent that it has more width, is more far-reaching, tighter and deeper.

Examples
On the competence side of organizational focus, surface regulations may be codified standards, in the form of definitions, formulae, standard operating

procedures, 'performance programs' (March and Simon, 1958), manuals, blueprints, job descriptions, or, when knowledge is more tacit, training programmes to develop tacit understanding from shared practice. In the deep structure it may be basic notions of process or structure, knowledge, action, the relation between the two, principles of mathematics, physics, and so on. On the intermediate level it may be more specific but still general principles of organization or design, such as parallel versus sequential processing, simultaneous or sequential design and implementation, degree of systemic integration versus decomposition, principles of planning-push or demand-pull in production, and so on.

An example is the basic 'Fordist' notion of a production system oriented towards high volume, mass production of standard products, on the basis of a 'push' principle. Here, production is planned on the basis of demand forecasts, and resulting production schedules are handed down in a hierarchy of planning and execution, and production takes place in isolated steps of specialized work, with stocks as buffers between them. The basic underlying cognitive categories are those of hierarchy, centralized planning, a whole as designed from separate parts, efficiency as economy of scale and specialization, and individuality of action and work. By contrast, consider the Toyota system, oriented towards small volume production of differentiated products, on the basis of a 'pull' system (Coriat, 2002). Here, volume and configuration of production are guided by demand, in teams of workers jointly responsible for an integrated whole of quality, scheduling and execution of tasks, seen as an integrated flow of activities, without stocks between steps in the sequence, in 'just in time' production, de-specialization and integration of skills. The basic underlying cognitive categories are those of work as a collective, not individual activity, the whole as a flow between connected parts, efficiency as economy of time and flow, and work as an integration of skills.

On the governance side, surface regulations may be labour contracts, incentive schemes, reporting and evaluation procedures, labour conditions, hiring/firing and career policies. In the deep structure it may be underlying, more fundamental norms and values of conduct, concerning trust, loyalty, commitment, intrinsic or extrinsic motivation, reciprocity, consensus versus command and control, individuality or collectivity, hierarchy or autonomy, rivalry or mutual support, ambition or quality of life, and so on. On the intermediate level we find structural principles of (de)centralization, levels of hierarchy, density of connections, centrality of positions, and so on. and procedural principles of authority sharing, accountability and control, communication, decision making, and so on, and human resource principles such as lifetime versus ad hoc employment, specialization versus integration of skills, and segmentation versus integration of tasks. Note again that while surface regulation allows for variety on the deep level, regulation on the deep level entails more ideology and indoctrination, especially in regulation on the governance side. The more fundamental, durable, generic elements of focus, in organizational culture, constitute the core of organizational identity.

This is the view of organization as a system for 'sense-making' (Weick, 1995), 'collective mind' (Weick and Roberts, 1993), system of 'shared meanings' (Smircich, 1983).

Derived Properties

One property of focus that derives from its basic dimensions is cohesiveness of focus, which increases with the number of activities or capabilities that fall under the focus (width), the extent to which each activity or capability is regulated (reach), and the tightness of regulation. Cohesiveness denotes the extent to which people are tied together under the focus. Inclusiveness of focus denotes the extent to which an individual is tied up in the focus. It relates to the range of people's life world covered by organizational focus. It increases with the extent that people are involved in more activities in the firm, have more roles, contribute more capabilities, each falling under the focus (width), with greater reach, greater tightness and greater depth (yielding greater indoctrination). Organizations have a strong culture to the extent that it is more inclusive, that is more cohesive and deeper. In other words, whatever people do in the organization (whether they have few or many roles), it is regulated with great reach, tightness, and depth.

With the dimensions of organizational focus we can be more precise about the contrast between firms and markets. Markets yield cognitive restrictions that are less inclusive, that is minimum width, reach, tightness and depth of focus, in both competence and governance. That would be impossible to coordinate, in central planning, and when tried would yield stagnation: the fixing of ideas, meanings, standards, division of labour to maintain exploitation would disastrously limit the scope for exploration. That, not complications of planning, caused the downfall of central planning.[3]

The notion of inclusiveness of focus connects with the distinction, mentioned earlier, that Simmel (1950 [1917]) made between a person's function in an organization, which takes up only part of his personality, and his full personality, and Ring and van de Ven's (1994) distinction between roles that people play in organizations and behaviour 'qua persona'. In an inclusive focus, role and persona get closer. Variety among people is constrained, in small cognitive distance. Extremes of this are found in cliques, and especially in clandestine, secluded or secret societies (Simmel 1950

[1917]: 345–76). Outside freedom, to engage in external relationships, is constrained by high inclusiveness of organizational focus, with few dimensions of the life world left that are not in some way already regulated within the group. Inside freedom is constrained by the tightness of focus, with little room to deviate from narrow norms. Both inside and outside sources of variety, and hence of innovation, are highly constrained.

Under an inclusive focus, tightness may become self-imposed. When high inclusiveness forms an obstacle to outside relationships, and people are cut off from sources of fresh or different ideas, they will tend to gravitate towards meanings shared inside the organization, which increases tightness, not because it is imposed by focus, but because it emerges from decreasing cognitive distance. Thus inclusiveness and tightness together tend to reinforce themselves.

Using the notion of cognitive focus, I now return to the core issue of this book: what is the role of organizations?

The Role of Organizations

If capabilities are connected between A and B, and between B and C, and not between A and C, there is a need for A and B to have some cognition in common, and for B and C, but there may be no need for A and C to have anything in common. This situation may arise in sequential interdependence (Thompson, 1967). Under pooled interdependence (ibid.), B, C and D may all share a common resource A, as a resource they tap from, or a resource they contribute to, in a 'star' or 'hub and spokes' configuration. Here they must all have some cognition in common with A, but not necessarily with each other.

Mintzberg (1979) argued that firms face two fundamental and opposing requirements: division of labour and coordination. The classical function of organization is to pool and coordinate differentiated activities that are technically related, to profit from economies of scale, scope or time, to the extent that they are inseparable, that is cannot without great loss of efficiency be spread across separate organizations. Since this is well-trodden ground, these considerations are not discussed here, but summarized in Appendix 3.1. It is also fairly clear that there is little argument to pool completely unrelated and unconnected activities or capabilities within a firm. So, the question is how far one should go in combining different but complementary activities or capabilities within a firm, rather than connecting them between firms.

This is the classic question, ever since transaction cost economics, of why the firm exists as an organization that integrates different activities or capabilities. Why not have autonomous, independent capabilities, and set up sufficient mutual understanding and agreement between them ad hoc, only when the need arises?

One reason for integration in a firm is technical complexity and systemic coherence. A system of production is systemic or complex to the extent that there are (1) many components that are (2) densely connected, in ties of complementarity that are strong in the sense that connections concern a wide range (3) of actions with (4) narrow tolerances on interfaces in order to preserve systemic coherence. As a consequence, in a complex system a small local change, in some component, may trigger multiple changes elsewhere, reverberating through the system, to yield a very different systemic configuration.

This well-known principle from systems theory has been revived in recent literature (Teece, 1986; Langlois and Robertson, 1995; Levinthal, 2000; Postrel, 2002) because of its importance for the stability of organizational systems and for differences between firms within an industry. I will return to this later. Transaction cost economics recognized technological inseparability (Williamson, 1975) as a reason to integrate activities within a firm. Skinning an animal for leather cannot be separated from skinning the same animal for meat. It takes two hands to clap and two people to move furniture. However, Transaction cost economics has neglected the systemic coherence indicated here.

More systemic coherence requires more cohesiveness of focus. A greater number of components requires greater width of focus, a wider range of interaction requires a greater reach of focus, and narrower tolerances require greater tightness of focus. A less cohesive focus, in a de-coupled system, may yield loss of efficiency, but has dynamic advantages. It facilitates the outsourcing of components and the keeping of only components that include the organization's core capabilities and complementary resources that are inseparable from them. It increases the scope and variety of possible linkages, and greater flexibility in the configuration of activities or capabilities. One form of decoupling is modularization, that is by re-composing the system in components with a one-to-one correspondence with function and/or capability, and with standards on the interfaces between component activities (see Langlois and Robertson, 1995).

A second point to be considered here is derived from the notion of specific investments from TCE (transaction cost economics). If the set-up of sufficient cognitive alignment constitutes a specific investment, which cannot be used in other linkages, it is only efficient to make it under the prospect of sufficient duration or intensity of utilization to recoup the specific investment. Especially when the knowledge involved is tacit, the building of understanding takes time, in shared practice, and it is likely to be fairly specific to the linkage involved. This has an implication for the durability of linkages, but not yet for a durable combination of different capabilities within an organization. Collaborative relationships that are sufficiently durable to build up and utilize mutual understanding may also be achieved between rather than only within organizations (Nooteboom, 1999a).

A third, more crucial, cognitive argument for integration of capabilities within an organization derives from Schumpeter. Novel entrepreneurial ideas typically do not make sense in an established institutional order of dominant ideas, routines, recipes, logics and practices, in an industry (Spender, 1989; Bettis and Prahalad, 1995). Here, organization yields a sheltered niche for deviance of ideas that cannot be traded or connected outside, due to lack of comprehension, and need to be configured within the organization, on the basis of entrepreneurial vision and charisma to inspire followers.

A fourth point for organization, which applies also to established firms, is the following. The whole point of moving from specific activities to more generic capabilities, derived from Penrose, and indicated above, was to obtain more scope for novel activities, in novel uses of capabilities, and thereby have more flexibility to respond to increasingly rapid changes of threat and opportunity, in technology and markets. Now novel utilization of capabilities and the new configurations of capabilities to which this is likely to lead require renewed investment in mutual understanding and ability to collaborate, if that was not already in place. That, however, takes time, particularly when the knowledge involved is more tacit. As a result, to maintain scope and flexibility for novel utilization, and hence novel combinations of capabilities, it pays to have a further reaching, more cohesive scope of mutual understanding, and ability and willingness to collaborate, already in place, beyond linkages that are currently operational. This is an argument of speed and flexibility. To warrant and utilize such wider sharing of cognition, across not only actual but also potential, unpredictable new linkages, plus the need for a certain duration to achieve and utilize the investment involved, yields an argument for organization, with a range of capabilities that are more tightly and durably aligned by organizational cognitive focus. For the more ad hoc investment in linkages as the need or opportunity arises, organizations can employ inter-organizational alliances.

The cognitive argument for organization can be further sharpened with an analysis of the depth of cognitive focus. For the same reason that a focus on capabilities (Penrose: resources) yields more scope and flexibility of activities (Penrose: services from resources) than a focus on specific activities, cognitive alignment in deep structure rather than in surface regulation is more generative and flexible, yielding a wider scope of capabilities. This was illustrated in Figure 3.1. To use a metaphor, fundamental mental categories are like the roots of a tree, largely invisible in the subconscious, capabilities are like the branches, and activities are like leaves and blossoms that appear and die off. Deep level cohesiveness is more tacit than surface level rules, and hence requires more time to develop, and more time for incoming staff to adapt to, and is more specific, requiring longer term relationships to recoup the investment, and therefore is more a feature of organizations than of inter-organizational relationships that, on the whole, tend to be less durable, less cohesive and more superficially coordinated.

There is another reason for coordination on a deep level, especially on the governance side. That lies in the condition, noted already in the introductory chapter (Chapter 1), that work has become increasingly knowledge intensive, professional, and abstract, and thereby more difficult for management to monitor and evaluate, let alone measure. This makes rule- and contract based control more difficult, and creates an advantage for more intrinsic motivation that requires less monitoring and control, on the basis of underlying values of conduct, or bonds of empathy, or even identification, and routinization, that require more time to develop and more cohesion to function (Nooteboom, 2002).

A more cohesive, and even a more inclusive, focus may also cater to the social need of people to have a sense of belonging. As I will argue later, using insights from Simmel (1950), it may also be needed to raise the goals of people to levels higher than basic gratification. They do, however, have a downside, in organizational myopia, group think, limited scope for creativity, and lack of freedom, possibly subjugation, or even a form of serfdom.

In sum, the most fundamental function of organizations, in contrast with inter-organizational relations, is to provide a focus with greater width and greater depth, for the sake of coordination that can quickly shift to novel patterns of activity, and for motivation that is more intrinsic. A cognitively and culturally more cohesive group, within an organization, can more quickly alter patterns of collaboration that lie within its potential. Less cohesive inter-firm collaboration, with more cognitive variety, has a wider scope of potential novelty, but requires more time, in setting up surface regulation, to utilize opportunities. I propose, and will later argue in more detail, that this consideration yields boundaries of the firm and limits to firm size also in the long term. I will argue that as the range of capabilities to be coordinated increases, the resulting increase in width of focus entails an increase of reach and depth of focus, and that this increase of cohesiveness or even inclusiveness increasingly limits the cognitive variety and flexibility needed for ongoing innovation by novel combinations.

An example
For an example of an organization that is not a firm, consider universities. In terms of the present analysis, a university may be characterized as

follows. Its scope of activities and capabilities is prescribed and constrained by public regulation concerning educational programmes and accreditation, budgets, and conditions for academic qualifications. Apart from those surface regulations, there is preciously little regulation on the deep level of cognition, with scholars operating from a wide variety of disciplines, schools of thought, paradigms, criteria of good science, standards of excellence, attitudes to collaboration, language, and styles of conduct and communication. Alignment is restricted to elementary ethical principles to make results from research public, and not to cheat or engage in plagiarism. Those have an external function of legitimation rather than an internal function of coordination. In that sense, a university is a weak organization. Such lack of cognitive alignment is needed to allow for the cognitive variety needed for invention, but yields great effort, with a great deal of conflict, in setting up surface regulation for collaboration when the need or opportunity arises.

Universities form a paradigm case of the difficulty to monitor, evaluate and command activities, due to high levels of idiosyncratic professionalism, requiring a high degree of intrinsic motivation. That would plead for deep level governance, on the basis of shared ideals, but that is difficult to square with the limited cognitive alignment that is needed for invention. That sums up the drama of universities.

FOCUS AND CULTURE

Having stated my core argument, I now proceed to develop it in more detail. This section gives a further elaboration of the purpose of organizational cognitive focus, and the cultural content of focus in terms of symbols and role models. Here, the discussion is primarily about culture in the anthropological sense of the totality of norms and values developed in a certain group, second in the sociological sense of the habits and lifestyles that distinguish a group, and third in the sense of the stock of documented or otherwise embodied achievements from the history of an organization as a civilization: artefacts, documents, designs, decorations, myths, rituals and symbols.

Selection, Adaptation and Higher Goals

Next to intellectual coordination and coordination of goals, organizational focus also has functions of selection and adaptation. In selection, it selects people, in recruitment and often on the basis of self-selection of personnel joining the organization because they feel affinity with it. In adaptation, organizational focus socializes incoming personnel, with initiation, and focuses their capabilities, in training.

Cognitive focus is needed not only to align cognition, to some extent, but also to raise goals to a higher level than basic needs and instincts, consistent with, and supporting the goal of the organization. The logic for this is derived from the sociologist Simmel (1950 [1917]).

Simmel (1950 [1917]) and Maslow (1954) proposed that people have different levels of needs, motives and cognitive make-up, where lower level needs must be satisfied before higher levels can come into play (the principle of 'prepotency'), and people are more alike on deeper than on higher levels. In the classic categorization of Maslow, on the deepest level we find the most instinctive, automatic, unreflected and difficult to control drives of bodily physiology, such as hunger and sexual appetite, which are highly similar between different people. Next, we find needs of shelter, safety and protection. Next, love and affection. Next, social recognition, esteem and legitimation. Finally, on the highest level, individual expression and self-actualization. Higher levels are more idiosyncratic, and hence show greater variety between people, than lower levels.

While there is some empirical evidence for a hierarchy of needs (Hagerty, 1999), especially the principle of pre-potency is far from accurate. The 'higher level' need for esteem and self-actualization can lead people to make great sacrifices on the 'lower levels' of safety, shelter and food. Man has a strong, basic, and perhaps even instinctive drive, it appears, towards metaphysics, as exhibited in the form of religious rituals of burial in the earliest forms of Homo sapiens sapiens. That may even be part of the characterization of our species, in distinction with earlier hominoids. Also, while people may have the same needs on the physiological level of food and sex, the foods and behaviours they choose in order to satisfy those needs vary greatly. Apparently, higher levels find their expression in a variety of ways of satisfying needs on lower levels, in different 'life styles'.

Nevertheless, in spite of these qualifications and additions, it still seems true that there are different levels of needs and motives, and that people are similar on lower levels of more basic needs, perhaps including spiritual ones, and more varied on higher levels of more sophisticated needs. This connects with the notion of cognitive distance. If people make sense of the world on the basis of mental categories that are constructed from interaction with the world, they see and interpret the world differently to the extent that they have developed their cognition along different life paths. Cognition is similar to the extent that the corresponding phenomena are similar, as in mechanics subject to laws of nature, in object-oriented cognition, and is more different in cultural and social life, and in cognition oriented at abstractions.[4]

Simmel (1950 [1917]) proposed that, as a result, in a randomly composed group of people, what people have in common resides on lower, more basic, unreflected levels of needs and object-oriented cognition as the size of the group increases. What random masses have in common is basic needs and instincts. He also proposed that the larger and more heterogeneous the group, the more norms and rules of conduct for the group are negative, indicating what is forbidden or undesirable, rather than positive, indicating goals and actions to achieve them. The underlying principle of logic is similar to the principle that a theory (with universal propositions) can be falsified but not verified. It is easier to specify what has been found to be false (in the current context: impermissible) than to specify all that may be possible (here: desirable). To specify what is forbidden entails freedom to do what is not forbidden, while to specify what may be done is either partial, leaving options open, and is then not very functional, or it forbids what is not specified, and then is inherently conservative.

In sum, next to alignment of cognition, organizational focus may be needed to raise shared goals to levels higher than instinctive needs. However, such goals are specialized to the organization, and hence have a narrow scope. The good thing about that is that it limits the indoctrination of people in the organization, and leaves room for diversity. However, according to Coleman (1974, quoted in Scott 1992: 338), corporate actors, with their narrower goals, increasingly dominate society, and crowd out the non-organized interests of people. This has an effect of cultural, and perhaps also political, impoverishment.

Symbols

As indicated earlier, specific instruments of organization, such as procedures for reporting, decision making, recruitment, contracting and the like, need not be part of organizational focus but are guided by it in terms of underlying principles of responsibility, accountability, openness, formality or informality, degree of specification (reach), tightness or looseness and so on. Since deep level cognitive categories are highly abstract and tacit, they need to be reflected in some visible, symbolic form, such as iconic symbols, symbolic behaviour or rituals, to guide their use in the formation of more specific principles or regulations. For people to share cognition, in the wide sense employed in this book, mental categories need expression in language or other signs. Organizational culture, with its symbols, heroes, myths and rituals, aims to represent and engender a certain style of behaviour (Simmel 1950 [1917]: 341) whereby the individual becomes part of a collective intentionality. For both the internal functions of coordination and adaptation, with expression, crystallization, stabilization and direction of meanings, and the external function of setting up and maintaining image and legitimation, and the selection of staff, we find symbols such as logos, 'mission statements', advertisement and external reporting.[5]

Some tangible form is also needed to stabilize the mental processes underlying organizational focus. As such, organizational focus has the same function as the body has for individual cognitive identity. In the theory of embodied cognition (see Chapter 2, and, in particular, Damasio, 2003) it has been recognized that cognition, driven by multiple feelings, is diverse and volatile, and often limitedly coherent, and lacks a clearly identifiable, stable, mental identity of the ego, and that such identity, insofar as it can be grasped, is due, in large part, to the body as a coherent source of feelings and their underlying physiology. Similarly, cognitive activities in an organization require some embodiment to crystallize, direct and stabilize cognition and communication.

On the governance side, differences in focus are associated with different foundations of reliability. As discussed earlier, reliability may be based more on control by legal or hierarchical coercion, incentives and punishments, in short 'deterrence' (Maguire et al., 2001), or more on trust, going beyond control and calculative self-interest, with more intrinsic motivations from internalized values of conduct, in a striving for social belonging and legitimacy, or the building of empathy, identification or comradeship (Nooteboom, 2002). In the latter, the exercise of 'voice' (Hirschman, 1970) and openness (Zand, 1972) are crucial. However, as also discussed, since both trust and control have their limits, they are as much complements as substitutes (Klein Woolthuis et al., 2005), and the question is what mix of the two is taken.

This is related to the idea, indicated in Chapter 2, that people have multiple mental frames, such as a frame of guarding one's interest and a frame of legitimacy or solidarity, between which people may vacillate and shift, depending on how they interpret 'relational signals'. Social psychology yields a basis for a much deeper analysis of this, and of corresponding decision heuristics (Bazerman, 1998). Such deeper analysis yields a typology of 'trust building actions' (Six and Nooteboom, 2010). Organizational focus may be oriented more towards a self-interested mental frame or more towards a solidarity frame. It may favour some types of trust-building actions more than others.

For an illustration of how focus may stimulate trust, I take an example from Six's (2005) study of processes of building and breaking trust within two commercial service organizations. For one of the two organizations, part of the cognitive focus supporting a normative order, aimed at building and maintaining trust, was the precept that 'we don't talk about people but to them'. This aims to avoid malicious gossip and to further the 'voice' and openness that are conducive to trust building, in allowing people to defend and explain their behaviour before mutual suspicion escalates in avoidance and 'exit'.

Exemplars

As noted before, the multiple causal factors in production systems, indicated earlier, may be seen in terms of multiple Aristotelian causality, with a final cause (goals), efficient cause (actions), material cause (means), formal cause (know-how) and conditional cause (external conditions). Aristotle also recognized an exemplary cause, which serves as a model to be emulated. This may be part of cognitive focus. Note that the original meaning of 'paradigm' is 'exemplar' to be followed. An example is Adam Smith's famous illustration of a pin factory as an exemplar of economy of scale by division of labour, with different people specializing in different stages of producing a pin. This notion of exemplar is useful for several reasons.

A deep reason from cognitive theory was discussed in Chapter 2. Often, it is not possible to specify clear, canonical, necessary and sufficient, context-independent definitions or conditions for goals, actions, means, know-how and coordination between them. Often, what works arises from practice and can only be specified incompletely. This has been recognized in the literature on communities of practice (for example Brown and Duguid, 2001). It is also consistent with the discussion of the role of prototypes in the theory of meaning, and with the inevitability of some degree of tacitness of knowledge, discussed in Chapter 2. It suggests that managerial direction often consists of setting an example, or role model, rather than forms of coordination by the rigorous specification of inputs, outputs, processes or skills (Mintzberg, 1983). This has the advantage of a greater potential for conveying tacit knowledge and allowing for greater variety of interpretation in emulation. Thus, exemplary behaviour forms an important part of symbolic behaviour.

A second reason why the notion of exemplary cause is useful is that it may be seen to appear in the phenomenon whereby in industries dominant designs in technology and organizations are widely adopted as an 'industry recipe' (Spender, 1989) or 'dominant logic' (Bettis and Prahalad, 1995), leading to 'isomorphism' (DiMaggio and Powell, 1983), with organizations conforming to dominant designs. Strategically this may not be wise, since, as economics teaches us, there is less profit to be made in pure price competition between identical activities than in differentiated activities based on unique capabilities that are not easily imitated. On the other hand, conformance does yield more certainty, efficiency and legitimation.

COGNITIVE DISTANCE

For many, a theory does not become respectable until it is developed into formal models. And indeed, while a price is paid in loss of realistic detail, abstraction into models increases analytical grip and ability to rigorously derive implications. Therefore, the basic idea of organizational focus is now formalized in terms of the notion of cognitive distance (Nooteboom, 1999) and optimal distance. The less mathematically inclined reader can skip the formulae and read only the words.

Origins, Problems and Advantages of Cognitive Distance

Nothing in the definition of organizations, given earlier, requires that a firm or organization exist of more than a single person. It allows for single-person, owner-manager firms. Those also face problems of coordination between goals, actions, means, know-how and environmental demands and constraints, and the need for focus to deal with them. However, additional problems of coordination arise when there are more people in the organization, in particular problems of cognitive coordination.[6]

The constructivist theory of cognition set out in Chapter 2 implies that people who have developed their cognition along different life trajectories, in different environments, will, to a greater or lesser extent, see, interpret, understand and evaluate the world differently. This yields the notion of cognitive distance (Nooteboom, 1992, 1999).

As in modern times people have increasingly become footloose, travelling more often and further away, constructing their cognition in life trajectories that traverse not only physical space but also cyberspace, on the Internet, locally cognitive distance is likely to increase, and inter-locally it is likely to decrease.

In a modified form, cognitive distance also applies at the higher aggregation level of organizations, if we then define it as difference in organizational focus, that is differences in shared knowledge, language, meanings, perceptions, understandings and values and norms of behaviour.

Cognitive distance, whether on the individual or organizational level, is not amenable to any simple, one-dimensional measure of distance, since cognition has many dimensions, including both rational and emotion-based inference, judgement and decision making, as specified in social psychology, and briefly set out in Chapter 2. In particular, cognition has dimensions related to understanding and dimensions related to moral judgement, which interact but can be distinguished conceptually. In spite of this multi-dimensionality, measurement of cognitive distance is possible.

In empirical work, proxy measures of the cognitive distance between firms have been constructed on the basis of indicators from organizational data and technological profiles derived from patent data, and distance was calculated in terms of correlation between profiles (Wuyts et al., 2005; Nooteboom et al., 2007). An alternative is to locate technological position in a multi-dimensional space of characteristics, and calculate the Euclidean distance between them. However, depending on the context, distance in some dimensions of knowledge may matter more than in other dimensions. Here, there is room and a requirement for further elaboration, and for a consideration of alternative measures.

According to the principle of cognitive construction, cognition between people is similar to the extent that the corresponding phenomena on the basis of which cognition is constructed are similar, as in mechanics and other phenomena subject to laws of nature, and is more different in abstractions and in cultural and social life. This is related to the idea that for cognition people construct metaphors, which for more abstract thought are derived from more concrete, bodily, material experience with objects (Lakoff and Johnson, 1980), indicated in Chapter 2.

For collaboration between people, cognitive distance is both a problem and an opportunity. The problem is that with increasing distance the ability of people to collaborate, intellectually and behaviourally or morally, is less, which hinders effective and efficient collaboration. Ability to collaborate intellectually is close, but not identical, to the notion of absorptive capacity (Cohen and Levinthal, 1990). It entails not only the ability to absorb and make sense of what others do and say, but also, in opposite direction, the rhetorical ability to help others absorb what one does or says oneself, by the use of apt illustrations, examples or metaphor. The opportunity of cognitive distance is that it offers options for new knowledge and perspectives.

Now, if ability to collaborate declines, say linearly, with cognitive distance, and the innovative value of collaboration increases, say linearly, and the performance of collaboration depends on the interaction of ability and value of collaboration, say as the mathematical product of the two, then performance is an inverse U-shaped function of distance, as illustrated in Figure 3.3 (Nooteboom, 1999). If one interprets ability to collaborate as the probability to reap the value of collaboration, then the product of ability and value can be interpreted as the expected value of collaboration. This implies an optimal cognitive distance: large enough to yield value from complementarity but not too large for mutual understanding and agreement. This formalizes the earlier claim that the core problem of organization lies in a trade-off between the novelty value of cognitive variety and the need for some cognitive coherence to utilize the potential of novelty.

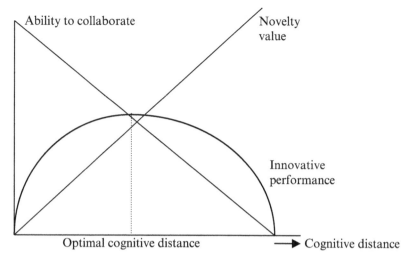

Figure 3.3   Optimal cognitive distance

The mathematical specification of the model is as follows:

The downward sloping line for ability to collaborate (A):

$$A = a_1 - a_2.CD, \qquad a_1, a_2 > 0 \qquad (3.1)$$

where *CD* is cognitive distance.

The upward sloping line for value (N):

$$N = b_1 + b_2.CD \qquad b_1, b_2 > 0 \qquad (3.2)$$

Multiplying Equations (3.1) and (3.2) results in the performance (L):

$$L = A.N = a_1.b_1 + (a_1.b_2 - b_1.a_2).CD - a_2.b_2.CD^2 \qquad (3.3)$$

If $a_1.b_2 - b_1.a_2 > 0$, this yields a parabolic, inverse U-shaped function of cognitive distance, with some optimal level of distance.

From Equation (3.3) it follows that optimal cognitive distance (*CD**) is:

$$CD^* = (a_1.b_2 - b_1.a_2)/2\,a_2.b_2 = \tfrac{1}{2}(a_1/a_2 - b_1/b_2) \qquad (3.4)$$

And corresponding optimal performance (*L**) is:

$$L^* = a_1.b_1 + (a_1.b_2 - b_1.a_2)^2/4a_2.b_2 \qquad (3.5)$$

From Equation (3.4) it follows that for optimal distance to be positive, we must again have $a_1.b_2 - b_1.a_2 > 0$.

The analysis implies a difference between reducing and crossing cognitive distance. This is related to the distinction between empathy, as the ability to place oneself in the position of someone who thinks differently, and identification, as thinking in the same way. In terms of the present analysis, reducing cognitive distance entails alignment on the deep level of cognitive categories, while bridging cognitive distance entails surface alignment between different cognitive perspectives, as illustrated in Figure 3.2.

In a refinement of the distance model we could separate competence and governance, as follows. The downward sloping line of collaborative capability would then split into a line for ability to share knowledge (competence), that is absorptive capacity, and a line for ability and willingness to collaborate (governance), and distance would split into distance in knowledge/skills and distance in practices, rules and norms of conduct, or underlying moral values.

Then it is plausible to assume that for governance distance has mostly a negative effect, and little positive effect of novelty value.[7] In other words, the slope of the novelty line (b_2) would be lower than for competence. While it is useful to have different, complementary knowledge, difference in views how to behave in relationships is mostly bothersome. Intuitively, one would expect optimal distance in views on collaboration to be small relative to optimal distance in substantive knowledge. Formally, this follows from formula (3.4): a decrease of b_2 decreases CD^*.

In sum, in this formal analysis, in a static setting of given curves of novelty value and ability to collaborate, an organization serves to optimize cognitive distance. This is achieved by organizational cognitive focus, with its cohesiveness calibrated to achieve optimal distance. However, note that the present analysis applies to any dyad of possible collaboration, while a firm consists of a whole range of possible combinations of capabilities and the people carrying them, within and between organizations, which makes the analysis more complicated, as will be discussed later.

Duration

What is the effect of ongoing collaboration on innovative performance? Familiarity no doubt breeds trust, as Gulati (1995) claimed. However, while trust is certainly good for the ability to collaborate, too much familiarity and trust may reduce variety in competence too much and thereby take out the innovative steam from collaboration. More precisely, cognitive distance will decline, and the curve of performance in Figure 3.3 will

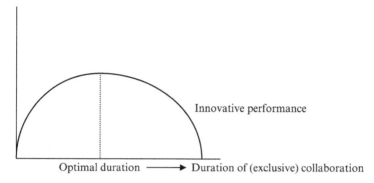

Figure 3.4   Optimal duration

Figure 3.5   Bridging a structural hole

be traversed from right to left, as the duration of exclusive collaboration increases. In other words, surface alignment between cognitively diverse partners may in time lead to more similarity in underlying cognition.

Thus, there is a derived hypothesis of an inverse-U shaped relationship between performance, particularly innovative performance, and the duration of exclusive collaboration. This is illustrated in Figure 3.4. Wuyts et al. (2005) empirically confirmed this for inter-firm collaboration for innovation in the pharmaceutical industry.

Note the qualification that the effect obtains for the duration of collaboration that is exclusive, that is it excludes the contribution from other parties beyond the dyad. To the extent that the partners in the focal relationship also have non-overlapping ties of collaboration with others, their knowledge and competence base may be continually renewed from different sources, maintaining cognitive distance between them. The argument brings us close to the argument of 'structural holes', propounded by Burt (1992), which indicates the value for learning of access to sources of knowledge not accessed by others, by bridging holes in the network of connections between them. This is illustrated in Figure 3.5.

Realism?

How realistic is the notion of optimal cognitive distance? The notion of cognitive distance is realistic in the sense that it has been measured, and the hypothesis of optimal cognitive distance has been tested econometrically, albeit in inter-firm collaboration for innovation rather than intra-firm collaboration (Wuyts et al., 2005; Nooteboom, et al., 2007). How this was done will be discussed in Chapter 4. However, the notion of optimal cognitive distance is hardly realistic in the sense of serving as an instrument for management. As noted, it arises, in different ways, on any interface between people, or between groups such as communities of practice, or between firms. It is not realistic to expect management to be able to reliably measure cognitive distance in competence as well as governance between all relevant pairs of people and communities, let alone identify ability and willingness to collaborate as precise functions of such distance, in order to pinpoint the location of optimal cognitive distance.

Nevertheless, the notion does serve as a useful heuristic device for analysing problems. In lectures and courses for a variety of junior and senior managers, I found that they immediately recognize the dual problem of competence and governance, the need to balance the trade-off between difference for novelty and similarity for ability to collaborate, the need to bring people closer together when collaboration fails, the opposite problem of stagnation when people become too close and work together too long, and the corresponding need to increase variety by rotation or renewal of personnel. They are also very well aware of the need for organizational-level alignment of cognition, in both competence and governance, and the role in that of organizational culture and role models.

The identification of optimal distance occurs more by trial and error, and by an evolutionary process of weeding out unsuccessful collaboration. Managers and workers, among others, can to some extent observe improvements or reductions of performance and goal achievement as a result of more or less alignment, adjust accordingly, and develop a feel for how far and in what way alignment should occur for different purposes under different conditions. This is the customary justification of optimality as a theoretical heuristic device, by an evolutionary argument, not as something that can be calculated, but as something that may arise from trial and error.

In sum, the merit of the notion of optimal cognitive distance lies primarily in its analytical and heuristic use in highlighting and illustrating problems and principles of alignment in a simple, clear and appealing fashion. For practice we must delve into the complexities and uncertainties of what goes on behind the simple notion, in evolutionary processes of adjustment.

Achieving Optimal Cognitive Distance

We can now see an organization, interpreted as a focusing device, as serving the purpose of reducing or increasing cognitive distance to improve results from the coordination of complementary capabilities. Given the wide notion of cognition used in this book, like cognitive distance cognitive focus has a competence and a governance side, and has perceptual, intellectual and normative content. It includes views of how people 'deal with each other around here'. The larger cognitive distance is, the more cumbersome and inefficient it is to achieve mutual understanding on perceptions of the environment, goals and priorities of the firm, relevant technologies, products, markets, actions in jobs and roles, and technical coordination between them, in 'dominant competencies' (McKelvey, 1982), on the competence side, and categories and instruments for alignment of interests, and conflict resolution, in a 'normative order' (Hannan and Freeman, 1977), on the governance side. Without cognitive focus of shared perceptions, meanings, understandings and values, too much effort, time and aggravation would have to be spent to disambiguate meanings, eliminate misunderstanding, set priorities, establish directions, coordinate activities, and negotiate the terms of collaboration.

Note again that the notion of organizational focus does not entail the need for people to agree on everything, or see everything the same way. Indeed, such lack of diversity would preclude both division of labour and innovation within the firm. As indicated earlier, there is a trade-off between cognitive distance, needed for variety and novelty of cognition, and cognitive proximity, needed for mutual understanding and agreement. In fact, different people in a firm will to a greater or lesser extent introduce elements of novelty from their outside lives and experience, and this is a source of both error and innovation (March, 1991; DiMaggio, 1997).

Indeed, distance may be too small, and then the organization would need to widen its focus and increase cognitive distance, by increasing the turnover of personnel, with an increased influx of staff at greater cognitive distance (March, 1991). Yet, to function as a coordinated system of actions, and achieve sufficient focus, with a sufficient limitation of cognitive distance, organizations develop and maintain their own specialized semiotic systems, in language, symbols, metaphors, myths, and rituals as part of organizational culture.

Similarly, Cook and Yanow (1996) also proposed that organizational culture is central to the notion of organizational cognition, in a constellation of intersubjective meanings, beliefs, and values, expressed in language, metaphors, acts, symbols, ceremonies, myths, in other words culture, which satisfy needs for identification but also exert pressures towards conformance. They illustrated their argument with a study of flute makers. This cultural concept of organizations connects with the notions of earlier authors that the fundamental task of organizations is to offer a shared code or language for shared understanding and communication. In economics this was proposed by Arrow (1974). Kogut and Zander (1992) similarly argued that organizations require a common 'code' for the rapid transfer of tacit knowledge within a firm, and for connecting complementary competencies, while protecting it from spillover to competitors. Going further back, it accords with Marshall's view of firms as organizational forms to enable knowledge.

My cognitive, cultural view of organization as a 'focusing device' (Nooteboom, 1999) is also similar to the view of organization as 'missionary' (Mintzberg, 1989), a system of 'shared meanings' (Smircich, 1983), 'sense-making' (Weick, 1995) or 'collective mind' (Weick and Roberts, 1993).

Shifting Ability to Collaborate

In the previous analysis, the model was static in the sense that ability and value of collaboration, analysed as functions of cognitive distance, were taken as given, so that the organization could only reduce or increase distance to achieve its given optimal level. Another possibility to consider is that the organization changes the parameters. One option is to try and shift ability to collaborate upwards, with an increased ability of people to understand and accept, in collaboration, people who see, think and act differently. That is a first type of organizational dynamic capability.

Postrel (2002) asked when communities of practice should invest in knowing about each other, and when they should go their own way. On the face of it, the answer is that they should invest in knowing about each other when activities of different communities are strongly coupled, or, in other words, when activities are 'systemic', and that one should go one's own way when activities are not or only loosely coupled, or 'stand-alone'. Only in the first case it is necessary to mutually adapt activities. Postrel shows that this intuition is not necessarily correct. If by going their own way, and investing only in their own knowledge and skill, specialist communities can extend the scope and flexibility of their activities, then they can thereby achieve fit to whatever other communities do. In terms of the present analysis, they increase their absorptive capacity and ability to collaborate. Nevertheless, even here there are some things they have to agree on, and some views, often tacit, which they need to share, on goals, norms, values, standards, outputs, competencies and ways of doing things, even if those are achieved not by coordination but by an extension

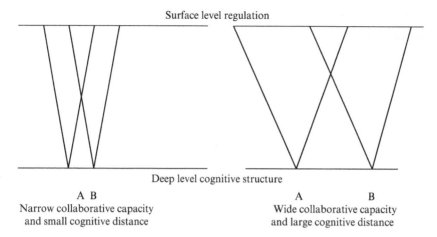

Figure 3.6   *Absorptive and collaborative capacity*

of the scope and flexibility of activities, as shown by Postrel. The question then is how allowance for full variety between communities, with no interference from organizational focus, might ensure that sufficient bridging between them arises? Some connection, in some cognitive proximity, must somehow be ensured, if activities are dependent upon each other. If not, why should those communities be part of the same firm? Penrose also proposed that purely financial holdings can hardly count as firms, for lack of coordination.

Yet, Postrel's point is an important one, and it applies to collaboration within as well as between organizations. An upward shift of ability to collaborate, in competence and governance, allows an organization to cope with more cognitive variety, and to thereby increase innovative capacity, while maintaining the coordination needed to utilize complementarities of competence. Such a shift may be achieved by a greater scope and depth of both intellect and skill, on the competence side, and ability to collaborate, on the governance side, as a result of past learning, either by analysis or by experience. In particular, increased ability to collaborate arises from experience in collaborating with people with different world views, behaviour and morality. Let us call the first competence capital (as an extension of intellectual capital, to include skills) and the latter behavioural capital.[8] An increase of such capital increases optimal cognitive distance and collaborative performance.

The principle is illustrated in Figure 3.6, which is derived from Figure 3.2. Here, an increased absorptive capacity, or ability to collaborate more widely, entails that categories on the deep level of cognition have an increased range of applications, with more opportunities for surface level regulations. With a narrow range, distance between categories of A and B has to be small, in order to create overlap for the sake of coordination, in the left part of the figure. With a wide range, on the right part of the figure, with a wider scope of understanding and ability to collaborate, overlap in surface regulation (crossing cognitive distance) is achieved at greater cognitive distance on the deep level.

In terms of the model in cognitive distance, an upward shift of collaborative ability entails an increase of the intercept (a_1) of the corresponding declining line in Figure 3.3. Suppose that:

$$a_1 = c_1 + c_2.TC, \; c_1, c_2 > 0 \qquad (3.6)$$

where TC is competence and/or behavioural capital accumulated from past learning from collaboration.

Then, from Equation (3.3) we find for collaborative performance:

$$L = c_1.b_1 + c_2.b_1.TC + (c_1.b_2 - b_1.a_2).CD + c_2.b_2.TC.CD - a_2.b_2.CD^2 \qquad (3.7)$$

For optimal cognitive distance, this yields:

$$CD^* = \tfrac{1}{2}(c_1/a_2 - b_1/b_2) + \tfrac{1}{2}(c_2/a_2)TC \qquad (3.8)$$

This shows how optimal cognitive distance increases with competence- and behavioral capital (TC). That yields lasting competitive advantage, in the ability to deal with larger cognitive distance and hence innovate more radically, since that capital takes time to build up and is cumulative.

The effect of the upward shift of ability to collaborate is illustrated in Figure 3.7. Complications arise when two parties have different absorptive capacities or more generally different abilities to collaborate. Let us assume that novelty value as a function of cognitive distance is the same. The party with the lowest ability to collaborate (A) has a lower optimal cognitive distance than the other party (B). The distance at which A can adequately collaborate is too small to be fully interesting for B. This complication may to some extent be resolved if B has the additional capability to 'draw' A out of its limitations. Recall the discussion in Chapter 2 of Vygotsky's 'zone of proximal development' (ZOPED), where a teacher can draw a pupil beyond its solitary ability to learn. This requires didactic and rhetorical skills, such as the clever use of metaphor to shift sense making, and the use of examples or illustrations to trigger understanding. When this fails, one may still seek recourse to

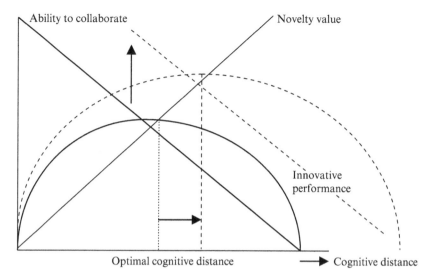

Figure 3.7   Upward shift of ability to collaborate

intermediaries that help cross cognitive distance. They must then have requisite absorptive capacity and experience in cognitive bridge building. This is one of several roles that intermediaries or go-betweens can play, as discussed in Chapter 4.

Decreasing Returns to Knowledge

In inter-firm collaboration for innovation, the inverse-U shaped effect of cognitive distance on innovative performance, in terms of patent production, and the effect of knowledge accumulation on absorptive capacity, as an important part of ability to collaborate, illustrated in Figure 3.6, was tested and confirmed empirically in an econometric study by Nooteboom et al. (2007). Details of the study will be given in Chapter 4. Here I note an unexpected but easy to understand additional effect that was found for knowledge accumulation. In addition to its effect on ability to collaborate, higher knowledge accumulation, yielding a wider scope of technological competence, also yielded a lower slope of the line for novelty value. As illustrated in Figure 3.8, this means that at a higher level of knowledge accumulation, one has to go further afield, at higher cognitive distance, to achieve a given level of novelty, and this effect increases with the level of novelty sought. This can be interpreted as a principle of decreasing returns to knowledge, or as a 'boredom effect': the more one knows, the more one

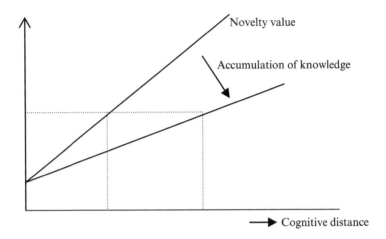

Figure 3.8   Decreasing returns to knowledge

has to seek out exotic, distant sources of knowledge to learn something new.

This effect, when applied to combinations within a firm, has implications for limits to the size of a firm, in decreasing returns to the range of capabilities, as will be shown later.

Focusing on Exploitation, Exploration or Both

A crucial condition for the cohesiveness of focus is whether the organization is oriented mainly towards exploitation, exploration or both (March, 1991). As indicated in the introduction (Chapter 1), depending on characteristics of markets, products and technologies, exploitation requires a certain clarity and stability of goals, standards, meanings, roles, tasks and skills, while exploration requires ambiguity of meanings and break-up of existing standards, roles, tasks and skills. The combination of the two, in the dual structure of an 'ambidextrous' organization (Duncan, 1976), is a paradoxical and arguably the most important task of management. If the exploitation system is systemic, as defined before, it is structurally difficult to combine them (Nooteboom, 2000). Even if it is structurally feasible, the combination in one firm may be difficult in terms of cognitive focus. In other words, the features of focus may depend on the extent to which the organization is oriented towards exploitation, exploration or both, and the extent to which the exploitation system is complex.

Typically, for efficient exploitation, faultless, detailed, fine-tuned collaboration is paramount, with a focus on mutual understanding and ability and

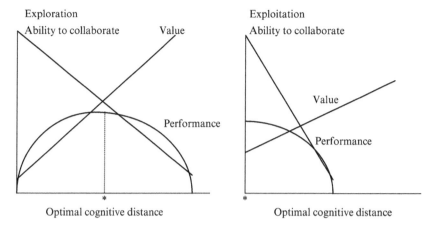

Figure 3.9   Exploitation and exploration

willingness to collaborate, with only moderate innovation, and hence little positive effect of cognitive distance on value (low b_2), and a relatively high level of value at zero cognitive distance (high b_1) and a sharp negative effect on ability to effectively collaborate (high a_2). By contrast, in exploration novelty value is paramount (high b_2), and there is more tolerance of ambiguity and of problems of mutual understanding and agreement (low a_2).

From formulae (3.4) and (3.5) it is obvious that for exploitative collaboration, where b_2 is lower and b_1 and a_2 are higher than for exploration, optimal distance is indeed lower. This is illustrated in Figure 3.9 There, parameters are chosen so that while cognitive distance still yields some value for exploitation ($b_2 > 0$), ability to effectively collaborate declines so sharply with distance, that resulting optimal cognitive distance is zero.

In exploration, optimal cognitive distance being relatively high, organizational focus, being less cohesive, that is having lesser reach and tightness, allows for more differences in cognition. Now, a firm can choose whether to focus on exploitation or on exploration. It can be very difficult to combine the two, with small distance for exploitation and large distance for exploration, in a mixed cognitive focus, but it is not impossible.

There appear to be two ways to design focus so as to combine exploitation and exploration. As indicated earlier, one is to go for a focus more on the deep level of fundamental categories, that allow for variety of capabilities, for both exploitation and exploration. This still leaves the need to translate the deep categories into more surface level coordination, in different ways for sites of exploitation and sites for exploration. Nevertheless, the shared underlying categories will help people from both types of site to understand each other to a greater extent than if they were outsiders, thus helping to develop and maintain connections in communication and exchange of personnel. However, note that such a deeper, more 'invasive' focus does tie personnel on a more fundamental level of cognition, entailing more indoctrination, in that sense, and requiring longer times of socialization of people into the organization, which may reduce the entry and exit of staff, which may in its turn limit variety for the sake of exploration.

An alternative is to try and limit coordination of cognition to where it is least different between exploitation and exploration. That is likely not to be the competence side, and may apply more to the governance side: how to deal with each other, in terms of the bases for intentional reliability (see Table 3.1). While people may then find it difficult to understand each other substantively, at least they trust each other, are sympathetic to each other's differences in substantive perceptions and knowledge, and in priorities, and are therefore willing to develop sufficient understanding for the task at hand. This commonality of behavioural style also facilitates the rotation of personnel between exploitation and exploration. In Chapter 5, in the analysis of dynamic capabilities, a more extensive and systematic discussion will be given of opportunities and problems to combine exploitation and exploration.

Whichever one chooses, exploitation or exploration, one may establish outside relationships for the other activity. The classic example is the drug industry, where typically small, radically innovative small technology based firms do the exploration, in discovering new active substances, and large pharmaceutical companies do the exploitation, in clinical testing, large volume production, and the utilization of distribution channels and brand name. There are many empirical studies that show this (for example Gilsing and Nooteboom, 2005).

However, problems are then likely to arise in the connection between exploitation and exploration, to the extent that exploitation requires the development of a new production process, process knowledge is highly tacit, and there is a close relationship between features of the product and of the process. That applies to a number of cases in biotechnology (Pisano, 2000) and to a large section of the semiconductor industry (Appleyard et al., 2002). In such cases exploitation and exploration may have to be combined in a single organization in spite of the problems involved. This will be taken up in Chapters 4 and 5.

Another complication in combining exploitation and exploration in one firm lies in capital markets. Exploitation attracts more conservative shareholders, aiming for security, while exploration attracts more adventurous shareholders, going for higher risk and profit. In February 2006, the Dutch conglomerate AKZO, combining paints, chemicals and pharmaceuticals, announced that it would hive off its pharmaceutical division for this reason, among others. The pharmaceutical division, being aimed more at innovation, attracted different shareholders from the paints and chemicals division, and it was difficult to satisfy both classes of shareholder in one corporation.

DEVELOPMENT, SIZE AND GROWTH OF THE FIRM

In this section I discuss the origin and stability of organizational focus, differences in the dimensions of focus at different levels or sizes of organization, and the resulting limits to the size and to the growth of the firm.

Origins and Conditions of Focus

I propose that in analogy to the cognitive identity of people in embodied cognition, according to the constructivist, interactionist view of cognition set out in Chapter 2, organizational focus, and the organization as a cognitive system more widely, arises out of the embodiment, in organizational arrangements of meanings, culture, structures and procedures, of outside experience, in an evolutionary process of development, along organization-specific trajectories through their environments. When resources are scarce and competition is tight, selection is likely, in the long run, to yield organizational cognitions and structures that reflect the exigencies of the environment of markets and institutions. Consider, for example, the view that stable environments tend to favour 'mechanistic' environments while turbulent environments tend to favour 'organic' ones (Burns and Stalker, 1961), or more specialist versus more generalist organizations (Hannan and Freeman, 1977).

This view of organizationally embodied cognition helps, I propose, to resolve the issue, identified in the literature on organizational cognition and learning, of whether it is proper to speak of cognition on an organizational rather than only on an individual level (Nooteboom, 1997). As shown by neural science as well as social psychology, the individual is less of a cohesive entity than we have always made out, and is only partly and to some extent only seemingly integrated. He or she is driven by feelings that are often conflicting and that are often given coherence and direction only in post-hoc rationalization. Organizations, on the other hand, are cognitively more cohesive than we have made out, in viewing organizations as mere aggregates of autonomous individuals. Individual cognition is constructed in interaction, in action contexts, and remains embedded, to some extent, in those contexts. What anyone knows, of relevance to the organization, is related to what he does in interaction with others, in that organization. Thus not only cognition on the level of the organization, but also individual cognition is to some extent collective. So, opposite to saying that organizational cognition is an aggregate, somehow, of prior individual cognition, as we were inclined to do in the past, we could now say that individual cognition is conditioned by, and embedded in, organizational cognition.

Organizational focus and cognition start with the imprint of the entrepreneur who started the firm, as a niche to develop his entrepreneurial ideas, protected from an uncomprehending environment, as suggested by Schumpeter. As noted before, this is also in line with Marshall's notion of the firm as an organization to 'make knowledge work'. Initial organizational focus and corresponding culture is maintained, propagated and extended in its utilization for collaboration, and in its use as a device for (self)selection and socialization of incoming staff, and the fact that it forms the environment from which novel cognitive construction takes place. Actions are repeated and given similar meanings by self and others (Berger and Luckmann, 1966), thus perpetuating and reconstructing focus. Actors make evident and persuade each other that the events and activities in which they are involved are coherent and consistent (Burrell and Morgan, 1979: 250, quoted by Scott, 1992: 250).

However, focus is subject to drift, due to interaction between staff, turnover of staff, and to occasional shifts, resulting from crises, caused, in particular, by shifts in the environment, or by new, challenging interpretations of the environment by influential new actors. Also, of course, its existence depends on population effects, in the weeding out by competitive selection.

As discussed before, an important condition for the features of focus is whether the organization engages in exploitation, exploration, or both. This depends on competitive opportunities and pressures, as a function of innovative and market turbulence in the environment, and on strategic choice. In the analysis of optimal cognitive distance, it was shown that for exploration optimal cognitive distance is larger than for exploitation, with a focus with relatively little reach and tightness. What is the difference in the depth of focus, between exploitation and exploration? One might expect that greater cognitive distance, that is less cognitive cohesion, would also entail less invasiveness, that is more surface level elements, yielding more freedom and room for variety and idiosyncracy of deeper level cognitive categories and values. However, a counterargument is that under the greater uncertainty of more radical innovation, focusing may have to be less specific, more generic, and that would suggest a deeper level of more fundamental categories.

Another condition for focus lies in the nature of technologies, skills and knowledge involved. Formal procedures depend on the extent to which knowledge is codifiable rather than tacit. For the sharing of more tacit knowledge, relationships of exchange or collaboration typically need to be longer and more intensive.

An important more formal feature of organizational form is of course legal identity, aimed at securing the interests of different stakeholders. Different forms of legal identity yield different requirements for organizational focus. Legal identity varies with the firm's stakeholders and their interests. Legal identity is needed to regulate ownership and decision rights, liability, contracting, and the like. For example, legal identity shields owners' personal assets from a firm's creditors (in limited liability), and, vice versa, shields a firm's assets from owners' creditors. It enables a market in shares, thus allowing for risk diversification for owners. It facilitates bankruptcy of firms. Here, firms distinguish themselves from organizations more generally. A firm is defined as an organization of capital and labour aimed at profit, in contrast with, for example, a foundation that is not aimed at profit, and where profits are re-absorbed in the organization. A firm with publicly traded shares faces other demands on cognitive focus than a small owner-manager firm.

Finally, focus depends on outside legal and cultural institutional conditions. In particular, what a firm can and needs to do in governance depends on contractual opportunities, norms and values of conduct, intermediaries of many kinds, political conditions, etc. Later, in Chapter 6, I will look in more detail at inter-industry differences in focus.

Stability of Focus

Organizational focus cannot be integrally and instantly re-shaped as a function of experience in competition, and to a greater or lesser extent this yields organizational stability or even inertia (Hannan and Freeman, 1989). Such stability is a well-established empirical phenomenon. In their study of large firms Patel and Pavitt (2000: 317) found that: '90% of firms have profiles of technological competence that are statistically similar between 1969–74 and 1985–90' which 'remains true even after taking account of acquisitions and divestments', and 'of 41 of the largest firms only one had a technological profile statistically different'.

There are several reasons for stability of organizational identity and focus. One reason is systemic. As indicated before, in a complex system, with many tight linkages between components, change in any element may endanger systemic integrity and would then require multiple changes elsewhere in the system to arrive at a new feasible configuration. Hence the more systemic a firm is, the less flexible and the more stable it will be, other things being equal.

A second reason is that cognitive focus yields absorptive capacity that tends to mostly confirm itself in its functioning, in a process of imprinting (Stinchcombe, 1965). Ways of seeing and making inferences yield habits that are relegated to subsidiary awareness, in routinization. However, as will be discussed later, in Chapter 5, there is a process by which absorptive capacity does transform itself in its functioning, so that there is some escape from inertia, in a dynamic capability, but this happens in a series of conditioned steps that require time. It is an empirical question to what extent the speed of that is sufficient to escape from selection pressures of competition.

Cultural identity and cognitive focus are maintained, in spite of turnover and exchange of staff, because in the entry into an organization there is, as noted before, self-selection according to expected fit to organizational culture, as well as adaptation by socialization into organizational culture, in introductory courses, meetings or rituals, and ostracism of those who do not conform. Furthermore, according to the idea of intelligence as internalized action the further development of cognition reflects the environment, in this case the organization, in which it takes place.

Nevertheless, in time firms grow and develop, and in the process focus shifts, certainly in content and communication. As firms develop from their founding, they go through stages of development, with corresponding obstacles (Bennis, 1969; Greiner, 1972). At first, in a new entrepreneurial venture, the entrepreneur participates in shop-floor activities and customer contacts, and coordinates on the basis of direct, personal supervision, in a simple organizational structure (Mintzberg, 1983). In view of this, knowledge does not need to be highly codified. The first and perhaps most salient obstacle arises when due to growth the entrepreneur has to delegate responsibility, withdraw from the shop floor, and organize division of labour, specialized support and staff functions, and codified, formalized, that is de-personalized, procedures of coordination and control across spatially and functionally separated activities. In other words, here the Schumpeterian founding entrepreneur has to become a manager or surrender authority to managers. Many entrepreneurs are unable to make that step, and then the firm may fail or may have to be sold. If the firm survives, then in organizational focus tacit values and uncoded norms may get codified. Direct supervision shifts either to the specification of inputs, processes, outputs, skills, or mission (Mintzberg, 1979, 1983, 1989), or to coordination by means of role models, often reflecting the entrepreneurs past actions, expressed in myths or heroic stories.

Levels of Organization

Generally, organizational focus will be strongest in single-person, owner-manager firms, weaker in work groups, wider yet in larger firms consisting of multiple groups, and weakest in multi-divisional firms, as a function of the diversity of capabilities involved.

In a single-person owner-manager firm, by definition cognitive distance is zero. There, organizational focus is inclusive. Personal life and business are highly interwoven. This arises in finance, with personal or family capital, profits as a source of personal income, and business risk as a personal risk. It often arises in housing, with the firm located at the home. It also arises in the goals of the firm. Focus also tends to be deep, with views and organizational ways and means tied up with fundamental cognitive categories and world views.

Organizational goals are more varied and more personal among independent, typically small firms than in large firms with publicly traded shares, for two reasons (Nooteboom, 1994). First, they have more opportunity for idiosyncratic goals than large firms that have to observe expectations and actions in stock markets, on the basis of short term earnings that determine share price and thereby opportunities for finance and take-over and risks of being taken over. To retain managerial positions and to manoeuvre for better ones, share price and hence profitability need to be closely observed. Small, independent firms, by contrast, with personal, family or bank finance can afford to have more idiosyncratic goals, as long as they pay their debts. Second, people become independent entrepreneurs for a variety of reasons that get reflected in organizational goals (Kets de Vries, 1977; Chell, 1985). They may flee from the authority imposed by employers, seeking self-employment. They may take refuge in self-employment from unemployment due to economic crisis combined with lack of social employment benefits, or discrimination of race, ethnicity or gender in labour markets. They may seek independence as a goal in itself or to achieve the opportunity to implement deviant ideas, satisfy personal preferences concerning niche products, or small-scale production with informal relationships and absence of bureaucracy.

Beyond a single-person organization lie communities of practice (Lave and Wenger, 1991; Brown and Duguid, 1991). It seems that for those width of focus is still limited, with a limited range of capabilities, while reach and perhaps depth of focus are still large, incorporating much of the life world of participants, in rich relationships, and focus may be tight, allowing for little deviance of conduct. However, this is not clear from the literature. The notion of communities of practice is so wide as to allow for a great variety of different kinds of community (Bogenrieder and Nooteboom, 2004).

One type, apparently closest to the original idea of a community of 'practice' (Brown and Duguid, 1991; Lave and Wenger, 1991) is a tight community where people interact on many issues (high reach), on a daily basis, with little ambiguity of meanings (tight), in the execution of a practice. Here, depth and hence invasiveness of focus tends to be large. Another type is that of a community of professionals from different contexts and locations of action, who exchange knowledge, such as scholars at a conference, for example. Here, unless contacts have developed into closer, more personal relationships, focus is strong in width and reach, and not very inclusive, but often tight, with people talking precisely about few things. Other groups can have large width and low tightness, with people talking vaguely about many things, such as practitioners from different practices talking about many aspects of their practice. Strangers typically talk vaguely about few things.

A cohesive group, with small internal distance in many dimensions of cognition, may be very efficient in a static sense, or in exploitation, but inefficient in a dynamic sense, or in exploration. To keep cohesive groups from cognitive inertia, it may be needed to rotate people across them, to keep up variety, that is to maintain some cognitive distance (March, 1991).

The small firm often has a limited range or portfolio of capabilities, yielding a limited range of technologies, products and competencies. The small firm typically coincides with a single community of practice, with its own legal identity, while in large organizations different component communities fall under a single legal umbrella. As a result, small firms are vulnerable, with limited diversification of risks, limited specialization in functions, limited economies of scale and scope, and limited career perspectives. They also have both the potential advantages and disadvantages of a cohesive scope. They often, though not always and not necessarily, have a cohesive focus, in thick and tight, often highly personalized relationships, with limited division of labour. High cohesiveness may also result from the cognitive stamp that the entrepreneur puts on his small organization, where he interacts directly with his personnel. In this way, radically innovative, small firms may isolate themselves and thereby close themselves off from the sources of application and further innovation.

This yields one of several paradoxes of the small firm. On the one hand, small size, with personalized, thick, informal relationships, integration of tasks among few people, and direct contacts, internally and outside, for example with customers, enables high flexibility and motivational power of identification with the firm. On the other hand there is potential for suppression of freedom and variety, and of isolation from the environment (see Nooteboom, 1994).

In larger firms, especially distance in job-related competence is larger, in a wider and deeper division of labour, but distance on the moral side of cognition is not necessarily larger than in a small firm. In fact, since in face-to-face work groups there is more informal, spontaneous social control of free-ridership (Simmel, 1950 [1917]), in the small firm the need for a more explicit moral focus is less. In larger organizations more attention may be needed to the moral dimension of organizational focus across different work communities. A difference in culture between large and small firms lies in the fact that with a more extensive division of labour, with coordination between greater numbers of people across possibly distant organizational units, knowledge and rules need to be codified to a greater extent than in small firms, where coordination can take place by direct supervision (Mintzberg, 1983).

The Multinational Corporation

The multinational corporation (MNC), with its presence of subsidiaries in a variety of countries, presents a special challenge for management and for theoretical explanation. If it is true, as proposed in this book, that the organization is a focusing device, and a cognitive system by embodiment, in organizational arrangements, of experience, then since the different subsidiaries develop their systems in different environments they will develop different cognition, in competence and governance, and this raises questions, and managerial problems, of diversity and conflict. Differentiation of activities and perspectives across subsidiaries and corresponding conflict, in particular between corporate headquarters and subsidiaries, is indeed a central issue in the literature in international business (Ghoshal and Nohria, 1997; Forsgren et al., 2005). Next to cognitive deviation, there are more objective strategic conflicts of interest. There is the familiar tension between on the one hand the drive to maintain corporation-wide standards and processes, for economy of scale, and on the other hand the opportunities for differentiation and innovation by deviating from established standards and processes (Doz, 1986).

According to the view of organizations proposed in this book, and the view of governance and the sources of reliability set out earlier, the problems should be tackled with a combination of the following principles. First, concerning competence a trade-off between variety, from the perspective of subsidiaries, allowing for cognitive distance, and cohesion for ease and efficiency of collaboration. Second, for governance a combination is needed of shared values/norms of collaboration and mutual dependence (Figure 3.1) with, though probably to a decreasing extent, a certain amount of hierarchical control.

Forsgren et al. (2005) conducted an empirical test of the effects of shared values and (im)balances of resource dependence between headquarters and subsidiaries, on the transfer of knowledge from the subsidiary within the MNC, and found significant effects of relations of dependence but not of shared values. This confirmed their expectation that it is 'hard factors' of power and mutual dependence that settle issues, not 'soft factors' of shared values. However, this result is not conclusive since shared values were not measured as such, that is as underlying fundamental notions as to how to conduct and govern collaboration, but as perceived identical interests in R&D marketing, production design and production, and that is different (Forsgren et al., 2005: 161). Clearly, there are differences in such interests, associated with the basic problem of cohesiveness versus variety in competence, but the question is whether the MNC as an organization helps to solve these problems by some shared views on how to collaborate and solve conflicts.

The MNC is also of particular interest in that it yields a specific case of how exploitation across different countries can yield exploration (Nooteboom, 2000), as a crucial dynamic capability. This will be taken up further in Chapter 5.

Limits to Size of the Firm

Firms can grow by increase of scale in given activities, that is more of the same, or by diversification, adding new activities or capabilities. According to Blau (1970), quoted in Scott (1992: 260), in the first case the percentage of administrative staff decreases, and in the second case it increases, due to increased problems of coordination and integration. According to Penrose (1959) that limits the rate of growth of the firm, in the need to assign more managers to coordination, thus limiting their assignment to further expansion, but need not in the long run yield a limit to the size of the firm. I will argue that it does.

Penrose focused on growth by diversification and by employing new services that belong to the potential of existing resources and their configurations. However, in ongoing growth at some point new capabilities have to be added. The number of distinct capabilities may also rise not in an extension of the scope of potential activities but in increased division of labour for the sake of efficiency. I expect that there are limits to size because under such increase of the range of capabilities, the organization faces a fundamental trade-off between variety and coordination. Either variety is maintained at the expense of coordination, and then at some point the question arises why the elements should be part of a single firm rather than being independent, or coordination is maintained at the expense of variety, which reduces innovative potential. In terms of organizational focus: as the range of capabilities is extended, focus widens, to the detriment of fast and efficient utilization of complementarities. In terms of cognitive distance: distance becomes too large, and while this yields new sources of novelty, the ability to utilize them by collaboration decreases, and distance goes beyond its optimal level. I now proceed to analyse the issue in more detail.

If the number of capabilities, and resources more generally, is n, then the number of possible connections between them is $n(n-1)/2$, and thus increases quadratically in n, if everything remains connected with everything else, yielding an accelerating increase of costs, including opportunity costs, of coordination, and, probably, noise in communication. This, of course, yields a classic reason for decomposition, in hierarchies or network structures such as, for example, a hub and spokes structure. Capabilities are clustered in local units, such as communities of practice (COP), which are in turn connected in divisions of firms, which are in turn connected in corporations. Is there a limit to this?

From the present cognitive perspective, problems of coordination increase with the dissimilarity of connected capabilities, within the different levels of organization. As the range of capabilities widens, to include capabilities that are less mutually complementary, organizational focus has to widen, but since it covers more diverse, less complementary capabilities, to achieve alignment among them each has to be more constrained. So either there is more constraint of variety or less cohesiveness. Furthermore, if it is true, as indicated earlier, on the basis of empirical research, that a principle of decreasing returns to knowledge obtains, so that as knowledge accumulates, novelty has to be sought at greater cognitive distance, then the dissimilarity of novel capabilities further increases, thus increasing problems of collaboration.

The costs of coordination are not just direct costs, but also opportunity costs of loss of cognitive variety, in the fact that in establishing mutual understanding, and willingness to collaborate, across an increasingly heterogeneous batch of capabilities, each of them gets more constrained in its scope of cognition. The paradoxical result then arises that while potential variety increases in terms of the scope of capabilities, in each of them actual variety decreases due to rising needs of common understanding. One alternative, to prevent escalation of costs and complexity of coordination, is to leave potential connections unutilized, but then the question arises why unconnected capabilities should be combined in a single firm. Would it make sense to have a focus only on the governance side, bundling activities or capabilities that are unconnected and yield no complementarity? The point of organizational focus is to facilitate fast and efficient collaboration.

Why facilitate collaboration, and incur the corresponding limitation of cognitive variety, if there is no collaboration to be had?

Next to cognitive considerations, mutual dependence is needed to complement trust on the basis of shared values/norm of conduct, as argued earlier, and illustrated in Figure 3.1. Unconnected capabilities, with little actual or potential complementarity, yield little mutual dependence as an incentive for collaboration.

This brings me close to Richardson's (1972, 2002) position that activities should be combined within a firm to the extent that they are similar and complementary, and should be relegated to outside relations to the extent that they are not. However, the analysis can be further refined.

A further question is whether coordination should be limited to surface level regulation, in the ad hoc coordination of specific activities when they arise. In that case, the question again is why that would be more efficient inside than between firms. Such ad hoc regulation has to be made anew each time that activities are re-configured. With a lack of deeper cognitive alignment, this takes time, in a working out of differences in cognition, in competence and governance. A faster alternative to ad hoc surface regulation is to build up a store of surface regulations that one might draw from as the need for any of them appears. However, it may be difficult to predict what combinations may arise, and for each of them what regulations they might need. With an increasing range of potential combinations their number would increase, and the question arises how much of all that effort will actually be utilized. Thus, for surface regulation among multiple capabilities, the best would generally be to await what concrete activities arise and improvise coordination accordingly.

The advantage of inclusion of a range of capabilities within one organization is that alignment of underlying cognition can be achieved, on a deeper, more generic level of cognition, yielding greater speed, scope and flexibility of generating surface regulations for novel combinations. The (specific) investment in such focus is worthwhile for its perspective, within a firm, for intensive and repeated utilization. Here is a remnant of TCE logic.

However, there are several drawbacks to this. First, it may be difficult to predict which capabilities will yield interesting combinations in an unknown future. Second, as the number of capabilities increases, cognitive alignment across all of them yields reduced variety in each of them, as indicated before. That effect is less to the extent that the capabilities and views are already more similar. Chemistry and biotechnology have more in common than chemistry and information technology. In other words, people can easily coordinate on the surface level to the extent that differences in underlying perceptions, views and convictions remain limited. As

underlying differences increase, indoctrinating people with shared perceptions, views and convictions smoothes their collaboration but reduces their
variety of cognition.

As a result, it seems that at some point it becomes better not to bring
further and more diverging capabilities under a single focus, and to take the
alternative of employing inter-firm collaboration, yielding a wider range of
potential capabilities that may yield interesting combinations, and the preservation of more variety in each of them, and to engage in the more ad hoc,
time consuming surface regulations for combination when and where the
need arises. However, without constructing a shared cognitive focus on the
competence side, integration in an organization may still be worthwhile for
a shared focus on the governance side, in shared views on how to deal with
each other. One can agree on that under great differences on the competence side. But that may also apply to collaboration between firms. Perhaps
one can find, with relative ease, partners who are diverse in competence but
like-minded on the governance side, yielding a basis for trust.

There is yet another consideration. Following the point made by Postrel
(2002), discussed before, and illustrated in Figure 3.5, one may maintain
cognitive distance and yet collaborate easily on the basis of a large absorptive capacity, and ability to collaborate more widely. Having large absorptive capacity, and seeking partners with such capacity, would reduce time
and effort in achieving requisite mutual understanding. Thus, having high
absorptive capacity, and experience in collaboration, and thereby being
an attractive partner, becomes a key dynamic capability and competitive
advantage. This applies both within and between firms. So, a firm might
include a great variety of competence and deal with it on the basis of large
absorptive capacity and ability to collaborate, in the units that may need
to connect with others, with ability to collaborate further supported by an
organizational focus only on the governance side.

However, that takes time, in an accumulation of knowledge, for
absorptive capacity, and of experience in collaboration with people who
think differently, for ability to collaborate. Also, recall that accumulation of knowledge requires partners at increasing cognitive distance to
learn something new, which may then further contribute to a widening of
variety within the firm, with its attendant coordination problems. In other
words: the solution may contribute to a worsening of the problem. Also,
having invested in large absorptive capacity and ability to collaborate,
one would want to utilize that dynamic capability in a greater variety of
different contacts, for which again outside relationships provide more
scope. An example here is scholars: the ones who have accumulated most
knowledge and most experience in collaborative research engage most
in varied collaboration outside their university. In this way, building

absorptive capacity within the firm, as a matter of human resource policy, may increase the problem of the most capable staff leaving the firm, before investment in them is recouped.

This rather elaborate analysis shows that it is not easy to refute Penrose. For every problem of firm size, a new potential solution crops up. However, it also appears that every time the end conclusion is that while a solution within the firm may be found, outside collaboration with other firms seems the better option.

In sum, a cognitive limit to firm size appears to lie in a trade-off between coordination and variety of cognition. The advantage of an organization is that by alignment on deeper levels of cognition it affords easier and faster coordination on the surface level of specific combinations of capabilities, but it does so at the price of reducing cognitive variety. In other words, organization tends to improve exploitation at the expense of exploration. The alternative is to engage in slower, more ad hoc, surface level adjustment while preserving cognitive variety, and the potential for that is greatest in outside collaboration with other firms. There may be ways out of this. While maintaining cognitive variety on the competence side organizations may still have a comparative advantage in providing a cognitive focus on the governance side. This applies most in low-trust environments, where indeed organization is most needed for a focus on the governance side. Another option to maintain both cognitive diversity and ease and speed of cognitive coordination is to build and maintain large absorptive capacity and ability to collaborate within the organization. But this requires considerable investment in the accumulation of knowledge and experience, and the question arises whether it would not be more attractive to extend the utilization of such dynamic capability in a greater variety of contacts, outside the organization.

Of course, these restrictions on firm size from the perspective of innovative, dynamic capability obtain only to the extent that innovation is a condition of survival. It is not a problem to the extent that the environment is stable, and the organization can block or exterminate competition, critics and institutional change. The Catholic church, for example, and many universities, have been successful at that for ages.

Limits to Growth of the Firm

To coordinate an increasingly complex whole of capabilities, one needs a sufficiently wide, far reaching and tight cognitive focus, especially on the normative, governance side to maintain ability and willingness to collaborate across such diversity of competence, often across diverse locations, in different cultural settings. This requires a certain strength and sophistication of organizational culture that requires time to develop as well as time for incoming staff to find their way and to adjust. Next to obstacles to size, this yields an obstacle to the speed of growth, which comes close to the limit to the rate of growth identified by Penrose.

Another limit to the rate of growth lies in the building up of absorptive capacity and ability to collaborate, as a dynamic capability to profit from wider cognitive variety, inside and outside the firm.

CONCLUSIONS

This chapter answers seven of the 17 questions listed in Chapter 1, and one only partially, as follows.

Question 1: Why do firms exist? What is the basis for organizational capability?
Answer: Organizations in general and firms in particular exist to limit cognitive distance, with a cognitive focus for coordination between complementary capabilities, with sufficient mutual understanding and motivation to collaborate.

Question 2: What is the (dis)advantage of firms relative to markets?
Answer: Firms exist to provide more cohesion (focus) for the sake of exploitation, while markets provide more variety for the sake of exploration. Organizational focus yields a constraint that can be compensated by outside collaboration. The duality of market and firm yields a solution to the problem of combining exploitation and exploration.

Question 3: What, if any, are limits to size of the firm?
Answers (apart from familiar arguments of scale or scope, are the following): The general argument is that there is a trade-off between coordination for efficiency and variety for innovation. As firm size increases by expansion of the portfolio of activities or capabilities, one can maintain coordination at the expense of room for variety, or one can maintain room for variety at the expense of coordination. In the first case there will be a decrease of innovation, and in the second case a decrease of the rationale for combining activities in one firm. In more detail, the argument is as follows. To the extent that increase of size yields increasing systemic complexity, in a portfolio of activities or capabilities, local change of only one component increasingly requires wholesale systemic restructuring, which yields a systemic obstacle to change. This yields an incentive for break-up into more autonomous components, for the sake

of dynamic efficiency, even if it yields a decrease of static efficiency. As capabilities are added and become increasingly dissimilar and less complementary, the extent and complexity of cognitive coordination needed to exploit their combinations increases non-linearly and increasingly reduces variety within each capability. This reduces the potential and speed of innovation. This yields a need to limit internal expansion and, instead, to maintain cognitive variety in outside relationships. If capabilities yield little complementarity they also yield little mutual dependence as an incentive for collaboration.

Question 4: What, if any, are limits to growth of the firm?
Answer: Apart from limits to size, the speed of growth is limited by the speed at which new staff can adapt to organizational focus. This comes close to Penrose's argument. Also, it takes time to build up absorptive capacity and ability to collaborate, as a basis for further expansion by combination with new capabilities.

Question 5: What are problems of coordination?
Answer: One problem may lie in complex coherence of complementary capabilities. A second lies in problems of mutual understanding and willingness to collaborate between complementary capabilities. Related to both, a problem lies in the combination of exploitation and exploration, which is difficult in complex systems and difficult to combine in a single organizational focus.

Question 6: What are capabilities to solve them?
Answer: Ability to achieve sufficient stability, mutual understanding and willingness to collaborate, for the sake of exploitation, while allowing for variety of knowledge and autonomy and spirit of competition, for the sake of exploration, within the firm or in collaboration between firms. This point is elaborated in Chapter 4, in the analysis of inter-organizational relationships, and in Chapter 5, in the analysis of dynamic capabilities.

Question 7: What is the basis for organization-specific capabilities?
Answer: Mostly organizational cognitive focus, starting from the imprint of a founding entrepreneur, rooted in deep level cognitive categories, implemented and communicated by means of symbolic pictures, objects, stories, slogans, events and behaviours, including role models.

Question 8: What causes stability of organizations?
Answer: First, elimination by competitive pressures of dysfunctional or unsuccessful deviations from established activities/capabilities. This

applies in particular under systemic complexity, where even local deviation rapidly becomes dysfunctional. Second, the fact that incoming personnel self-select or are selected and socialized according to the culture associated with cognitive focus. Third, the fact that further cognition is constructed under shared organizational conditions.

Question 9: What are dynamic capabilities?
Partial answer: One dynamic capability is a high intellectual capability (absorptive capacity) and behavioural capability to collaborate across cognitive distance, based on learning from earlier collaboration, in order to achieve higher optimal cognitive distance, that is operate efficiently at a higher cognitive distance. Another dynamic capability is to design and implement an organizational focus that provides sufficient alignment for exploitation, where needed, and yet is only limitedly cohesive, allowing for exploration, for example with a focus either on the deep level of fundamental categories, or with a focus only on the governance side. Further dynamic capabilities are developed in later chapters.

One last comment: With a risk of oversimplification, the whole argument about firms and markets may be summarized most succinctly in saying that organizations serve more for exploitation and markets more for exploration. This may sound counter-intuitive to economists, who have learned that the virtue of 'the' market is that it yields static *allocative efficiency* (allocation of scarce resources), which seems more exploitation related than exploration related. This possible enigma is eliminated when one recognizes the difference between statics and dynamics. Under static conditions (stable preferences and technology), in so far as they still obtain, market competition is needed as a matter of governance, to provide incentives for productive efficiency and to avoid monopolies. Under dynamic conditions of innovation, the present argument applies. There, markets are needed to supply variety needed for exploration, while firms are needed to realize and exploit innovations. Firms are needed for reasons of both competence and governance: to achieve sufficient mutual understanding and collaboration to realize opportunities from complementary capabilities.

NOTES

1. As noted also in Chapter 2, Aristotelian causality was rightly rejected in its application to physics, where especially final causality is misplaced, but in human affairs it fits perfectly.
2. Perhaps another way to look at organizational focus arises from the notion of 'tags' from the methodology (I hesitate to use the term 'theory') of complex systems. A system

consists of components that interact, and it is complex if the interactions generate emergent behaviour, particularly adaptive behaviour. Such systems carry tags, which serve two functions. One is to 'define the network by delimiting the critical interactions, the major connections' (Holland, 1996: 23). A second is to act as an identifier for other systems to 'decide' whether to connect or not. Here, it will be argued that the main 'delimitation of critical interactions' that characterizes and identifies an organization is a cognitive focus.

3. This is my view on the feasibility of a centrally planned economy, in the famous 'socialist calculation debate', with Hayek as a protagonist. My view is similar to Hayek's view on the impossibility of planning due to the dispersion of knowledge.

4. See the earlier discussion, in Chapter 2, on 'primary' and 'higher level' metaphors (Lakoff and Johnson, 1980).

5. This may be related to the notion of 'tags' as identifiers of complex adaptive systems (Holland, 1996) for other systems to decide whether or not to connect.

6. However, modern neural science indicates that even the self is fragmented rather than unitary, and problems of cognitive coherence and coordination arise on that level as well. In fact, this was presaged in philosophy, for example by Nietzsche (1885).

7. I say 'mostly' since the betrayal of trust may be a basis for developing greater wisdom in dealing with man.

8. I avoid the term 'social capital' here since later, in Chapter 4, that will be associated with structures of networks and positions in networks.

APPENDIX 3.1   ECONOMIES OF SCALE, SCOPE AND TIME

This appendix is an abbreviated version of a paragraph from Nooteboom (2004b) and summarizes familiar economies of size.

Economies of Scale

One form of economy of scale is division of labour: because people special-ize in a specific part of production they can perform the work more effic-iently. This applies, for example, to an assembly line, yielding sequential interdependence. Note that here the distinction between economies of scale and scope becomes somewhat ambiguous. One can speak of economy of scale in the sense that a large volume of the same product is produced. One can speak of economy of scope in the sense that different, complementary activities are distinguished, in specialization.

A second form of scale economy arises from indivisibilities of assets, such as 'threshold' and 'Babbage' effects (the latter was discussed also by Penrose, 1995: 68). A threshold effect arises because of some minimum capacity that gets better utilized at larger volumes of usage, such as an attendant in a shop or at another service point (Nooteboom, 1982), driver of a vehicle, teacher before a class. The Babbage effect arises when indivis-ible assets are connected in series, where the least common multiple yields a minimum efficient size.

Another form of scale economy is due to the mathematical fact that the content of a sphere is proportional to the cube of the radius, and its surface is proportional to its square, while content yields production capacity and surface is connected with costs of material and hence weight, in case of a vehicle air resistance and transportation costs, in case of a chemical reactor costs of cleaning and costs of heat loss. As a result, the revenue per unit of cost increases in proportion with size of production. It can easily be calculated that a doubling of size (production volume) yields a 20 per cent reduction of per unit cost.[1] The effect has therefore been called an 'engin-eering' economy of scale. It applies to process industries (oil, chemicals, some pharmaceuticals, some food industries), where it has been called the 'pots and pans effect', but it applies also to trucks and aircraft. The 20 per cent reduction of cost at a doubling of volume is a familiar rule in those industries.

Further effects of scale arise in markets, in 'network externalities', 'bandwagon effects' and 'contagion effects'. In network externality (also called the 'telephone effect'), the utility of some product depends on the number of others who choose a product with the same or a compatible technical standard. This can yield a 'snowballing effect' of a new standard that gains a head start before competing standards. This is a case of 'first mover advantage'. The standard example is the telephone: it is useful to the extent that others have a telephone that is compatible, in order to call and be called. Another example is the celebrated case of video recorders. In the 'bandwagon effect', consumers (or voters, politicians or managers) copy each other's choices. In the 'snob effect' it is the other way around: copying the choice of others is avoided. In the diffusion of a new product, early adopters exert a demonstration effect upon potential later adopters ('contagion'). This yields the familiar S-shaped ('logistic') curve of diffusion. Such contagion may occur at a distance or, mostly with stronger effect, in direct contact, by 'word of mouth'. Here, it matters who the source is. One is more inclined to follow people in similar positions or roles (role equivalence or equivalence in network position; see Burt, 1992).

Economies of Scope

Economy of scope follows from different activities using the same resources, in different ways, or at different times, and thereby improving their utilization, or from different activities complementing each other in the production of resources. An example is the utilization of a distribution channel for a variety of products. Economy of scope yields an argument for combining activities in an organization only if the effect of scope is inseparable. For example, hide and meat are inseparable in the living animal. Now consider the process of slaughter. After separation of hide and meat, the former can be separated off in the leather industry, and the latter in meat processing. There may also be (in)separability in place and time. Consider a steel factory. After melting the steel, it saves energy to directly process it in the rolling of steel, which requires, preventing heat loss, that the rolling plant is located next to the melting plant. The heat that comes off the subsequent cooling of steel plates may be used for other processes, such as heating hothouses for plants, which then are also most economically located near the steel plant.

Economies of Time

The effect of economic cycles on capacity utilization tends to be multiplied upwards in a supply chain. A small decline of demand at the downward end of the chain requires some time to register and adjust to, in the next upward link, which then needs to reduce activity more sharply, and this effect is multiplied up the chain. This has been called the 'car queue' effect: a slight deceleration can build up to a sharp brake, or a collision, further up the queue. As a result, firms up the chain, for example in the production of raw materials, suffer from cycles most.

When under-utilization of capacity is endemic, and widespread across producers, the need arises to reduce fixed costs. This is especially important in process industries, where fixed costs are high and furthermore 'sunk' in the market, and thereby create exit barriers. In such cases, there is a threat of ruinous price competition under conditions of excess supply, because assets cannot be reduced or sold off. Therefore the emergence of excess capacity should be avoided. A problem here is that in some industries (oil, basic chemicals) for strategic reasons governments, not to become dependent on other nations in times of crises, stimulate domestic production capacity. This yields all the more reason not to create even more excess capacity when entering some country, but to utilize existing capacity.

Another economy related to time arises in experience effects. According to the 'experience curve', unit cost declines as experience, measured as cumulative (uninterrupted) production increases. This is due to increasing skill, better division and co-ordination of work, a fine-tuning of processes by elimination of redundancies, and other process improvements. Such an experience effect can also become a liability, by yielding an exit barrier to new, competence destroying technology, thus locking a firm into existing practice.

A special form of experience derives from learning. According to the interactionist/constructivist theory of knowledge set out in Chapter 2, learning is based on existing mental categories, which are in turn based on past learning. As a result, learning is cumulative, with increasing returns to experience. That is why liberalization of markets is not a sufficient condition for developing nations to catch up. Since they are behind in their knowledge, they cannot compete in the utilization of opportunities from liberalization, and due to the cumulativeness of knowledge, this gap can only widen. This effect was analysed earlier, in the formal discussion of optimal cognitive distance and the effect on it of absorptive capacity. There, it was also noted that there are decreasing returns in that as knowledge increases it becomes increasingly difficult to find yet further new knowledge.

Threshold Costs

Another time-effect, which yields an economy of scale and scope, is due to the presence of the fixed 'threshold' costs, mentioned earlier. These may be due to the fact that productive capacity is not feasible or viable below some minimum level (is indivisible), such as a person, or a machine. They may also be due to minimum set-up costs, for an installation for physical production, a research facility or some service capacity. Such thresholds arise, in particular, at service facilities such as a point of sale at a shop, a call desk, driver of a truck, teacher before a class, specialist support staff in a firm. For staff (attendant, driver, teacher), the threshold cost is one person during availability of the service, for each separately staffed service point. Threshold staff or facilities are under-utilized during low levels of demand (low customer visits, empty truck, low class attendance), and this yields a scale effect. At higher levels of demand, additional labour may be added part time, only during peak hours.

Threshold costs have increased dramatically. This is the case, for example, in research and development of advanced technology, and as a result of that in the development and production of many products that employ such technology, such as semi-conductors, aircraft, cars, consumer electronics, biotechnology. Formerly, products in consumer electronics could be made with low fixed costs and cheap labour, in the manual assembly of components in boxes. With the onset of miniaturization, this practice was no longer viable, and had to be replaced with the use of robots for assembly, which entails considerable threshold cost.

Effects in Markets and Transactions

In marketing also, there are substantial 'threshold costs': in distribution channels and brand name. In distribution there are set-up costs of laying a pipe-line or track, building a warehouse, building a station or airport, having an attendant at a service point, sending a truck along a certain route. For the development of a brand name one must invest heavily in advertising and other forms of promotion. The fixed cost of an ad on national TV is more easily recouped for a product that is marketed nationwide than for a local product. The need to market a specialized product world wide, in order to gain sufficient economy of scale to compete, creates a need for a worldwide brand name, with correspondingly higher fixed costs. Recently, relatively novel effects of scale were reported to arise in the insurance business: novel opportunities arise in direct marketing and tele-marketing, but this requires large threshold outlays for hardware, software and the building up of data bases.

There are also several scale effects in transaction costs (Nooteboom, 1993). One is due to 'threshold costs' of contact (search costs) and contract (evaluation and setting up a contract or other agreement), which weigh more heavily at small firm sizes. Furthermore, to the extent that knowledge is tacit there is less documentation as a basis for assessment and evaluation of competencies, needs, reliability and so on. As discussed in Chapter 1, tacit knowledge also reduces absorptive capacity, and knowledge is especially tacit in small firms. When knowledge is tacit, it tends to be self-evident, and not subject to rational criticism, until it has been sufficiently externalized in codified knowledge. Note that thus tacit knowledge gives a double jeopardy: less information for evaluation and control, and a lesser basis for critical reflection and debate. As discussed, there is limited absorptive capacity until tacit knowledge is made explicit, and this is not always possible. However, tacit knowledge also has the advantage that it does not spill over as easily as codified knowledge. That is an advantage especially to small firms, since it is relatively difficult for them to protect their innovations. Patents, for example, are relatively expensive for them.

NOTE

1. If revenue for a spherical unit of production is proportional to volume v, which is proportional to the cube of radius r (r^3, so that r is proportional to volume to the power $1/3$), and total cost is proportional to the square of the radius, then unit cost is proportional to $1/r$. The ratio of unit cost between two installations, with r_1 and r_2 then is $r_2/r_1 = (v_2/v_1)^{1/3}$. Thus, If $v_2/v_1 = 2$, the unit cost ratio is 0.8.

4. Organization between organizations

INTRODUCTION

As noted in Chapter 1, nowadays a theory of the firm should include an account of the boundaries of the firm and inter-organizational relationships (IORs). After the analysis of the firm in Chapter 3, the present chapter turns to IORs. There is an enormous literature on that, and a complete survey would go too far. The focus here is on the fundamentals related to theory of the firm. First comes a discussion of the boundaries of the firm. Second a discussion of the sources of innovation in IORs, in particular the effects of cognitive distance, absorptive capacity, and the duration of relationships. The chapter proceeds with an analysis of the governance of collaboration, and the role of trust and of intermediaries. Next, taking all this into account, the analysis goes beyond dyads of firms to consider effects of the structure of multiple interacting organizations, of the position of an organization in such a structure, and of the strength and content of ties. A central issue here is a debate on the strengths and weaknesses of strong ties. The analysis ends with an attempt to integrate a variety of apparently contradictory effects. Next to theoretical analysis, much evidence will be presented, from a variety of empirical studies. Some of the text is derived from Nooteboom (2004b).

BOUNDARIES OF THE FIRM

This section gives a summary of the basic principle proposed here concerning the boundaries of the firm and the need to collaborate between firms, especially from the perspective of innovation. Second, building on Chapter 2, it gives a closer analysis of the basic principles of learning and innovation in interaction between firms. Then it gives a look at further details of entrepreneurial or managerial choice and at complications in drawing the boundary between activities and capabilities within and between firms.

The Basic Principle

The analysis in Chapter 3 suggests that the boundary of the firm should follow from a trade-off between on the one hand variety of capabilities within the firm for novelty creation (exploration) and on the other hand coherence for its utilization and further improvement (exploitation), taking into account the option of mobilizing complementary sources of innovation outside the firm, in collaboration with other organizations. A more or less cohesive focus within the firm, generating some limit to cognitive distance, to enable fast and efficient utilization of opportunities in the connection of complementary capabilities, may be complemented with more ad hoc and slower combinations with a greater variety of outside capabilities. In other words, while organizational focus inevitably yields some degree of myopia, it may be compensated by outside cognitive variety, in 'external economy of cognitive scope' (Nooteboom, 1992). The mix of limited variety and coordination in the firm is achieved by means of organizational cognitive focus, with a competence and a governance part, for, respectively, ability and motivation to collaborate. As explained in Chapter 3, organizational focus has dimensions of width, reach, tightness and depth. Organizational focus is instituted and maintained by means of administrative processes, practices and routines that are rooted in organizational culture, which includes the use of symbols and symbolic behaviour, including exemplary behaviour from role models. Governance does not rely on cognitive focus only. It is based also on mutual dependence, routinization, personal empathy and identification, contract and, to a decreasing extent, on hierarchy.

This statement is a normative one. In fact, many firms are not primarily innovation oriented and still define themselves in terms of activities rather than capabilities; and boundaries of the firm are also affected by other considerations than innovation and growth. For example, there are familiar arguments of economy of scale, scope and time, which are summarized in the appendix to Chapter 3. Firms may be forced to conduct activities inside because appropriate partners for outside collaboration are lacking, or they may be forced to collaborate outside if merger or acquisition is not feasible. Firms do not internalize activities, or do not engage in alliances, when it is forbidden by competition policy. Public organizations may not be allowed to outsource activities for reasons of public equity, justice or accountability.

There is no universal best point of optimal trade-off between variety and coordination. It depends on contingencies of institutional environment, organizational capabilities and strategic choice. In strategic choice, firms may opt for a focus on exploitation, with less internal cognitive distance, and a more cohesive focus, and seek a connection with outside exploration. Conversely, they may opt for exploration, maintaining a less cohesive focus, and transfer innovations they explored to outside partners that engage in tighter coordination for the sake of exploitation. As noted in Chapter 3, the classic example is biotechnology, with small, technology-based firms focusing on exploration of new materials or processes, and exploitation being conducted in large pharmaceutical firms.

Firms may try to combine exploitation and exploration internally, under a single organizational focus, in an 'ambidextrous' form of organization. This is difficult but not impossible. How difficult it is depends on a number of contingencies, such as the extent to which exploitation is systemic and thereby disallows exploration within the exploitation system because that would upset the integrity of the exploitation system. If, on the other hand, exploitation is based on more stand-alone activities, and is already oriented at differentiated production for different applications and customers, exploitation and exploration are easier to combine. In a small organization, exploration and exploitation may be combined on one shop floor, with the entrepreneur monitoring the connection between the two and intervening for their coordination as the need arises. As discussed in Chapter 3, when exploitation and exploration need to be separated, they may still be connected under a single organizational focus that is directed mostly at the deep level of basic cognitive categories that allow for specific capabilities and 'surface regulations' that differ between exploitation and exploration, and yet form the basis for fast arrangements for coordination. The focus may be limited mostly to the governance side, leaving room for great variety on the competence side. In all these cases, focus still imposes some restrictions on variety, and further variety would need to be sought outside the firm, in IORs. The latter form the focus of the present chapter.

Outside institutions for the organization and governance of collaboration between firms may be lacking, such as reliable legal ordering, reputation systems, technical standards, or ethics of conduct. Firms may lack the absorptive capacity or capability to collaborate at a significant cognitive distance. All this will be examined in the course of the present chapter.

Learning by Interaction

This section builds on the analysis of learning by interaction given in Chapter 2. One may learn by communication or imitation, in absorbing knowledge or capabilities from others, or one may learn experientially, by discovery from experience. Note that 'absorbing' here entails cognitive reconstruction in the assimilation of observed behaviour. Schumpeter proposed that inventions arise from 'novel combinations'. In Chapter 2 it was indicated how new ideas may arise from association between pre-existing ideas. Using ideas from Piaget, it was shown how mental 'reciprocation' between different existing practices constitutes an important step in the discovery process.

Here, the principle is applied to organizations and their practices. Failure to survive with existing practice and capabilities triggers attention to what others are doing that appears to be successful where one's own practice appears to fail. This may lead to the incorporation of elements from others' practices into the design or architecture of one's own practice, in experimentation with hybrids. Hybrids are likely to yield inefficiencies and constraints imposed by the basic architecture, design or logic of established practice that yield obstacles for the fuller utilization of the emergent potential of novel elements. If in interaction reciprocation is indeed reciprocal, with different agents incorporating elements from each others' practices in their different basic logics of action, comparison of success and failure may yield insights into the adoption of novel principles of design that better accommodate promising old and novel elements. Here, learning by experience is a social process of interaction for reciprocation. Note that here 'novel combinations' go further than just re-arranging elements from different sources, and entail a transformation of basic logics or architectures into a new synthesis, as well as transformations of the elements involved.

In this perspective, absorptive capacity (Cohen and Levinthal, 1990) consists of an existing system of ideas and capabilities. More knowledge and experience yields a broader basis for association with outside ideas. The notion of cognitive distance refers to differences in elements and logics or architectures of thought and practice. There must be such difference for association by reciprocation to occur. But if the difference is too large, observed practices and expressions of ideas cannot be assimilated, and reciprocation is impossible. This leads to the idea of an intermediate, optimal cognitive distance, as presented in Chapter 3 and applied and further developed in the present chapter.

Firm Size

The size of the firm is limited by its boundaries, as summarized above and analysed in Chapter 3. Here we look at characteristic differences between large and small firms. As is well known in the literature on small business, there is widespread self-employment, in small and medium sized enterprises (SME), from a variety of motives and conditions. As noted in Chapter 3, self-employed, in small firms, have more opportunity as well as more varied motives for idiosyncratic goals and styles of organization. The literature has offered the following motives:

1. 'Push' factors (self-employment as a need):
    (a) social maladjustment, inability to accept authority, heterodoxy (Kets de Vries, 1977);

    (b)   conditions of unemployment, inability to access labour markets due to ethnic or religious discrimination, lack of social security benefits for unemployment and old age (the hypothesis of a 'flight' into self-employment, Stanworth and Curran, 1973; Scase and Goffee, 1980);

    (c)   personal crisis that triggers a switch in the course of life (illness, bereavement, identity crisis, divorce) (Chell, 1985); and

    (d)   pressure to take over father's firm.

2.   'Pull' factors (self-employment as an attraction):

    (a)   ambition, will towards self-realization, creativity, power, or wealth;[1]

    (b)   opportunity: offer from a friend or family member to participate in his venture, availability of finance (for example from family), chance access to assets or markets; and

    (c)   wish to be independent, or to maintain a small scale, personalized form of business or a traditional craft.

According to some estimates, only between 10 and 20 per cent of self-employed are of the heroic, Schumpeterian type of entrepreneurship (Williams, 1977; van den Tillaart et al., 1981). The rest, then, are driven by one or more of the other motives. Then, boundaries of the firm may be more determined by the motive to stay small and informal than by what is most expedient for innovation and growth.

Motives arise from personal inclinations and experience, in combination with institutional conditions. In Chapter 3, mention was made of the effects of capital structure and capital markets on goals and styles of entrepreneurship. In less developed countries there may be more unemployment and there is less social security, which engenders the push factor towards self-employment in the flight from unemployment, in search of alternative means of caring for family. This is the well-known 'refuge hypothesis'. In some countries there is more ethnic and religious discrimination in labour markets than in others. In more developed countries, on the other hand, with benefits for unemployment and old age, pull factors of self-realization are more prominent. Attitudes to risk vary across cultures. Clearly, the emergence and survival of small, independent ventures depends on conditions of technology (effects of scale) and market (entry barriers, intensity of price competition). In small business, there is room for a variety of motives, due to funding by banks or venture capitalists or from informal, family-based sources, which impose less tight and uniform norms of performance than do equity markets.

All the motives indicated have been found in a variety of empirical research. Here only a small, illustrative sample can be given. In an international comparative study of 2500 entrepreneurs in nine countries, Pompe et al. (1986) found that in highly developed European countries (UK, Germany, Netherlands) and Japan more than half of self-employed were motivated by self-realization, compared with around 10 per cent in lesser developed countries (Cameroon, Colombia, Brazil and Indonesia). Dissatisfaction with employment occurred more in Europe than in less developed countries outside Europe. A further discussion of the literatures on those subjects lies beyond the scope of the present book.

Degree of Innovativeness

It is an old quandary in Schumpeterian economics whether small, independent entrepreneurial firms or large, integrated firms contribute most to innovation. According to Schumpeter (1909, 1939, 1942), in early capitalism the innovative entrepreneur ('Mark I') was an independent outsider, setting up his own new venture, without vested interests in established technologies, products and markets. In later capitalism, entrepreneurship ('Mark II') increasingly required large teams of specialists that only larger firms could afford. Rothwell (1985, 1986, 1989) proposed that both types of entrepreneurship (Mark I and II) have a role to play, and that there is 'dynamic complementarity' between small and large firms, in innovation, with small and large firms being strong and weak in opposite ways. Small firms have 'behavioural' advantages: motivation to accept risks and low income in early stages of innovation, close contact with customers and employees, flexibility of small emergent firms that haven't yet hardened into organizational shapes to fit established, 'dominant' practices. Large firms have advantages in resources: revenues from established activities to fund innovation, a wider range of activities to pool risks and cross-subsidize new ventures, specialized human and other resources, market access (distribution channels and brand names), and established political and social capital.

In view of dynamic complementarity, one would expect that large firms typically produce the scientific inventions that require large R&D teams with specialists, while small, outside firms will be quicker in bringing inventions into practice, in new products (exploration), and large firms carry new products into efficient, large-scale exploitation. Clearly, the division of labour between small and large firms depends on institutional conditions, such as limits in the integration of activities in large conglomerate firms imposed by anti-trust policy (Nelson, 1993).

The analysis is borne out by many empirical studies (for example Blair, 1972; Davis et al., 1985; Wijnberg, 1990; Acs and Audretsch, 1990). Acs and Audretsch (1990) and Vossen and Nooteboom (1996) found that while small firms engage less in R&D than large firms, when they do they do so at a greater level of intensity. Examples of inventions that were developed and commercialized by small firms are: electric light (Edison), the telephone (Alexander Graham Bell), aeroplanes (Wright brothers), micro-computers (Silicon Valley), self-service retailing (Nooteboom, 1984), and computer-aided design (Rothwell and Zegveld, 1985).

In the present context, these phenomena confirm predictions from the analysis in Chapter 3. They illustrate the advantage of flexibility and speed of utilization afforded by a narrower range of capabilities, and a more cohesive organizational focus, offered by smaller firms. They also illustrate the advantages of a broader range of capabilities, with a wider scope, and more resources for R&D, offered by larger firms, at the cost of a lower speed of innovation.

Of particular importance, in the analysis of the boundaries of the firm, is the classic phenomenon of entrepreneurial spin-off, where an entrepreneur who develops a radically new idea that does not fit into the established arrangements, in particular the established cognitive focus of the firm, and then has to break out and set out alone. This can be seen as evidence for the hypothesis that firms need to limit organizational focus. Here, this limiting is performed by facilitating spin-offs for initiatives that become too eccentric to the focus. Spin-offs will be discussed in more detail in the extended discussion of 'dynamic capabilities' in Chapter 5.

Firms and Clusters

Increasingly, debates on effects of firm size have become somewhat out-dated because small firms have learned to compensate for their weak-nesses by collaboration in networks (or clusters, or industrial districts). Alliances, clusters, 'industrial districts' or networks[2] of firms are also forms of organization, but they are not firms or organizations in the sense of being an 'autonomous administrative planning unit' (Penrose, 1995: 15). If they have a legal identity (for example as a cooperative or association) it is generally different from that of a firm, until collaboration takes the form of an equity joint venture. Large firms are learning to compensate for their weaknesses by a greater or lesser decentralization of units within the firm (Bartlett and Goshal, 1989). Large firms can operate more or less as internal clusters, of communities, departments, divisions or subsidiaries, while they remain firms. Next to legal form, the difference between decentralized firms and clusters of firms lies in the 'cohesiveness' of cognitive focus. This brings me back to the basic thesis of this book, of the firm as a cognitive focusing device. In greater decentralization, organizational focus is weakened in competence (variety of capabilities) and to some extent also in governance (modes of organization), but as discussed earlier at some point the question arises what the sense is of keeping disintegrated activities within the firm, given the alternative of coordination between independent firms. One way to maintain focus is to facilitate spin-offs, as indicated above.

From the logic developed in Chapter 3, the solution for small firms to compensate for their weaknesses in alliances or networks, and the solution for large firms to decentralize or disintegrate have limitations. Networks of firms have a less cohesive focus than individual firms do, and this slows down the utilization of potential combinations. However, lesser cohesiveness enables greater variety, and autonomy of component firms allows for flexibility in the configuration of firms, where firms that no longer fit, in new constellations for new conditions, drop out.

To enable a faster and more efficient utilization of potential combinations of capabilities, firms may develop a joint cognitive focus for individual relationships or for the cluster or network as a collective, supported by elements of a shared culture, but this tends to be less cohesive than the focus within a firm. Apart from the obvious and important difference in legal identity, the difference of such networks compared with organizations is that ties are weaker, with lesser duration and frequency of interaction, greater cognitive distance, fewer specific investments, and lower scope of content, which yield greater flexibility of configuration and diversity, which is advantageous especially for exploration. To preserve that comparative advantage, one would expect any cognitive focus on the network level to be limitedly cohesive, that is not to be very wide, have limited reach, and be less tight. Note that concerning the strength of ties we are talking of averages here, from which deviations will arise: some individual relationships across firm boundaries may have greater frequency or personal bonding than many intra-organizational relationships. Such bonding may indeed become a problem, from the firm's perspective. Between specialist professionals from different organizations cognitive distance may be smaller than between them and others in their own organizations.

Any person within an organization will be involved in multiple relationships, under a cognitive focus that is strongest overall, across the different dimensions of focus, within a community of practice, weaker elsewhere in the organization and weaker still between organizations. For example, a professional society with members across firms will have a focus that is very narrow (oriented only at that specific profession), with little reach (leaving open aspects of professional conduct), low strictness (allowing for variety of practice that makes meetings interesting), and rather a deep level (concerning fundamental principles of professional knowledge and ethics).

Deep level focus takes a long time to develop and may be in place in local or regional settings with a homogeneous culture, with a long history.

In fact, that condition may be one of the most important reasons for regional clusters and industrial districts to play their celebrated role. When these conditions are not satisfied, a condition for developing such an often relation- or community-specific focus, supported by elements of shared culture, is the expectation of sufficient durability of the community to make such investment worthwhile. And then, this does reduce its flexibility of configuration. A compromise may be found in establishing a focus for a core group of firms, with a more flexible periphery of more loosely connected firms.

Zuchella (2006) discussed the role of focus in industrial districts. In fact, her definition of clusters and industrial districts includes a system of shared values. The analysis includes the problem of myopia that such focus may entail, yielding an obstacle for ongoing exploration. This may require outside connections with other clusters in different countries, in 'multiple embeddedness'. This issue of external linkages of local clusters will return later.

Thus, we find a hierarchy of cohesiveness of focus, from the firm via clusters or districts to markets of only ad-hoc connected firms. Recall, from Chapter 3, that within the firm there is increasingly cohesive focus as we descend from the firm level down to the level of communities of practice. In small firms, however, that hierarchy of levels is not deep, and the firm level is close if not equal to the level of communities. There is much more to be said about innovation in networks of firms, such as clusters and industrial districts, and effects of network structure and density and strength of ties. That will be taken up later in this chapter.

On the side of large firms, decentralization, uncoupling and autonomy of units for the sake of greater variety and flexibility of configuration, have their limits. One reaches a point where it no longer makes sense to have the units within a single firm.

COGNITIVE DISTANCE

This section summarizes some empirical tests of hypotheses concerning the effect of cognitive distance, here between firms, in collaboration for innovation. On this aggregation level of organizations cognitive distance denotes difference in organizational focus. This paragraph first positions innovation in wider goals of collaboration, and then proceeds to give some details of empirical tests of hypotheses concerning optimal cognitive distance, absorptive capacity, and optimal duration of collaboration. Those hypotheses, and to a limited extent also results from the empirical studies reported here, were already indicated and used in a more general context, not only in collaboration between firms but also in collaboration between individuals, in Chapter 3.

Goals of Collaboration

There are many reasons why firms need outside relationships with other firms, as shown in the extensive literature of inter-firm alliances, which is too large to survey here (for such a survey, see for example Nooteboom, 2004b). There are reasons of strategy (collusion, eliminating a competitor), efficiency (scale and scope), market positioning (fast market entry), and access to complementary capability, outside organizational focus of 'core competence'. Part of the latter type of reason is the need for outside relationships for innovation, in the development of new products, production processes, markets, or forms of organization, and for learning, in the development of new capabilities. That is the focus of the present book. That subfield is also covered by a large literature (Lundvall, 1988; Porter, 1990; Prahalad and Hamel, 1990; Hamel, 1991; Kogut and Zander, 1992; Nooteboom, 1992; Hagedoorn, 1993; Hagedoorn and Schakenraad, 1994; Nooteboom, 1999; Ahuja, 2000; Rowley et al., 2000; Hagedoorn and Duysters, 2002; Duysters and de Man, 2003). The basic idea that for innovation firms need to open up to outside relationships, which goes back at least as far as Lundvall (1988), has recently received a new buzz-word label of 'open innovation' (Chesbrough, 2003).

In outside means and conditions for innovation, not only alliances are relevant, but also conditions of national innovation systems (NIS) and conditions of location ('externalities'), in regional innovation systems (RIS). There are large literatures on both, and these also will not be systematically included in the present book, but some essential effects of location cannot be ignored. Inter-firm relationships for learning and innovation clearly go beyond inter-organizational dyads, to include network effects, that is effects of the structure and the content and strength of ties between firms, and interactions between structure and strength of ties. That is taken up later in this chapter. The present paragraph focuses on the design and governance on dyadic relationships.

Optimal Cognitive Distance

Especially from an evolutionary perspective on innovation (Nelson and Winter, 1982), heterogeneity or variety is a crucial source of innovation, and this has been taken up in the alliance literature (Stuart and Podolny, 1996; Almeida and Kogut, 1999; Rosenkopf and Nerkar, 2001; Fleming, 2001; Rosenkopf and Almeida, 2003; Ahuja and Katila, 2004). However, that literature does not explain how, precisely, heterogeneity produces innovation.

Like variety more generally, heterogeneity in inter-organizational relationships has three dimensions that are seldom explicitly distinguished. One is the number of firms involved, the second is the pattern of ties between them, and the other is the difference, in particular cognitive distance, between them. Here the focus is on cognitive distance. Between firms, in contrast with people, cognitive distance is the difference between the cognitive foci of firms, with two main dimensions of technological knowledge/competence and moral principles for internal governance. Effects from the number of interacting firms and the pattern of ties between them are discussed in later sections.

A large stream of literature has indicated only the problems rather than the benefits of such cognitive distance. In a study on alliance formation in the semi-conductor industry, Stuart (1998) argued that the most valuable alliances are those between firms with similar technological foci and/or operating in similar markets, whereas distant firms are inhibited from cooperating effectively. In a similar vein, the diversification literature argues that most is to be learned from alliance partners with related knowledge and skills (Tanriverdi and Venkatraman, 2005), or from areas that firms already possess capabilities in (Penner-Hahn and Shaver, 2005). In a survey of key customer relations of 180 young technology-based firms, Yli et al. (2001) hypothesized that relationship quality, in terms of goodwill trust and shared norms and reciprocal expectations, would have a positive effect on knowledge acquisition, but found a significant negative effect. In the literature on international business also, a pervasive view is that cognitive distance is a problem to be overcome. Johanson and Vahlne (1977, 1990) employed the notion of 'psychological distance', which is seen as having an adverse effect on cross-cultural communication. When learning is discussed, in that literature, it is mostly seen as learning to cope with transnational differences, by accumulating experience in cross-border collaboration (for example Barkema et al., 1997), rather than taking those differences as a potential source of learning to change home country products or practices.

The principle of optimal cognitive distance, set out in Chapter 3, applies also to inter-organizational relationships (IORs). According to this principle, there is an inverted-U shaped relationship between innovative performance and cognitive distance. As indicated, here cognitive distance refers to difference in organizational cognitive focus between organizations, in competence as well as governance. The former has been operationalized and measured in terms of technological profiles of firms, derived from patent data, with different scores, relative to industry averages, per patent class. The distance between them can then be measured in terms of correlation coefficients (Wuyts et al., 2005; Nooteboom et al., 2007). An alternative would be to locate n-item profiles as points in n-dimensional space and calculate the Euclidean distance between them (Los, 1999). For distance in governance one should have indicators on the use of alternative instruments of governance and/or underlying principles. No ready database for this seems available, and it appears that dedicated data would have to be collected for it, to be connected to data on innovative performance in collaboration. With some success, Wuyts et al. (2005) used proxy variables from existing firm data, such as firm size, profit margins, and degree of diversification.

Wuyts et al. tested the hypothesized inverse-U shaped effect of technological and organizational distance (see Figure 3.3), here applied to the likelihood of alliance formation, on a data set of alliances established in 1981–6 between 67 of the world's largest 150 firms that operated in ICT industries, and did not find the hypothesized inverse-U shaped effect of technical distance but did find such an effect, somewhat surprisingly, in view of the imperfection of the proxy measure, of organizational distance. This test was not very conclusive, for two reasons. First, the dependent variable was not innovative performance from collaboration, as required by the hypothesis, but the likelihood of alliance formation, which was supposedly dependent, at least in part, on expected innovative success. However, the alliances involved ranged across a wide spectrum of goals, and were not all aimed at innovation as the main goal. Furthermore, even when innovation was the main goal, the hypothesis requires managers to anticipate innovative success, in terms of optimal cognitive distance, which is perhaps too much to expect. In other words, this test was rather a long shot. Nevertheless, the result of a significant inverse-U shaped relation between likelihood of alliance formation and difference in type of organization remains interesting. Wuyts et al. also tested for an effect of alliance duration, but this will be discussed in a later section.

A more direct and adequate test of technological distance on innovative performance of alliances was conducted by Nooteboom et al. (2007), on the basis of a data set on patent production (taken as a measure of innovative performance), and a measure of technical distance constructed from patent portfolio's, as indicated above, on data from 994 alliances between 116 companies in the chemicals, automotive and pharmaceutical industries in 1986–97. There, with appropriate control variables, the inverse-U effect of cognitive distance was unambiguously confirmed. A complication here was that a firm's number of new patents, in any given year, could not be attributed to specific alliances of that firm, and could only be related to the totality of those, and thus had to be related to average technological distance across all alliance partners of the focal firm.

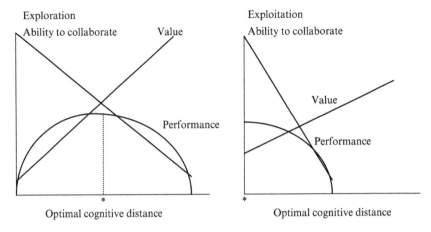

Figure 4.1   Exploitation and exploration

Nooteboom et al. (2007) included a test of the difference between exploration and exploitation, with the expectation that for exploration the
positive effect of cognitive distance is more pronounced, while for exploitation the negative effect is more pronounced, as argued in Chapter 3, and
reproduced in Figure 4.1.

With the data, a distinction was made between patents that were more
exploratory to the firm, defined as patents in patent classes that the
firm did not already engage in, with exploitative patents in classes that
the firm already engaged in. The results clearly confirmed the expected
differences.

Absorptive Capacity and a Boredom Effect

Nooteboom et al. (2007) also tested for the effect of absorptive capacity,
based on knowledge accumulation, on the location of optimal cognitive
distance, as hypothesized in Chapter 3, and reproduced in Figure 4.2. The
hypothesis is that knowledge accumulation has a positive effect on the
intercept of the downward sloping line representing collaborative ability
as a function of cognitive distance.

The database used was the same as described in the preceding section.
Knowledge accumulation, or 'technological capital' (TC), as a determinant
of absorptive capacity, was measured as the number of patents that a firm
obtained in the previous five years. The mathematical specification of the
resulting model was given in Chapter 3. This shows that according to the
hypothesis the model would include, next to a negative effect of the squared
cognitive distance (yielding an inverse-U effect), a positive interaction

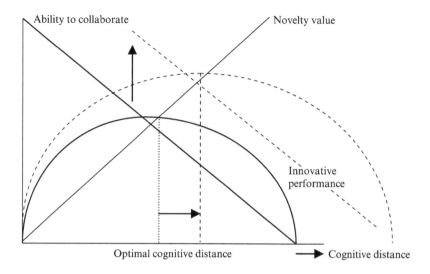

Figure 4.2   Upward shift of ability to collaborate

effect between technological capital and cognitive distance. In fact, the empirical analysis found a negative interaction effect. As demonstrated mathematically in Appendix 4.1, this can be explained if an increase of technological capital at the same time yields a downward rotation of the upward sloping line for novelty value. That would lead to a negative inter-action effect of technological capital and cognitive distance, as observed, and an additional positive interaction effect between technological capital and the squared term in cognitive distance, which was corroborated by the empirical study.

In sum, evidence is found that technological capital does indeed increase absorptive capacity but at the same time decreases the impact of an increase of cognitive distance on novelty value. As indicated in Chapter 3, the latter indicates a principle of decreasing returns to knowledge, or a 'boredom effect': the more one knows, the further afield, at greater cognitive distance, one needs to look to find something new, which is plausible. The result-ing effects and interactions between cognitive distance and technological capital are illustrated in Figure 4.3, according to the model estimate, for the range of observations. Note that at the highest level of technological capital, optimal cognitive distance is zero. Apparently, according to the underlying interpretation of the model, when one has a very broad and deep stock of knowledge outside collaboration has lost it value of novelty, for lack of partners that can help to innovate further, and the best one can do is exploit that knowledge base with partners one can easily do business

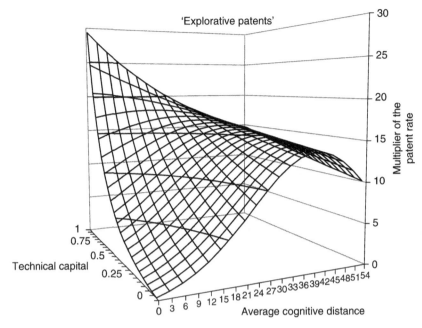

Source: Nooteboom et al. (2007).

*Figure 4.3   Exploration performance as a function of cognitive distance
            and technical capital*

with. In other words, then the sources of novelty for exploration are
entirely internal to the firm.

Optimal Duration

Wuyts et al. conducted a test of the hypothesis of an inverse U-shaped
effect of the duration of a relationship, set out in Chapter 3. The rationale
of this is that to the extent that a relationship lasts, and is exclusive, that
is occurs in isolation from other sources of renewal, cognitive distance is
reduced, that is partners start to think more alike and to know the same
things. However, they were not able to incorporate the qualifier variable
of non-overlapping outside sources. When those occur, connected organizations 'bridge structural holes' (Burt, 1992), and are continually refreshed
with new knowledge, whereby, by hypothesis, they maintain cognitive
distance to maintain innovative potential in their relationship.

    From portfolios of R&D agreements between 18 major pharmaceu-
tical companies and small biotech companies, from 1985, the duration of

relationships was measured only indirectly, with a proxy variable in the form of the dispersion of partners, defined as the ratio of the total number of different partners over the total number of agreements. If a firm's portfolio of agreements is characterized by low levels of partner dispersion, this firm tends to cooperate more frequently with the same partners, thus yielding higher duration of relationships. It is inherently difficult, in any feasible sample of alliance data across time, to have reliable data on the duration of alliances, since for many observations one will know the starting date but not the ending date of the alliance.

The dependent variable, as a measure of innovative performance, was the number of patented drugs of chemical type 1, according to FDA concepts, which represent a new technology different from the established technologies, as they involve an 'active ingredient that has never been marketed before'. An example of such a chemical type 1 drug is Novartis' Zometa drug, approved in 2001, which involves a completely new active ingredient (zoledronic acid) for treating the deterioration of cancer patients' inner bone structure (hypercalcemia of malignancy). Drugs based on a previously approved active ingredient are not considered a technological innovation. The FDA provides this detailed information only for drugs approved from 1991 on. The pharmaceutical firms from the sample received approval for 64 drugs of chemical type 1 in the period 1991–2000. The model was a test of the likelihood of such a type 1 drug as a function of partner dispersion, with appropriate control variables. With this empirical set-up Wuyts et al. confirmed the inverse-U shaped effect.

COMPLICATIONS

This section discusses complications that may arise in collaboration, within and between organizations, due to problems in connecting activities or capabilities. In particular, it can be difficult to separate exploitation and exploration.

Inseparability and Stickiness

Outsourcing of capabilities that fall outside the core of the firm, that would stretch organizational focus too much, is subject to a number of conditions. One is that in order to maintain coordination with outsourced activities, one requires the maintenance of sufficient absorptive capacity, to judge its quality and to enable efficient connections. This explains the otherwise puzzling phenomenon that firms outsource activities but still maintain capabilities in that area, on the basis of ongoing R&D, design, prototyping or pilot production (Granstrand et al., 1997).

It may also be inherently difficult to outsource certain capabilities. This may arise, in particular, under conditions of systemic complexity, where technical or cognitive elements are hard to separate organizationally, without loss of efficiency, speed or quality of fit. Earlier, in Chapters 1 and 3, problems of combining exploration and exploitation were noted, and the option was suggested of specializing in one and outsourcing the other. However, technically and cognitively it may be very difficult to separate the two. This can occur, for example, in the connection between the development of products and of processes to produce them, when process development requires intimate experience-based knowledge of both product features and features of production, to the extent that such knowledge is 'sticky'.

In Chapter 2, several causes of sticky knowledge were noted. One was tacitness of knowledge, yielding a problem not only in limited opportunities for externalizing and codifying it, for the purpose of transfer, but also for absorption, since tacit knowledge is difficult to replace on the basis of rational critical analysis. A second cause of stickiness may be the high embeddedness of knowledge in specific action contexts, and context dependence of the meanings of terms. In particular, stickiness arises to the extent that knowledge is 'presentational' rather than 'representational' (Shanon, 1993; see Chapter 2). Presentational knowledge is highly embedded in context, and lacks the representational properties of 'compositionality', with a whole that is composed of well-defined elements joined together in accordance with rules of well-formedness, a clear separation of content and medium of articulation, whereby the medium is of no relevance, and both the constituents and the dimensions upon which they are defined are distinct and well differentiated.

When it is feasible to overcome the stickiness of knowledge, but knowledge adaptation is still costly, the question may be who adapts to whom. Von Hippel (1999) suggested that that side should adapt whose knowledge is most complex and frequently used. When customers have highly diverse needs or desires and capabilities, especially when that knowledge is also highly tacit, while producers can specify modules and features of the product, and ways to configure them, then rather than customers transferring their complex, idiosyncratic information to the producer, the producer should transfer information to customers, for each of them to adapt or configure the product to his own knowledge and needs. This is recognizable in trends to involve customers in the customization of products, such as the configuration of features of a car, the booking of a voyage from the website of a tour operator, the design of insurance policies and the processing of claims, and so on. This yields an additional principle for drawing the boundaries of the firm in terms of knowledge and capability.

Illustrations

Brusoni (2006) gave an example in the chemical engineering industry. He distinguishes between 'division of labour' and 'division of knowledge'. While chemical plants are highly modular, and hence decomposable, and hence partially outsourceable, there are different ways of doing decomposition, with important differences in outcomes. The complexity lies in the coupling between systems of reaction processes, separation processes, energy, control and safety. To optimize design requires a thorough understanding of systemic effects of alternative decompositions. Given a choice of decomposition, the elements can be outsourced, but the capability to decompose and synthesize elements in different ways cannot. As a result, some re-integration of capability and activity took place after chemical producers had fully outsourced the production of chemical plants.

Pisano (2000) gave an example in biotechnological process technology compared to chemical synthesis technology, in: (a) theoretical understanding of the basic processes; (b) ability to precisely and fully characterize intermediates and final products; and (c) knowledge of the second order effects of scaling up from experimental to operational production. As a result, 'biotechnology process development relies ... on trial and error and iteration of the process design *after* the process is transferred out of the laboratory' (op cit.: 135). Given these conditions, 'At some organizations, the plant was viewed as an integral part of the development process and a critical venue for experimentation. Others kept the plant relatively isolated from the development process; preferring instead to do most development in the laboratory and pilot plant' (op cit.: 137).

One company had previously focused on product development, and had mostly outsourced process development, and now started to integrate the entire development process. Then they ran into the familiar problem, in connecting exploration and exploitation, of 'the huge gulf between the interests of research scientists focused on finding novel products and the capabilities required to get a process up and running in an actual plant' (op cit.: 138). The company next instituted a process development group, where a pilot plant is integrated with the commercial manufacturing plant. This required the build-up and integration of a broad base of scientific capabilities in process technology disciplines. For that, they could build on the knowledge accumulated by the initial process development group. A second company resisted disruptions of ongoing manufacturing for the sake of development, not to disturb the continuity of clinical testing to satisfy demands from regulatory agencies, and faced the consequences of lack of integration between exploration and exploitation. A third company went further in separating production and development, by outsourcing, but ran into the problem of sticky knowledge, with the contractor lacking the subtleties of process knowledge.

A similar problem was identified by Appleyard et al. (2000), in the semi-conductor industry. There also, product innovation is highly intertwined with process innovation, 'requiring that the receiving fab (fabrication unit) have an equipment set that is identical to that on which a new process is developed in the development facility. Even stringent requirements for equipment duplication . . . cannot eliminate all significant differences' (op cit.: 189). A solution was attempted, here also, in integrating development in a hybrid development/production facility where the pilot is eventually implemented at a commercial scale, and was transferred only then to a operational high-volume production facility, with substantial personnel rotation and equipment duplication (op cit.: 198), and the process remains in parallel operation in the hybrid facility for at least 12 month after the transfer, as a back-up for any unforeseen problems of transfer. However, a remaining problem of this arrangement lies in disincentives for experimentation in the manufacturing environment, which may eventually impair its performance (op cit.: 201).

These examples serve to illustrate how difficult it may be to separate exploration and exploitation, within and between firms, and the need, in that case, to establish an organizational focus that accommodates both. This is typically supported by rotation of personnel across the two to support mutual understanding and ability to collaborate.

INTER-ORGANIZATIONAL COLLABORATION

Apart from substantive problems in connecting knowledge, on the competence side, there are problems of governance, and corresponding problems in diverging views on collaboration. Problems of governance arise from relational risk, here between organizations. This section analyses the risks and discusses instruments for governing them. This is a large subject, with a correspondingly large literature, which cannot be fully treated here. A summary will have to suffice, for which use will be made of Nooteboom (1999, 2002, 2004b). The analysis is needed for itself, in view of the general need to combine competence and governance, and for the later analysis of network effects, in view of the differential effects of network structure, position in networks, and strength of ties on both competence and governance.

Relational Risk

There are three kinds of relational risk: of holdup, spillover and mishap. As defined in transaction cost economics (TCE), the problem of hold-up results from dependence in the form of switching costs: if the relationship breaks, costs have to be incurred anew. Switching costs are caused, in particular, by investments that are specific to the relationship. While there is much justified, fundamental criticism of TCE, especially under conditions of innovation, this central notion of specific investments is still highly relevant. Rather than losing importance, the notion of specific investments gains importance in the context of innovation. Next to the types of specific investment recognized in TCE (in location specificity, time specificity, tangible asset specificity, and human asset specificity), in innovation specific assets are needed to develop mutual understanding under conditions where knowledge is in flux, and to build up personal trust under conditions where uncertainty hinders governance by contract, and reputation mechanisms are not yet in place. Both types of investment, in mutual understanding and trust, tend to be highly relation-specific.

In relationships, one may also lose a hostage, mostly in the form of sensitive information. There are also opportunity costs of dependence: the loss of the value that the current partner offers relative to the next best alternative. This depends on the availability of alternative partners, or the possibility of conducting an activity oneself, and the extent that the partner offers something unique. In other words, it depends on the extent that a partner has a monopoly in his offering, or monopsony in his access to markets.

The 'hold-up' risk is that the partner may opportunistically exploit asymmetric dependence to demand a higher share of jointly produced added value, under the threat of exiting from the relationship. TCE claims that when the risk is high, it requires organizational integration to control it (Williamson, 1975). Next to full integration, within a firm, there are intermediate forms of semi-integration by means of detailed 'bilateral governance' (Williamson, 1985). When the frequency of transactions does not warrant the investment in detailed bilateral governance, one can employ a third party for arbitration, in 'trilateral' governance. Hold-up risk is purely a matter of intent, not of competence. One is not opportunistic by accident. In the literature on trust, two forms of opportunism are recognized. One is active, in lying, cheating, extortion and so on. Another is passive, in free riding, and lack of attention or commitment (Nooteboom, 2002).

Spillover risk entails that knowledge that constitutes competitive advantage, as part of core competence, reaches competitors and is used by them for imitation and competition. That is of particular relevance in innovation.

The risk may be direct, in the partner becoming a competitor, or indirect, in networks, with knowledge spilling over to a competitor via a partner. In the past, many firms have been overly concerned with spillover risk. First of all, one should realize that to get knowledge one must offer knowledge. The question is not how much knowledge one loses, but what the net balance is of giving and receiving knowledge. Second, when knowledge is tacit it spills over less easily, or is more 'sticky' (von Hippel, 1988; Brown and Duguid, 2001) than when it is documented. However, even then it can spill over, for example when the staff or the division in which the knowledge is embedded are poached, or when the staff involved have more allegiance to their professional colleagues, also in rival firms, than to the interests of the firm (Grey and Garsten, 2001), or professional vanity leads them to divulge too much in meetings with outside colleagues. Furthermore, the question is not whether information reaches a competitor but whether the competitor will also be able to understand it, that is turn it into knowledge, and to turn that into effective competition. For this it needs to be understood, and the competitor's absorptive capacity may not enable that (Cohen and Levinthal, 1990). There may be 'causal ambiguity' (Lippman and Rumelt, 1982). Next, it needs to be effectively implemented in the organization. And finally, if by that time the knowledge has shifted, spillover risk drops out. Spillover may be intentional, as when sensitive information is used as a hostage, but it may also be accidental, due to carelessness or mistakes in guarding sensitive knowledge.

Third, relational risk may lie in mishaps, such as accidents, misunderstandings or mistakes. This is more a matter of competence than of intentions.

Trust

In the literature on inter-organizational relationships, there is a big and ongoing debate on the question to what extent governance is a matter of control, on the basis of the deterrence of opportunism, by contract or hierarchy, or can go beyond that, in trust based on solidarity or benevolence. According to TCE, it is impossible to reliably judge possible limits to other people's opportunism, and therefore trust does not yield a reliable safeguard (Williamson, 1975: 31–7). If trust goes beyond calculative self-interest, it yields blind, unconditional trust, which is not wise and will not survive in markets (Williamson, 1993). From a social science perspective, many others take the view that trust is viable, without necessarily becoming blind or unconditional (Macauley, 1963; Deutsch, 1973; Granovetter, 1973; Ouchi, 1980; Gambetta, 1988; Bradach and Eccles, 1989; Helper, 1990; Hill, 1990; Bromiley and Cummings, 1992; Murakami and Rohlen,

1992; Dyer and Ouchi, 1993; Ring and Van de Ven, 1992, 1994; Gulati, 1995; McAllister, 1995; Chiles and McMackin, 1996; Noorderhaven, 1996; Nooteboom et al., 1997; Das and Teng, 1998, 2001; Nooteboom, 1999, 2002). A committed partner does not immediately exit from the relationship in case of unforeseen opportunities or problems, but engages in 'voice' (Hirschman, 1970; Helper, 1987).

The literature on trust is too voluminous to review here. An essential point is that trust is a four-place predicate: a trustor (1) trusts a trustee (2; an individual, organization or institution), in some respect of behaviour (3; competence, truthfulness, resources, intentions), depending on circumstances (4) (Nooteboom, 2002). The distinction between trustor and trustee highlights the essentially interactive nature of trust (Hardin 2002). The distinction between people and organizations as trustors and trustees was discussed for example by Zaheer, McEvily and Perrone (1998).

The third dimension, the distinction between trust in competence or resources and trust in intentions, recognized by many, is important for the causal ambiguity (Nelson and Winter, 1982: 123) that it yields. Expectations may be disappointed due to a variety of causes, such as mishaps, a gap in competence, lack of commitment or outright opportunism. When an expectation is disappointed it is not directly clear which cause is at work. There is room for misinterpretation of events that can have tragic consequences. A relationship may break down because ego infers opportunism of alter while in fact the cause of disappointment was a mishap, or a gap in competence.

The fourth dimension of trust, its circumstances, indicates that trust has its limits. While counter to Williamson (1993) trust can go beyond calculative self-interest, it does have its limits, depending on the trustee's resistance to temptations and pressures towards opportunism, which depend on situational contingencies of opportunity and threat to survival (see Pettit, 1995), and should not be blind in the sense of unconditional.

Governance

In Chapter 3, a distinction was proposed between reliance/reliability, which includes control, and trust, which goes beyond control, with a table (Table 3.1) that specifies sources of reliability, between and within organizations. Between organizations there are instruments of control in legal contracts, incentives from mutual dependence, hostages, reputation, and sources of trust in shared ethical norms and values of conduct, routinization of conduct, and personal empathy and identification. Within organizations an important function of cognitive focus is to provide shared norms and values of conduct. In inter-organizational relationships, with their lesser coherence and continuity, and greater cognitive distance, there are generally fewer such norms and values. However, such sources may be developed to some extent. Since this tends to constitute a relation-specific investment, a condition is that there is a perspective for sufficient duration. Note that the building of trust can go too far, particularly when it takes the form of full identification or routinization, which may cause blindness to risks and novel opportunities of innovation in alternative relationships. The table in Chapter 3 does not include the possible services of intermediaries or go-betweens. These are specified in a later section in the present chapter.

There is no single best instrument or recipe for governance. Instruments need to be carefully configured as a function of a range of conditions, concerning the goals of alliance partners (for example innovation), their experience (with each other and with others), differences in outlook (cognitive distance), the range of activities and content of a tie (related to goals and conditions), the type of technology involved (systemic, modular, stand-alone), type of knowledge (degree of tacitness), market conditions (type and degree of competition), and institutional conditions (legal infrastructure, availability of a reputation mechanism, availability of trusted third parties). Of course, the chosen instruments should complement each other, and should not be in conflict. A central question here is whether trust and control are substitutes or complements. Can one afford less contract when there is more trust? Or does one always need both, since both are limited? Can the two reinforce each other? Klein Woolthuis et al. (2005) showed that trust and contract can be both substitutes and complements. Both have their limits and the one needs to begin where the other ends.

The context of innovation makes special demands, and imposes limits, on the configuration of instruments. The high uncertainty involved in especially radical innovation entails that the specification of contracts is problematic and can constrain the scope of innovation when imposed anyway. Under the high flux of knowledge and entry and exit of players that is typical of especially early stages of radical innovation, reputation mechanisms and reliable third parties (reliable in both competence and fairness) may not yet be in place. If all those instruments from Table 3.1 are unavailable, one is left with the sources of benevolence, on the basis of institutionalized ethics or personalized trust. However, such generalization would be too hasty. What instruments are available depends on details of ties and structure of the network, to be analysed later in this chapter.

Go-betweens

There are a host of different types of intermediaries whose task it is to help judge performance and to provide intermediation or arbitration in conflicts. Shapiro (1987) called these intermediaries 'guardians of trust', Zucker (1986) saw them as part of 'institutions based trust', and Fukuyama (1995) used the term 'intermediate communities'. Many of these serve to develop and police technical or professional standards, with certification systems. There are also roles for go-betweens as consultants in the management of IOR's (Nooteboom, 2002).

One role of these, recognized in TCE, is that of arbitration or mediation in 'trilateral governance'. When there is relational risk, but transactions are insufficiently substantial or frequent to warrant the cost of developing intricate forms of 'bilateral' governance, with instruments described above, it may be efficient to establish only simple agreements and submit to arbitration or mediation.

A second role is to assess the value of information before it is traded, to solve Arrow's 'revelation problem': if one wants to sell information, the partner will want to assess its value by looking into it, but then he already has the information and might no longer pay for it. This problem can be solved in several ways. One is the use of licences, with a limited payment up front, and later payment in proportion to the emerging yields of the information. Another is to let a go-between assess the value of the information for the potential buyer.

A third role for a go-between is to create mutual understanding, helping to cross cognitive distance. As indicated earlier, this is especially important when there is asymmetry between partners in their absorptive capacity or ability to collaborate. A fourth role is to monitor information flow as a guard against spillover. The reason for this role is that if partner A does the monitoring himself, in the firm of partner B, then this scrutiny inside B's firm may increase the spillover from B to A. A fifth role is to act as a guardian of hostages. Without that, there may be a danger that the hostage keeper does not return the hostage even if the partner sticks to the agreement. The third party has an interest in maintaining symmetric trust and acceptance by both protagonists.

A sixth, and perhaps most crucial role is to act as an intermediary in the building of trust. Trust relations are often entered with partners who are trusted partners of someone you trust (Sydow, 2000). If X trusts Y and Y trusts Z, then X may rationally give trust in Z a chance. X needs to feel that Y is able to judge well and has no intention to lie about his judgement. This can speed up the building of trust between strangers, which might otherwise take too long. This is particularly important in view of the dynamics of the build-up and breakdown of trust. New relationships might have to start small, with low stakes that are raised as trust builds up. This may be needed especially when extended contracts are not feasible or desirable, as is the case particularly in innovation.

The disadvantage of such a procedure is its slowness. A go-between may provide help for a more speedy development. Intermediation in the first small and ginger steps of cooperation, to ensure that they are successful, can be very important in the building of a trust relation. The intermediary can perform valuable services in protecting trust when it is still fragile: to eliminate misunderstanding and allay suspicions when errors or mishaps are mistaken as signals of opportunism.

A seventh role, related to the sixth, is to help in the timely and least destructive disentanglement of relations. To eliminate misunderstanding, to prevent acrimonious and mutually damaging battles of divorce, a go-between can offer valuable services, to help in 'a voice type of exit'. An eighth role is to support a reputation mechanism. For a reputation mechanism to work, infringement of agreements must be observable, its report must be credible, and it must reach potential future partners of the culprit. The go-between can help in all respects.

NETWORKS

There is a large literature on inter-firm networks in innovation, which cannot be fully included here. Here, the focus is on issues of cognition. What are the effects of the structure of networks, the position of a firm in it, and the nature and strength of ties between firms, on ability to innovate by collaboration, and on relational risks and their governance?

From Dyads to Triads

Inter-organizational relationships go beyond dyads. There may be multiple participants in collaboration, and indirect linkages in networks. Those have implications for the value, risk and governance of relations. One may value a partner not for himself but for the access that he provides to others. In an alliance, one may need to assess the risk that the partner may be taken over by a competitor, possibly in an indirect way, in which he takes over a majority shareholder of the partner (Lorange and Roos, 1992). Spillover risk can be indirect, via partners to competitors. If one already has partners, adding a new one might raise spillover risk for existing partners. A dense network and strong ties may help absorptive capacity and governance but may inhibit novelty potential.

Simmel (1950 [1917]) showed that a fundamental shift occurs in going from dyadic to triadic relations (see also Krackhardt, 1999), and that beyond that, with more than three players, no further fundamental change occurs, and the analysis can be conducted in some combination of dyads and triads. In dyadic relations no coalitions can occur, and no majority can outvote an individual. In a triad any member by himself has less bargaining power than in a dyad. The threat of exit carries less weight, since the two remaining partners would still have each other. In a triad, conflict is more readily resolved. When any two players enter conflict, the third can act as a moderator or 'go-between'. On the other hand, he may also opportunistically exploit his position as a go-between.

One stream of literature on networks suggests that players who span 'structural holes' can gain advantage (Burt, 1992). If individuals or communities A and B are connected only by C, then C can take advantage of his bridging position by accessing resources that others cannot access, and by playing off A and B against each other. As a result, the third party is maximally powerful and minimally constrained in his actions. Burt (1992) employs the notion of *tertius gaudens,* or laughing third, proposed much earlier by Simmel (1950 [1917]).

However, as Krackhardt showed, Simmel also indicated that under some conditions the third party is maximally instead of minimally constrained. This occurs when the third party bridges two different cliques, with dense and strong internal ties, who entertain different values and norms, while both can observe the actions of the third party. The third party then has to satisfy the rules or norms of both cliques (the intersection of norm sets), and thereby is constrained in his or her actions. If the two sets have no intersection, interests cannot be reconciled, and the third party is in an impossible situation. The key factor that determines whether the bridging party is minimally or maximally constrained is the degree to which his actions are public, or at least known to both A and B. If not, then the situation described by Burt obtains, and the third party is minimally constrained. If the actions are public, he or she is maximally constrained. Membership of multiple cliques then yields a position of potential power, but also constrains the use of it. This often applies to managers or boundary spanners who bridge different departments or organizations. It can apply to the manager of a joint venture who still has allegiance to the parent who remains the employer.

However, Simmel (1950 [1917]: 160) also showed that if, in such a structural position, the party in between is less dependent on the two parties that are connected, and the third party's position does not depend on reconciling them, he or she may again be minimally constrained by arguing that since it is impossible to follow the demands of both other parties, one has the right to go one's own way. The example Simmel gave was that of William the Conqueror who was confronted with two irreconcilable law systems of his Norman sponsors and the Anglo-Saxon population he conquered, and used this to impose his own will.

While Simmel claimed that beyond three not much new happens in terms of structural logic within the group, he did recognize a number of effects of network size, but these will be left aside in this chapter. In more recent sociology much study has been devoted to the effects of the density and strength of ties in networks, and I will now focus on that.

Density and Strength of Ties

A central debate in the network literature was whether in networks for innovation ties should be sparse and weak (Granovetter, 1973; Burt, 1992), or dense and strong (Coleman, 1988). The argument in favour of sparse and weak ties is that in frequent and intense interaction between many actors, in a dense structure, much of the information circulating in the system is redundant. An example Granovetter used, in personal networks, was the discovery of new employment opportunities, through acquaintances with which one has only sporadic contacts. If A is connected to B, and B is connected to C, then A does not need a direct connection to C because information can be accessed from C through B (Burt, 1992). The cost of redundancy, in setting up and maintaining ties, increases with the strength of ties. Thus, according to Burt (1992), efficiency can be created in the network by shedding redundant ties and selectively maintaining only a limited set of ties that bridge 'structural holes'. Then, time and energy are saved for developing new contacts to unconnected nodes. Apart from efficiency, bridging structural holes also provides advantages of 'brokerage'. Also, strong, that is intense and long lasting ties, can lead to reduced variety and hence reduced potential for learning. Or, in other words, and more precisely, strong ties can lead to too little cognitive distance. Originally (Granovetter, 1973) density and strength of ties were conflated, while later it was recognized that they represent separate features (Burt, 1992). It is conceivable that sparse ties may be strong and that dense ties may be weak (Reagans and McEvily, 2003).

According to Coleman (1988), by contrast, dense and weak ties ('cohesion' or 'network closure') facilitate the role of social capital such as the build-up of reputation, trust, social norms, and social control, for example by coalition formation, to constrain actions, which facilitate collaboration, as suggested by Simmel.

In this debate the empirical evidence is mixed. McEvily and Zaheer (1999) found evidence against redundancy in an advice network, for the acquisition of capabilities. Ahuja (2000) found evidence against structural holes, for innovation in collaboration. Walker et al. (1997) found evidence in favour of cohesion, for innovation in biotechnology. In view of these apparently inconsistent findings, subsequent studies have taken a 'contingency' approach (Bae and Gargiulo, 2003), investigating environmental conditions that would favour the one or the other view (Podolny and Baron, 1997; Ahuja, 2000; Rowley et al., 2000; Podolny, 2001; Hagedoorn and Duysters, 2002).

In fact, this apparently contradictory evidence is not surprising. The two opposite claims concerning density and strength of ties may well both be true. As noted by Burt (2000: 373): 'the closure and hole arguments are not as contradictory as they might seem . . . The ambiguity stems in large part from the different roles that social capital plays in the study populations.' More precisely, I propose here, they simply represent different aspects of collaboration: on the one hand a competence dimension, in terms of the access to new knowledge, the combination of complementary competencies, joint production of new knowledge, and the creation of Schumpeterian 'novel combinations', and on the other hand a governance dimension of managing relational risks of opportunism and spillover or loss of appropriability of returns on innovation. Concerning competence, particularly in exploration of novel opportunities, one may need weak ties, in the bridging of structural holes. For governance, one may need cohesion. This was also Ahuja's (2000) argument: structural holes are less likely to be beneficial when overcoming opportunism is critical for success. When combining competence and governance perspectives, there are arguments both in favour and against density and strong ties, in innovation and knowledge transfer (Uzzi, 1996, 1997).

Another cause of the ambiguity of outcomes in empirical studies lies in the neglect of the content of ties (Gilsing and Nooteboom, 2005). Hansen (1999) made a distinction between acquiring knowledge about and knowledge from others, that is between the identification of the location and usefulness of knowledge, and the transfer or sharing of knowledge. He, and earlier Uzzi (1997), argued and found empirical evidence that strong ties promote the transfer of complex knowledge, while weak ties promote the transfer of simple knowledge.[3]

The following subsections analyse in more detail the effects of network structure and strength of ties.

Network Structure

Gilsing and Nooteboom (2005) offered several new hypotheses as modifications and additions to the extant literature on the effects of network structure. Network structure has a number of features, such as density of ties, (degree) centrality, that is the extent to which some firms have more direct ties than others, and stability of ties.

A first hypothesis is that in contrast with the strength of weak ties argument networks for radical innovation or exploration (March, 1991;

Nooteboom, 2000) require density of ties. There are three arguments from considerations of competence. First, under the radical uncertainty of exploration it has not yet been established what knowledge, and hence what sources, are relevant. As a result, one has to hedge one's bets concerning what sources to tap, including sources that may turn out to be irrelevant. This is an argument for redundancy in type of sources. Second, there is high volatility of existence of firms and their network membership, so that firms that give access to knowledge now may not exist tomorrow. As a result one has to hedge one's bets concerning what firms will remain in existence. One may need to maintain a tie with C even if one also has a tie with B who also has a tie with C, to cover for the risk that B drops out for access to C. This is an argument for redundancy in ties. Third, under the conditions of a large variety of knowledge, or potential knowledge, in exploration, with large cognitive distances, one may need a third party to help understand a given party, by supplementing one's absorptive capacity, or to check the accuracy of information. This is an argument for redundancy for triangulation. The argument that density enables triangulation was proposed earlier by Rowley et al. (2000). However, they argued that it was most important in exploitation, while Gilsing and Nooteboom argue that it is most important in exploration. In exploitation knowledge has become more diffused and standardized and less help is needed from others to understand it.

Fourth, there is an argument by default: in exploration costs of redundancy matter less. They are typically smaller and less relevant than in exploitation. Under exploration, (specific) investment in a tie tends to be smaller, in mutual understanding, designing and executing experiments, building and testing prototypes, in comparison with investments for exploitation, such as investment in scaling up, efficient production systems with corresponding division and coordination of labour, distribution channels, brand name, and the like. Note that there is room for contingency here. In some industries, such as aerospace, prototyping and testing may require investments that are as high, or even higher, than for production. Second, costs are less relevant. As the innovation literature argues, in exploration competition is aimed at technical and commercial viability, while low cost emerges as a competitive advantage only later, after the market has materialized and price competition increases from new entrants who jump on the bandwagon of new market success (Abernathy, 1978; Abernathy and Utterback, 1978; Abernathy and Clark, 1985).

There are also arguments in favour of density from considerations of governance. As indicated before, the literature (Coleman, 1988) proposes that density favours the functioning of social norms, social control, coalitions, sanctions, and reputation mechanisms. These mechanisms of social control are particularly needed in exploration, in view of the limited feasi-bility of contractual control, due to uncertainty concerning the content and conditions of a contract and limited ability to assess and control contract compliance. On the other hand, from a governance perspective density also brings risks. Having a partner who has multiple partners increases his opportunities for switching, which may increase his hold-up power, with more 'opportunities for opportunism'. Density also opens up more avenues for spillover, which may increase risk of loss of competitive advan-tage. However, as argued by Nooteboom (1999), in radical innovation change of knowledge may be so fast that spillover risk becomes negligible. Hold-up risk from multiple partners is limited if it is balanced, that is if all actors have such multiple partnerships, as tends to be the case in a dense network.

Concerning other features of network structure, stability of the network should be low, reflecting frequent exit and entry of network participants, for the sake of novel combinations (see the simulation model in March, 1991). Moreover, under such conditions of radical innovation, with uncer-tainty concerning what elements will emerge and survive in what configur-ation, centralization is less relevant. Centrality may also yield an obstacle to re-configuration of ties, in attempts to maintain the power invested in established, centralized positions.

For more incremental innovation, in exploitation, the arguments con-cerning network structure go in the opposite direction. The cost of redun-dant ties matters since competition has shifted to price, and the size of costs is also likely to be high. Since it is now clear what knowledge is relevant, who has it, and network membership is more stable, there is less need to hedge bets by redundancy of ties. Since knowledge is more stable and dif-fused there is less need for triangulation. Concerning governance, reduc-tion of uncertainty allows for more governance by contracts, lessening the need for dense ties for the sake of a reputation mechanism. As a result of the emergence of dominant designs and the stabilization and diffusion of knowledge, network stability can be larger, and centrality in the network may be needed for efficient coordination in division of labour, in hub-and-spoke type structures. This depends on industry contingencies. Centrality or some density is needed, in particular, if technology is systemic, to ensure that the different components of the system remain in tune with each other (Langlois and Robertson, 1995).

Tie Strength

Tie strength has a number of dimensions. According to Granovetter (1973: 1361), in personal networks there are four dimensions of tie strength:

'amount of time, emotional intensity, intimacy (mutual confiding) and reciprocal services'. Gilsing and Nooteboom (2005) proposed the following, modified dimensions: scope of shared activities, that is the range of issues or 'multiplexity' incorporated in the tie, frequency of interaction, duration of the relationship, trust and openness, and the extent of formal, contractual control. The scope of a tie refers to its content. Scope may refer to width and depth of knowledge shared, but also to the range of different contents of knowledge, concerning technology, materials, sources, markets, government regulations, finance, accounting and gossip on the technical or intentional reliability of potential or actual partners.

The following hypotheses were proposed for exploration networks. Duration should be low, since long duration would conflict with the need for network flexibility, for the sake of Schumpeterian novel combinations, and it may lead to too much reduction of cognitive distance as a source of innovation. Short duration must then be compensated by high frequency of interaction to recoup the specific investments relevant in exploration. High frequency is also consistent with the speed of developments associated with radical innovation and efforts to win innovation races. The limited viability of contracts in exploration, due to uncertainty, and the need to share tacit knowledge, in intensive and frequent interaction, plead for high trust and openness and low contractual control. The wide range of uncertainty that characterizes exploration, and the importance of reputation mechanisms, argued before, plead for a wide scope of ties: there are multiple issues to find out and talk about.

Again, the hypotheses concerning networks for exploitation go in the opposite direction, although there are industry contingencies. In exploitation specific investments tend to be larger, with a longer economic life, requiring longer duration of relationships to recoup investments, while longer duration is less of a problem due to less volatility and the emergence of dominant designs in technology and organization. Dominant designs and codification and wider diffusion of knowledge yield less need for a high scope and high frequency of interaction. Due to less uncertainty contracts are more feasible, and they are more needed because due to lesser scope and frequency of interaction trust and openness are less, and due to lesser density of networks, argued before, reputation mechanisms are weaker.

AN INTEGRATED MODEL

This section reports on attempts to integrate the multiple effects discussed in the earlier sections. What are the combined effects of cognitive distance, network structure, position in a network, and strength of ties, from a perspective of both competence and governance, on exploitation and exploration? This is a tall order, and no final, complete results can be supplied as yet. However, progress in this direction is being made.

Interaction between Structure and Strength of Ties

Note that while density and strength of ties are distinct categories, there is interaction between them (see Rowley et al., 2000). For example, for governance one can use contracts or trust/openness (in tie strength), or, alternatively, density for the sake of social control (structure), in a reputation mechanism. Another example is that when specific investments are needed, to recoup those one needs either high frequency or long duration (strength), while the latter entails a certain stability of the network (structure). Here elements of structure and strength can substitute for each other. This gives an opportunity to reconcile the otherwise contrary effects of 'weak ties' versus 'closure'.

What is the empirical evidence, in the extant literature? Rowley et al. (2000) made the customary hypotheses that in exploration density and strength of ties are negatively related and in exploitation are positively related to performance, and they concluded that 'our results do not strongly support the theoretical arguments regarding the main effects of strong ties or density . . .'. They did find evidence for the interaction effects between tie strength and structure. Hagedoorn and Duysters (2002) found a positive effect of 'multiple, redundant ties' under exploration and Beerkens (2004) found empirical evidence for dense ties in exploration in three industries: chemicals, cars and pharmaceuticals. Gilsing and Nooteboom (2005), in two qualitative case studies of exploration and exploitation in multi-media and biotechnology, found considerable evidence in favour of most of their hypotheses, contrary to previous literature, but not for all. Here, the focus is on the anomalies of the latter study and their interpretation.

Most of the anomalies were in exploration in biotechnology, in interaction between small biotech firms and universities. One of the theoretical arguments was that in exploration knowledge is more tacit, which complicates knowledge diffusion and the build-up of a joint understanding (competence), and also limits the use of contracts for formal control (governance). However, it turned out from the biotechnology case that while in exploration knowledge was indeed highly tacit in the exploration process, exploration outcomes were highly codified, which, counter to the assumption, enabled governance by formal contracting and monitoring. Another empirical anomaly in biotechnological exploration was the moderate centralization of the network structure, and the narrow scope of ties. The explanation of the latter lies in the highly science-based nature of biotechnology, which makes the role of universities and research institutes a more central one and eliminates the need to explore subjects related to organization, production, marketing and distribution. The most important anomaly in biotechnological exploration was that network structure was stable and, correspondingly, ties had long duration. However, closer analysis showed a structure that satisfied theoretical considerations, but in an unforeseen way, in a dual, 'small world'-like structure (Watts, 1999), with a dense and stable core community 'at home', yielding high absorptive capacity to utilize less durable and less dense ties to such communities elsewhere. In this way, the potential for inertia in long local ties was compensated by continual influx of novelty from more flexible outside ties.

In exploitation in multimedia, anomalies were: fairly high density and frequency of interaction. Related to that, governance can still be informal and trust-based, and serve as a complement to formal control. This deviation from hypotheses may be attributable to the fact that in the integration of a systemic technology some exploratory activity was still going on, in exploitation, which put limits on the codifiability of knowledge. Then, also in a setting of exploitation, high frequency is warranted and governance needs to be of a more informal type.

An important characteristic of knowledge that varied between both industries was the extent to which it was systemic versus stand-alone knowledge (Teece, 1986). This yields an important feature of the content of ties. This issue has received limited attention in the literature on networks and alliances (but see Teece, 1986; Langlois and Robertson, 1995). It yields important, relatively new insights. In multimedia, high density was needed to preserve systemic integrity of the emerging technological architecture while the combination of high frequency, short duration, wide scope and informal governance created cognitive diversity. In other words, stability of structure was needed in view of the systemic nature of technology, while potential disadvantages of that were compensated by features of the ties.

In sum, how structure and strength of ties enable and constrain learning and innovation in inter-firm networks depends on the extent to which knowledge is tacit versus codified as well as on the degree to which it is systemic or stand-alone. When knowledge and technology are systemic, this can require frequent interaction and informal governance even towards exploitation. Also, while knowledge can be tacit in exploration, the results of exploration can be codified, allowing for contractual control even in exploration. The most important conclusion perhaps is that in exploration local stability and density of structure, with ties of long duration, can be complemented by more sparse and flexible outside ties, in a small-world structure.

The findings seem in line with the findings by Beerkens (2004) on the role of redundancy in networks in exploration and exploitation in chemicals, cars and pharmaceuticals. The findings concerning the interaction between structure and strength of ties is in line with the findings of Rowley et al. (2000). The results on industry effects are in line with a recent study by Hagedoorn et al. (2005), who found that understanding the phenomenon of repeated ties, as a dimension of tie duration, requires a careful consideration of the specific industrial context. Overall, the analysis yields some explanations of the ambiguity of empirical results in previous literature, as discussed in the introduction. The analysis shows that for this it is important to look at the interaction of structure and strength of ties from the perspective of both competence and governance.

Interaction between Distance, Network Structure and Position

As noted before, variety or heterogeneity has three dimensions: number of firms, the pattern of ties between them, and cognitive distance in pairs of firms. Concerning the pattern of ties we have features of the whole network, such as network density, and features of the network position of individual firms. Here, there is a notion of 'social distance' between any two firms, defined as the number of intervening firms on the shortest path between them. Concerning the network position of a firm, one can consider the centrality of the firm in its ego-network, that is the network among only the direct relations of the firm. This is related to the notion of efficiency, that is the lack of redundancy in the ego-network: to the extent that direct relations of a firm have ties not only to the focal firm, but also to each other, the focal firm takes up a less central position, and the network among the firm's relations is more redundant and less efficient. Another concept of centrality is betweenness centrality, that is the extent to which the firm lies on a cross-roads of shortest paths between all the other firms in the network. The latter is related to the extent that the firm bridges structural holes in the network.

Gilsing et al. (2008) extended the econometric model of Nooteboom et al. (2007), by adding to the effects of cognitive distance (D) the effects of overall network density (D) and betweenness centrality (C) of the focal firm. Here, cognitive distance has been labelled, more appropriately, 'technological distance', to reflect the fact that it measures only differences in technical competence as reflected in patent characteristics, and thus does not include more governance related competence, for which no variable could be constructed. Use was made of the same data, discussed earlier (Nooteboom et al., 2007). Here, the overall network is defined as all the ties that exist, in the form of inter-firm alliances, between the firms in the sample. For details of the method and the results I refer to the paper. Here I focus on the interpretation of the results. The same basic logic was used: innovative performance (L), here only in exploration, defined as the production of patents new to the firm, is hypothesized to be proportional to the mathematical product of ability to absorb/collaborate (A) and exploratory potential or novelty value (N). New here are the hypotheses that in addition to the positive effect of technological distance (D) on exploratory potential (N) and its negative effect on ability to collaborate (A), we have:

- a negative effect of overall network density (D) on exploratory potential (N), and a positive effect on ability to collaborate (A); and
- a positive effect of betweenness centrality (C) on potential (N) and a negative effect on ability to collaborate (A).

The argument is as follows. Concerning the effects of network density, in agreement with the logic proposed by Burt, overall density yields redundancy in access to new information, and hence lowers novelty value. In agreement with the logic proposed by Gilsing and Nooteboom (2005), density aids absorptive capacity by pooling different absorptive capacities, to enhance understanding of the meaning and value of information, and to help testing its validity by triangulation. Here it is not only the opportunities for triangulation in the ego-network of direct relations of the focal firm, but also the opportunities that they, in turn, have from their relations, and so on throughout the network.[4]

Concerning the effect of betweenness centrality, in agreement with the logic proposed by Burt, it indicates the extent to which the focal firm bridges structural holes, which favours access to new information. However, it also may also yield information overload of the firm, reducing its ability to absorb the diverse knowledge coming in also from firms at large social distance, that is coming in via multiple intervening ties, with an accumulation of distortions and noise, due to multiple misunderstanding, partial absorption, selection, interpretation and augmentation along the way.

The mathematical specification of the full model is given in Appendix 4.2. Similarly to the original model of only cognitive distance, the model implies inverted U-shaped effects on performance of density and centrality. It also implies multiple interaction effects. According to the model, cognitive distance and betweenness centrality are substitutes: they both increase novelty value and decrease absorptive capacity. They are both complements with respect to density, which has opposite effects. In the empirical study, the hypotheses are all confirmed in terms of signs and significance of

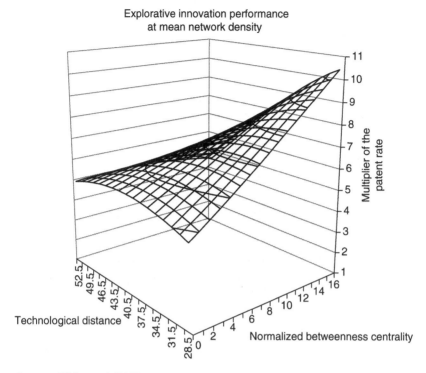

Explorative innovation performance
at mean network density

Source:　Gilsing et al. (2008).

Figure 4.4　*Exploration performance as a function of betweenness*
　　　　　　　centrality and cognitive distance, at mean network density

effects of variables (see Appendix 4.2), except one: the hypothesized interaction effect between cognitive distance and network density was positive,
as hypothesized, but not statistically significant. Yet the other coefficients
involving the two variables (their independent linear and quadratic effects)
were in line with the hypotheses. Some of the effects, calculated according
to the model estimate, are given in Figures 4.4 and 4.5. The graphs cover
the range of observations. They demonstrate alternative strategies as a
result of interaction effects.

Figure 4.4 shows that within the range of observations at mean network
density, with high betweenness centrality, yielding problems of absorptive
capacity, one cannot afford to also have large technological distance to
direct partners.

Figure 4.5 shows that even at the mean level of betweenness centrality
one needs a certain amount of network density to yield requisite absorptive

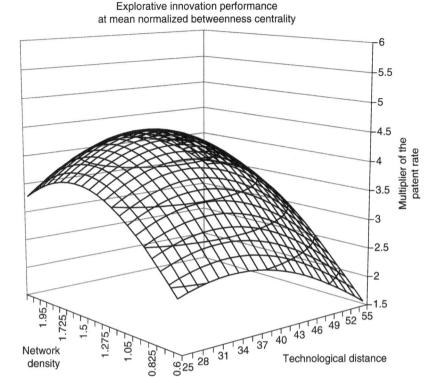

Explorative innovation performance
at mean normalized betweenness centrality

Source: Gilsing et al. (2008).

Figure 4.5   *Exploration performance as a function of network density and*
cognitive distance, at mean betweenness centrality

capacity, and an intermediate level of technological distance is best at all
levels of network density.

CONCLUSIONS AND RESEARCH AGENDA

The notion of cognitive distance, derived from the present cognitive theory
of the firm, has demonstrated its fruitfulness in empirical research on innovation by collaboration. More broadly, the theory has helped to develop
hypotheses on effects of features of networks, of structure and strength of
ties, on innovation by collaboration.

Answers to the research questions listed in Chapter 1 are as follows:

Question 9: What are dynamic capabilities?
Answer: This question was answered, in part, in Chapter 3, with the claim that one important dynamic capability is the intellectual and behavioural ability to collaborate with other organizations, at sufficient cognitive distance. Much of the present chapter was dedicated to the further analysis of that capability. To this is now added the capability to design networks of optimal density, if such design lies within the power of an organization, or to select such a network, and to select or develop an optimal position of centrality, carefully traded off with the effects of cognitive distance and density.

Question 10: What determines the boundaries of organizations?
Answer: For a firm as a legal entity boundaries are determined by legal regulation of property, liability and authority. For a firm as an organization, as a form for coordinating activities, and for 'making knowledge work' (Schumpeter, Hayek), the boundary is determined by organizational cognitive focus: the activities and capabilities that fall within the reach of organization-specific meanings, understandings and culture.

Question 11: Why do organizations collaborate with others?
Answer: to repair organizational myopia caused by organizational focus, by means of complementary cognition, at a cognitive distance too large to realize efficiently within the firm.

Question 12: How is inter-organizational collaboration governed?
Answer: by some appropriate mix, given goals and external conditions, of instruments that yield reliability (control and/or trust). There are instruments of control in contractual limitation of opportunities for opportunism, material incentives to refrain from opportunism, the use of reputation mechanisms, hostages and balance of mutual dependence. There are also factors of trust, beyond control, in shared values and norms of conduct, and in relation-specific routinized behaviour, empathy and identification.

Question 13. What are the effects of network features on the conditions and results of collaboration between firms?
Answer: On the competence side, novelty value of relationships is reduced by density of the network and long term exclusive ties, and is enhanced by cognitive distance and betweenness centrality. Absorptive capacity is reduced by cognitive distance, betweenness centrality, and short term, infrequent interaction and lack in investment in mutual understanding. Governance is enhanced by network density, centrality of a firm in its ego-network, and long-term, high trust ties.

There is vibrant activity of ongoing research of innovation in IORs, in which the literatures on inter-firm alliances, with an emphasis on strategic behaviour of firms, and the literature on networks, with an emphasis on structural effects, are coming together in the study of strategy in networks. That constitutes progress. Important for innovation is the distinction, in recent research, between two dimensions of variety: number of actors and the pattern of ties, and cognitive distances between them. A shortcoming in much research still is the neglect to combine issues of competence and governance. That combination yields analytical complexity, but is needed to understand the otherwise contradictory results concerning positive and negative effects of network structure and strength of ties. One possibility might be to further extend the integrated model with network effects on governance.

The combination of competence and governance is also of great importance for policy. Focus only on governance can eliminate the variety and flexibility needed for innovation, while focus only on innovation can create havoc with firm interests, in unforeseen relational risks. Another point that is important for policy concerns trade-offs between variety and homogeneity and between stability and change. Variety, in numbers and cognitive distance, is beneficial for radical innovation, but a certain homogeneity and cognitive proximity is beneficial for collaboration. Hence one should make trade-offs and look for optimal variety and distance. Similarly, a certain flexibility and variability of relations is needed for innovation, but also a certain stability, to elicit and enable investments in mutual understanding and trust. Hence one should make trade-offs here as well, in looking for optimal rather than maximal flexibility.

Another lesson, related to the combination of competence and governance, concerns the interaction between structure and strength of ties. Problems resulting from measures taken in the one may be compensated by measures taken in the other.

Another lesson concerns contingencies of industry, in relation to contingencies in type of technology (systemic, stand-alone), type of knowledge (more or less tacit), and the different effects of tacitness in products and tacitness in production.

A particularly interesting avenue for further research appears to lie in the notion of 'small worlds' (Watts, 1999). There is empirical evidence, and theoretical argument, in favour of dense and stable local communities, with strong ties, which have more sparse, weak and flexible ties with more distant, similar communities. Perhaps this yields a link with the research of communities of practice (Amin and Cohendet, 2003). In inter-organizational relations, there is a challenge to conduct research that includes the combined effects of cognitive distance, within and between local communities, local density and strength of ties, within communities, and inter-community sparsity and variability of ties.

More attention is required for triads. On the whole, the literature has tended to focus on either two actors (dyads) or many (networks). While some attention has been given to triads, they have remained under-researched (Madhavan et al., 2004). Burt's (1992) studies of bridging structural holes, and studies of roles of third parties or go-betweens (Shapiro, 1987; Nooteboom, 2002) entail three parties, but there the third party takes up a special intermediary position external to the relation between the other two actors. Simmel's (1950 [1917]) more extensive analysis of triads, in which any two can form a coalition against the third, who may then switch from the position of *tertius gaudens* emphasized by Burt to a problematic position of being caught 'in the middle' (Krachhardt, 1999). As shown by Simmel, in a triad any one can help to solve problems between the other two, and there may be effects of rivalry between two in gaining favour from the third, and so on. This could yield a source of inspiration for more extensive analysis of triads. The importance of triads goes beyond governance, and has implications for competence. This was already part of the earlier analysis: in a closed or transitive triangle, where each has a tie to the other two, two sides may triangulate their understanding of the third. There are also spillover effects. If A has a tie with B and B has a tie with C, and C is a potential competitor of A, then knowledge transferred from A to B may spill over to C, and for A's control of spillover it matters a great deal whether or not A also has a tie with C. These are just some indicative examples of the importance of triads.

Knoke and Chermack (2005) showed that there is not only the issue whether ties are uni-directional or symmetrical, which tends to be neglected, but also to what extent ties are acknowledged. A may claim a tie to B, as recipient or sender, which is not acknowledged by B. This can have important implications that seem to have been wholly neglected.

There may be useful spillover from insights from inter-organizational relations to relations between units within organizations. This will be picked up in Chapter 5, in the further analysis of dynamic capabilities of firms.

Involvement in IOR's has implications for intra-organizational focus. When in an IOR focus becomes stronger to reduce or cross cognitive distance between the organizations, this is likely to require a weakening of focus within the organizations to allow for it. In particular, within the firm one may need to leave certain activities alone (reduce width of focus), or constrain them in fewer respects (reduce reach), or to relax tightness, or to reduce its depth to allow also for deviations on more fundamental levels of cognition.

A cognitive theory of the firm

Finally, an important issue is the dynamics of networks: explanation of the change of the structure and strength of ties over time. This also will be taken up in Chapter 5, after the analysis of a general 'logic' or heuristic of discovery. In combination with the above analysis of structure and strength of ties that will yield a basis for an understanding of network dynamics.

NOTES

1. According to economists, economic agents strive for maximum profit. According to Spinoza's notion of *conatus*, people (and other forms of life) strive to realize their potential. In fact, that idea goes back as far as Aristotle. According to Schopenhauer people strive for survival. According to Nietzsche this is not so: people often knowingly lower chances of survival, from a will to power. I think Spinoza's notion of *conatus* is the most accurate. People strive to realize their potential, and that may be different for different people.
2. I take regional clusters and industrial districts to be synonymous, and to denote networks with an important aspect of local embedding.
3. Hansen (1999) associated simple knowledge with codified knowledge (information) on opportunities regarding where specific knowledge was located and by whom. Complex knowledge was associated with more tacit knowledge on in-depth technological issues.
4. An alternative might be to take so-called Bonacich or eigenvalue centrality (Bonacich, 1987), where direct relations are weighted by their relations, which are weighted in turn by their relations, and so on.

APPENDIX 4.1 SPECIFICATION OF THE MODEL OF OPTIMAL COGNITIVE DISTANCE WITH BOTH COLLABORATIVE ABILITY AND NOVELTY VALUE A FUNCTION OF KNOWLEDGE ACCUMULATION

In Chapter 3, the mathematical specification of the basic model was as follows:

The downward sloping line for ability to collaborate (A):

$$A = a_1 - a_2.CD, \qquad a_1, a_2 > 0 \qquad \text{(A4.1)}$$

where CD is cognitive distance

The upward sloping line for value (N):

$$N = b_1 + b_2.CD \qquad b_1, b_2 > 0 \qquad \text{(A4.2)}$$

Multiplying Equations (A4.1) and (A4.2) results in innovative performance (L):

$$L = A.N = a_1.b_1 + (a_1.b_2 - b_1.a_2).CD - a_2.b_2.CD^2 \qquad \text{(A4.3)}$$

Now, suppose that:

$$a_1 = c_1 + c_2.TC; \qquad c_1, c_2 > 0 \qquad \text{(A4.4)}$$

where TC is technological capital, that is accumulated knowledge

Then, from Equation (A4.3) we find:

$$L = c_1.b_1 + c_2.b_1.TC + (c_1.b_2 - b_1.a_2).CD + c_2.b_2.TC.CD - a_2.b_2.CD^2 \qquad \text{(A4.5)}$$

If TC decreases the positive slope of the line for novelty value (b_2)

Let $b_2 = f_1 - f_2.TC$ $\qquad$ (A4.6)

Then, from Equation (A4.3) we find:

$$L = a_1b_1 + (a_1f_1 - b_1a_2).CD - a_1f_2.TC.CD - a_2f_1.CD^2 + a_2f_2.TC.CD^2 \qquad \text{(A4.7)}$$

APPENDIX 4.2 SPECIFICATION OF THE INTEGRATED MODEL OF COGNITIVE DISTANCE, CENTRALITY AND NETWORK DENSITY

$$A = a_1 - a_2.CD - a_3.C + a_4.D \tag{A4.8}$$

$$N = b_1 + b_2.CD + b_3.C - b_4.D \tag{A4.9}$$

Where: A = ability to collaborate, N = novelty value, CD = technological distance, C = betweenness centrality, D = network density

$$L = A.N = a_1.b_2 + (a_1.b_2 - a_2.b_1).CD + (a_1.b_3 - a_3.b_1).C + (b_1.a_4 - a_1.b_4).D$$

$$- a_2.b_2.CD^2 - a_3.b_3.C^2 - a_4.b_4.D^2$$

$$- (a_2.b_3 + a_3.b_2).CD.C + (a_2.b_4 + a_4.b_2).CD.D + (a_3.b_4 + a_4.b_3).C.D \tag{A4.10}$$

Where: L = performance in exploration.

5. Dynamic capabilities

INTRODUCTION

The present chapter is dedicated to a further analysis of dynamic capabilities (Teece et al., 2000), that is capabilities to develop or change capabilities. These entail learning, that is the change of knowledge and change of competencies more generally, including organizational capabilities. Learning can entail the adoption of knowledge from others and development of new knowledge. Development of new knowledge can arise from intellectual inference, from interaction with others and from own experience, and usually arises from a combination and interplay between the three. Ideas arise from thought, experience and debate, and they yield experiments, alone or in collaboration with others, which yield new ideas. Collaboration and debate are important especially from the constructivist, interactionist perspective of knowledge used in this book and set out in Chapter 2. Here, differences in cognition, in cognitive distance, form a source of variety as a basis for innovation. In preceding chapters several dynamic capabilities have already been discussed. In Chapter 3 there was an analysis of the capability to employ organizational cognitive focus that enables a combination of exploitation and exploration within and between organizations. A second capability is the ability to find or develop outside partners at sufficient cognitive distance, and the intellectual and behavioural capability to collaborate across such distance, taking into account issues of both competence and governance. In Chapter 4 the capability was added to design networks of optimal density, if such design lies within the power of an organization, or to select such a network, and to select or develop an optimal position of centrality, carefully traded off with the effects of cognitive distance and density. The present chapter proceeds as follows. First comes a discussion of entrepreneurship as a fountain of dynamic capability, and novel opportunities for it. Second, there is a further discussion of different forms of learning, with a summary, extension and application of a 'logic of discovery' derived from Nooteboom (2000).

ENTREPRENEURSHIP

There is an enormous body of literature on entrepreneurship that has grown over the past 30 years but goes back to a variety of early economists. Much contemporary literature repeats earlier insights that are worth recovering. First a survey is given of notions concerning entrepreneurship, and connections between them. Second comes a discussion of effects of firm size, and complementarities and transitions between large and small firms. Third comes the theme of continuity and discontinuity in innovation.

Forms of Entrepreneurship

In the history of economics one finds a variety of notions of entrepreneurship, proposed by a range of classical and Austrian economists: Adam Smith, Marshall, Cantillon, Say, Bentham, Thünen, Mangoldt, Menger, von Mises, von Hayek and, later, Kirzner. In more recent literature, discussions and surveys have been provided by, among others, Kets de Vries (1977), Stanworth and Curran (1973), Scase and Goffee (1980), Casson (1982), Hébert and Link (1982), Chell (1985), Weinberg (1990), Chell et al. (1991), Nooteboom (1994), Thurik (1996), van Praag (1996) and Blaug (1997). The following entrepreneurial roles have been identified:

- innovation (Bentham, Thünen, Schumpeter and perhaps Say);
- creative destruction by novel combinations (Schumpeter);
- arbitrage: the identification and utilization of opportunities for matching supply and demand (Cantillon, Smith, Menger, Mizes, Hayek, Kirzner);
- the provision of capital (Marshall);
- creating or entering new markets (Mangoldt, Schumpeter); and
- the configuration and management of production factors for efficient production (Say, Marshall, Mizes).

It has been argued that the provision of capital is not part of entrepreneurship, since capital can be obtained from capital markets, and that management is not part of it, since that can be hired (Blaug, 1997). However, in view of the 'real' or fundamental, Knightian uncertainty involved in entrepreneurship, and the idiosyncracy of perception and initiative that characterize entrepreneurship, outside supply of capital can be problematic, so that the entrepreneur has to supply his own at least in part (Casson, 1982). Management is not routine, certainly in the early stages of exploring Schumpeterian novel combinations, where the entrepreneur has to supply his own leadership and management. In this chapter it will be argued that the later development and adaptation of organization also constitute a non-trivial entrepreneurial task. So, it seems that the provision of capital and management are still part of an entrepreneurial process. A key question is how 'episodic' change, in Schumpeterian 'creative destruction', is related to more gradual change, in incremental innovation and in the arbitrage function of entrepreneurship.

Associated with different roles of entrepreneurs, different characteristics and competencies have been identified, as follows:

- acceptance of radical uncertainty (Knight, Schumpeter);
- alertness, perceptiveness, open-mindedness, imagination, vision, idiosyncratic perception and initiative (Kirzner), independence (Schumpeter), internal 'locus of control' (an attitude that one is not at the mercy of external change but can influence one's environment);
- judgement, sense of realism, decisiveness;
- perseverance, ambition or need for achievement; and
- charisma, strength of personality; capability of leadership (Schumpeter), managerial capability (Marshall).

One of the paradoxes of Schumpeterian entrepreneurship is that on the one hand for radical innovation one must have a certain amount of stubbornness and single-mindedness to pursue ideas that everyone else considers absurd, while on the other hand one must maintain self-criticism and sensitivity to signals of error. Another paradox is that on the one hand one must maintain strong, inspirational leadership, and on the other hand when the firm is successful and starts to grow one must be able to delegate tasks and responsibility.

According to Schumpeter entrepreneurs form an elite, while according to (other) Austrian theorists (especially von Mizes) entrepreneurship is widely dispersed. The need for charisma is related to radical (Knightian) uncertainty. Engaged in radically novel ideas, for markets that do not yet exist, the entrepreneur needs to be able to inspire followers, partners, employees and providers of capital, to carry them along in a risky venture with unknowable outcomes. According to others, entrepreneurship is a widespread, daily phenomenon. Clearly, this depends on whether one defines entrepreneurship as radical innovation or as including even small feats of arbitrage.

This chapter addresses the question how we may connect these widely diverging roles, characteristics and motives of entrepreneurship. Do the different types of activity have to be combined at the same time, or are they required at different times, in some development process, by different people perhaps?

Firm size: Transitions and Complementarities

Concerning the more innovation oriented entrepreneur (creative destruction), Schumpeter (1909, 1939, 1942) recognized two types. According to him, in early capitalism the innovative entrepreneur 'Mark I' was an independent outsider, setting up his own new venture, without vested interests in established technologies, products and markets. In later capitalism, entrepreneurship 'Mark II' increasingly required large teams of specialists that only larger firms could afford. Therefore, a question is how aspects of innovation and diffusion are related to firm size and other firm characteristics. Rothwell (1985, 1986, 1989) proposed that both types of entrepreneurship (Mark I and II) have a role to play, and that there is 'dynamic complementarity' between small and large firms, in innovation, with small and large firms being strong and weak in opposite ways. Small firms have 'behavioural' advantages: motivation to accept risks and low income in early stages of innovation, close contact with customers and employees, flexibility of small emergent firms that haven't yet hardened into organizational shapes to fit established, 'dominant' practices. Large firms have advantages in resources: revenues from established activities to fund innovation, a wider range of activities to pool risks and cross-subsidize new ventures, specialized human and other resources, market access (distribution channels and brand names), and established political and social capital.

In organizational development, successful new, small firms encounter growth obstacles (Bennis, 1969; Greiner, 1972). At first, in a new entrepreneurial venture, the entrepreneur participates in shop-floor activities and customer contacts, and coordinates on the basis of direct supervision, in a simple organizational structure (Mintzberg, 1983). In view of this, knowledge does not need to be highly codified. As success emerges and sales volume grows, the distance between the entrepreneur and operational activities increases, and the entrepreneur must institute division of labour, specialized support and staff functions, and codified, formalized procedures of coordination and control across spatially and functionally separated activities. In other words, in the development of the firm there is the need of a transition from Schumpeterian to Marshallian entrepreneurship. Failing to see this, or to accept it and make room for managers, many entrepreneurs fail to make the transition. Then, they may be taken over by more managerially oriented firms. Organizational focus may need to be changed to accommodate this.

In view of dynamic complementarity, one would expect that large firms typically produce the scientific inventions that require large R&D teams with specialists, while small, outside firms will be quicker in bringing inventions into practice, in new products (exploration), and large firms carry new products into efficient, large-scale exploitation.

The analysis is borne out by many empirical studies (for example Blair, 1972; Davis et al., 1985; Wyatt, 1985; Wijnberg, 1990; Acs and Audretsch, 1990). Examples of inventions that were developed and commercialized by small firms are: electric light (Edison), the telephone (Alexander Graham Bell), aeroplanes (Wright brothers), micro-computers (Silicon Valley, Apple), self-service retailing (Nooteboom, 1984), and computer-aided design (Rothwell and Zegveld, 1985).

The present book builds on the notions of exploration and exploitation, derived from Holland (1975) and March (1991). In order to survive in the short term, firms must efficiently exploit current resources (assets, capabilities and competencies). In order to survive in the long term they must develop new resources. Thus, to survive now and later, they need to combine exploitation and exploration, either within the firm or in networks of firms. That is a paradoxical task. Exploitation typically requires division of labour, which requires stable roles and standards, and absence of ambiguity, while exploration requires a break-up or shift in those dimensions of organization. According to the principle of dynamic complementarity, small firms have a comparative advantage in exploration and large firms in exploitation. Exploration requires more acceptance of uncertainty and lack of resources, perseverance, and charisma to carry others along in that uncertainty, and flexibility to deal with emerging novelty. Exploitation requires the massing, matching and managing of diverse resources.

In specialization in exploitation or exploration, small firms may exploit small niche markets, or residual markets for crafts, or they may engage in exploration of novel opportunities where their flexibility and speed yield a competitive advantage. Large firms may specialize in basic inventions, large systemic innovations, or exploitation of innovations developed elsewhere, in scaling up and large scale marketing and distribution or in take-overs of small firms that fail to cross the threshold from an entrepreneurial to a managerial firm. Clearly, the division of labour between small and large firms depends on institutional conditions, such as limits in the integration of activities in large conglomerate firms imposed by anti-trust policy (Nelson, 1993), on policies to suppress entry barriers and policies to support or facilitate small firms.

Dynamic complementarity, then, may take several forms:

- Small firms pass on the results from exploration to large firms, for the sake of exploitation. This is observed, for example, in the transfer of pharmaceutical innovations from small biotech firms to large pharmaceutical firms, as discussed in Chapter 4.

- After exploration, small new firms grow into large ones, overcoming the obstacles involved, to achieve the advantages of size needed for exploitation. An example is Apple computers.
- After exploration, small firms that fail to overcome growth obstacles are taken over by large firms.
- The innovations of small firms are imitated by large ones, which then slowly push out the smaller, less efficient firms, due to economies of scale. An example is self-service retailing, which in most countries was initiated by small, independent firms (with the exception of Switzerland), followed by large, integrated chain store firms, to which the small independents tried to respond with forms of collaboration (buying cooperatives, voluntary chains, and franchising, see Nooteboom, 1984).

The case of retailing illustrates a well known point that small firms may, at least to some extent, compensate for their lack of resources by collaboration, in networks (Johannisson, 1986), to establish scale, specialization, diversification of risk, and market access. The need for personalized networks depends, among other things, on lack of institutions, such as a reliable legal system. Birley et al. (1991) showed that in Italy a relatively large amount of time is spent in building and maintaining networks. Conversely, large firms may compensate their disadvantage of sluggishness by allowing for more or less autonomous or modular units, for the sake of exploration. Thus, the notion of dynamic complementarity shifts from that between small and large firms to that between more or less integrated organizational forms, within and between firms.

Here, we find the beginning of an analysis that assigns different features of entrepreneurship to different stages of development, in innovation and organization. However, the distinction between exploration and exploitation is too stark. Between radical, frame-breaking innovations and mere application, there are incremental innovations, and shifts from product innovation to innovation in production and organization.

Continuity and Discontinuity

A central theme, in the literature on innovation, entrepreneurship and organizational change, is that of continuous versus discontinuous change. In the literature on organizational change, Weick and Quinn (1999) proposed that there are two distinct traditions: one that takes change as discontinuous or 'episodic', and one that takes change as continuous and cumulative. Purportedly, episodic change breaks the inertia of established practices and structures, is caused by external shocks, and proceeds according to managerial design and planning. Continuous change, by contrast, arises from an accumulation of small changes, in a 'redirection of what is already under way' (Weick and Quinn, 1999: 366), and is emergent rather than planned. Episodic and continuous changes are presented as alternatives, and no clue is given of how they might be connected.

An episodic view is presented in the notion of 'punctuated equilibria' (Tushman and Romanelli, 1985; Tushman and Anderson, 1986; Romanelli and Tushman, 1994; Gersick 1991). Here, long periods of stability, on the basis of existing 'dominant designs' (Abernathy and Utterback, 1978), are punctuated only intermittently by radical breakthroughs. No explanation is given of the origin of such breakthroughs. Are they created out of nothing, or do they emerge, somehow, from experience?

Similarly, in the economic literature on innovation and entrepreneurship, (neo)Schumpeterian innovation theory is clearly episodic: inventions, which remain unexplained, creatively destroy established order, and then converge on dominant designs that form the basis for a newly developing practice. Related to this, in evolutionary theory the creation of variety by invention was seen as analogous to mutations in biological evolution, yielding novel forms that are subjected to selection in markets, with surviving innovations propagated by growth and imitation. As in Schumpeterian theory, evolutionary economics offers no explanation of the origins of invention.

Nevertheless, a great advantage of evolutionary theory is that it offers an approach to the development of new forms that is not based on design and planning, in contrast with views on episodic change, in (even recent) management literature (see Weick and Quinn, 1999, referred to above), as somehow designed 'from above', by management, under pressure from exogenous shocks that remain unexplained. However, while evolutionary theory has generated important perspectives, it also has its limitations and may even be misleading, for example in its neglect of invention (Nooteboom, 2001; Witt, 2005; Nelson, 2006). Criticism of evolutionary theory is discussed in some detail in Chapter 6.

The entrepreneur according to Schumpeter has variously been characterized as being non-adaptive, causing disequilibrium, in creative destruction, and yielding increased uncertainty in markets (Cheah and Robertson, 1992). The entrepreneur according to (other) Austrians (Menger, Hayek and more recently Kirzner, 1973, 1985) is adaptive, reacting to exogenous shocks of change, utilizing inventions and drawing markets towards equilibrium in the sense of diffusing innovations and matching supply and demand. Here again, we find the split between episodic and continuous change. Consider the following quote (Kirzner, 1973: 127) 'For Schumpeter the entrepreneur is the disruptive, disequilibrating force that dislodges the market from the somnolence of equilibrium; for us the entrepreneur is the equilibrating force whose activity responds to the existing tensions and provides those corrections for which the unexploited opportunities have been crying out'. In this arbitrage view of entrepreneurship Kirzner is close to Cantillon. While Kirzner's entrepreneur is more 'alert' to new possibilities than other people, this is 'not really a theory about how agents create new data, but how they react to new data' (Foss, 1994: 111). The question is how entrepreneurial action can also yield 'new data': how entrepreneurs can break through existing categorical imperatives.

However, like the distinction between exploration and exploitation, the distinction between Schumpeterian, disequilibrating, and Smithian/ Austrian, equilibrating entrepreneurship is too stark. There are cases of entrepreneurship that are difficult to assign to either type, because they contain elements of both. An important type of innovation, between Schumpeterian entrepreneurship and entrepreneurship according to (other) Austrians, is product differentiation. It can be reconstructed as bridging gaps between supply and demand in Lancasterian product characteristics space (Lancaster, 1966), by offering novel combinations of available product characteristics that are closer to pockets of demand. This is Austrian in that no new characteristic appears, and gaps are bridged in characteristics space by varying the intensities of characteristics in their mix. Differentiation becomes more Schumpeterian when it consists of the addition of a new dimension to characteristics space, which subjects user preferences and the positioning of existing products to a jolt (Péli and Nooteboom, 1999). An example would be adding colour to toothpaste, which used to be uniformly white, or to cars, which according to the famous dictum of Henry Ford used to be available 'any colour as long as it's black'. Another example of an innovation that contains elements of both Schumpeterian and Kirznerian entrepreneurship is the example of railroads discussed by Schumpeter (1939). Uncertainty is reduced as railroads diffuse, and entrepreneurship in this area becomes increasingly routine. But now consider the 'ice station' innovation of beer brewer Annheuser Bush (AB). By combining railroad transportation with the cooling of beer by means of 'ice stations', AB greatly extended the feasible distance between market and production, thereby allowing for economies of scale in brewing. This innovation that may seem Schumpeterian was produced as a combination of well diffused, settled technologies of railroads and cooling, in an identification of possibilities from existing technology and practice that might as well be seen as Kirznerian.

Note also that diffusion does not consist in a simple mechanical 'working out' of a single innovation. Generally, new applications require adjustment or 're-invention'. Often, new applications are achieved in combination with complementary innovations in technology, marketing, organization, infrastructure and institutional conditions.

> For use on ships, the steam engine required further innovations and improvements, such as the screw to replace the paddle. Seawater deposed salt in the boiler which caused explosions. That required separation of the water that cooled the condenstor and water in the condensator. Wooden ships were too small for large engines required for efficient use. That required a transition to steel ships. (Mokyr, 1990: 128)

Different firms have different, partly firm-specific constellations of resources and capabilities, partly embedded in teams, organizational structure and culture, associated with the firm's cognitive focus, where adoption of innovation is seldom a mere slotting in, and typically requires a reconstruction of existing structure, process and sometimes even cognitive focus. What is established on an industry level may require quite fundamental shifts on the firm level. That is why in the measurement of innovation a distinction is made between products or processes new for the world, for an industry and for a firm. In short: diffusion requires innovation on the part of users.

In the literature of innovation and organization, there is ample empirical evidence of apparently discontinuous breakthroughs and ruptures, pleading for the episodic view of change (Tushman and Anderson, 1986). The question now is how discontinuity arises, on what basis, and whether there might be continuity in it, or at least intermediate steps or stages. Breakthroughs and inventions must arise, somehow, from experience and learning. How does this work? Or, in other words, how does exploration arise from exploitation? In the present book, answers are sought from a theory that proposes different stages in a 'cycle of discovery' (Nooteboom, 1999, 2000).[1] One may think that such a theory of discovery is logically impossible, since it would entail the prediction of discovery, and if discovery could be predicted it would no longer constitute discovery. But this is mistaken: we may well be able to specify processes of discovery without thereby claiming to be able to predict its outcomes. This takes us to theory of learning and discovery, to be discussed in a subsequent paragraph.

Novel Opportunities

Several new conditions yield a host of opportunities for entrepreneurship, with implications for dynamic capabilities.

One condition is that ICT has massively reduced important economies of scale and entry barriers to markets. Reduction of costs of search and communication has greatly facilitated collaboration between firms, needed especially by smaller firms in view of their lack of specialized labour and staff support. Greater transparency of markets, in presenting and searching products on the Internet, has reduced market entry barriers for new and smaller firms. Firms can more easily set up on a small scale and can remain small for quite some time, by outsourcing production, distribution, invoicing and administration. The speed of innovation has increased, giving advantage to the higher potential flexibility and speed of smaller firms. A second condition is increased prosperity, which has yielded a rising demand for differentiated products (up Maslow's pyramid of needs), yielding new small niche markets for small firms to flourish in. This is not to say that all advantage has shifted to smaller firms. There are still economies of scale in some production (for example in most process industries), in distribution and brand name, and in institutional influence (in law-making, design and implementation of government schemes).

In 'platform organizations', producers offer a platform of modules from which users can configure their own good or service, or can route their questions or submit information, or a platform for outsourcing, where potential suppliers can scan and analyse requirements and submit their tenders. Platforms are not necessarily restricted to the products of a single producer. A company like e-Bay, for instance, hosts many different types of producers, some fully-fledged businesses, some family firms, and others amateurs or enthusiasts. As shown by von Hippel (2005), some producers go further and offer users 'toolkits' for exploration, which offer means for product-design, prototyping and design-testing. For example: software for users to design their own semiconductor chips. Here, users can combine existing elements offered by producers with elements added from their idiosyncratic context of use.

The fundamental logic of platforms lies in the asymmetry of knowledge between users and producers (von Hippel, 2005). Users have idiosyncratic and highly tacit knowledge of their experiences and their needs, while producers have knowledge and experience in providing solutions to needs. Transfer of need information from users to producers, in market analysis, is costly, partial, reductive, slow and faulty. It is costly in transaction costs of selecting potential customers and communicating with them. It is partial in that much of the knowledge is tacit and for that reason difficult to identify and capture. It is reductive in that it tends to yield averages that filter out the outliers in experience and ideas that may be the most interesting and innovative. It is faulty because in interpretation information is added and knowledge is transformed to fit the absorptive capacity of the producer. The totality of these problems has been labelled as 'stickiness' of information (von Hippel, 1999). As a result, in terms of communication and interpretation it is much more efficient to leave information on needs where it originates, and to supply modules from which users can configure their own custom-made product. This presumes, of course, that the product modules yield the required potential, and can indeed be consistently combined in unforeseen ways, and that users know how to configure them. For the latter, one will need to supply instructions, and they, in turn, may need to be customized for different users. For this, one needs continual feedback on user experience, in the development of modules and instructions. Some products can more easily be broken down into modules than others.

The tipping point between traditional forms and the platform lies in the relative complexity of user- and producer innovation. User production is more efficient when user information is more complex, with greater variety of user needs, and more sticky than producer information on how to configure a product. The logic applies not only for the initial configuration of a product, but also for its subsequent maintenance and repair. For that, producers would have to keep records of what exactly it supplied to a given customer, including any special parts, while users have that information directly accessible (von Hippel, 2005: 49).

All these conditions further enhance the opportunities for a strengthening of organizational focus, with more outside collaboration to tap into outside variety.

In open source communities, a further step is taken: here there are no longer separate producers, and users together take care of production. This arises especially in the production of non-physical products, such as software (for example Linux, Apache, Sendmail) or information (for example Wikipedia), for two reasons. First, one no longer needs producers with specialized hardware, and users together have the solution knowledge needed in the system. Second, without physical goods one can use the full potential of the Internet and does not need anything beyond that. Users produce ongoing additions or improvements to an existing system, enabled, when needed, by free access to the underlying source code. The condition usually is that they attach their name to the contribution, their contribution can be used and modified freely by other participants, and that they may not incorporate the contributions from others in products they sell. This may be guarded by a 'General Public License' (GPL), supported by Internet Mailing Lists (IML) whereby infringements are tracked and communicated.

Do we here have a form of organization without any cognitive focus at all? When we compare a software creating community such as Linux, where participants share a professional outlook, and there is self-selection on the basis of professional skill, with a much wider, apparently totally unfocused, amateurish community such as Wikipedia, it turns out that quality is higher and more consistent, and quarrels and disagreements are far less frequent in Linux than in Wikipedia (Nooteboom and Went, 2008). This suggests that even in open source communities some restriction of focus and conditions for participation appears to be needed.

LEARNING

In this section a summary is given of different types of learning: adoption of new knowledge or competence by communication or imitation, learning by collaboration and learning in the sense of discovery from experience.

Learning by Communication

One can learn by adopting existing ideas, insights or skills from others, by communication or imitation. Since one is dealing with existing knowledge or competence that is typically well-tried, tested and consolidated in 'dominant designs', this form of learning can be planned and programmed. However, such learning by adoption is seldom a matter of mere replication. The theory of embodied cognition set out in Chapter 2 implies that in imitation and communication information is transformed in its absorption, and in that sense always entails an element of both loss and creation. In expression by the 'sender' tacit knowledge can never be fully codified and externalized, so that expressed knowledge is always incomplete, and in absorption, or assimilation, knowledge is complemented and supplemented from the existing cognitive framework of the 'recipient'. Thus adoption of knowledge by communication is always imperfect, and can yield unintended and unnoticed variation. This is a source of misunderstanding and error, but also of innovation by variation.

Furthermore, what is 'left out' by the sender and what is 'added' by the receiver, and how this is done, depends on clues from the context. Thus, meaning is always context dependent. That indicates the fundamental importance of the experiential context of learning, even if it is learning by adoption from others.

A relevant concept here is that of 'scaffolding' (Hendriks-Jansen, 1996; Shanon, 1993), discussed in Chapter 2. The context of practice and learning, including the people involved, disambiguates meaning (a universal becomes specific by its place in a sentence, in a context of action), triggers relevant associations and cuts irrelevant ones, from a 'seamless web of belief' (Quine and Ullian, 1970). Classic examples are mothers that stimulate appropriate responses from infants (Hendriks-Jansen, 1996) and teachers who draw out pupils beyond their current level of performance (see Vygotsky, 1962: 'zone of proximal development'). Another example is the role of tools in apprenticeship in the construction of corresponding mental schemas. This entails conformance to local practice and perceptions that also causes, in due course, myopia and blindness to the extraneous, in a reduction of cognitive distance.

This, I propose, is related to the notion of 'legitimate peripheral participation' from the literature on 'Communities of practice' (Lave and Wenger, 1991). Newcomers to such a community remain at the periphery for a while, to develop absorptive capacity for the local jargon, expression of tacit knowledge in gestures and practices, symbolic behaviour, rules of the game, and norms of legitimacy, by 'indwelling² in the experiences, perspective, and concepts of other participants' (Von Krogh, 1998: 114), with incumbent members providing the necessary scaffolding.

On the side of the 'receiver', communicative ability requires appropriate absorptive capacity, geared to the 'sender'. On the side of the sender, it requires the rhetorical ability to trigger understanding by the 'receiver'. In Chapter 4 I discussed how tacit knowledge may form an obstacle to absorption, since tacit knowledge tends to be unconscious and therefore taken for granted and therefore not open to rational criticism. This obstacle may be reduced by an ability to make tacit knowledge more explicit, in a Socratic ability of mental midwifery ('maieutics'). The creative use of illustrations and of metaphor can also do wonders in triggering the grasp of the unfamiliar. By definition, a metaphor frames the foreign in terms of the familiar.

Apart from mutual understanding, on the competence side, there are issues on the governance side, in learning by adoption. In adoption between firms there are potential concerns of risks of spillover, that is loss of appropriability, with corresponding instruments for their control, as discussed in Chapter 4. In adoption between individuals within organizations there may also be concerns of spillover, in competition for careers, psychological safety (Edmonson, 1999), and risks of reputation and of mutual dependence (Bogenrieder and Nooteboom, 2004). It is part of dynamic capability to also deal with such problems of governance.

In conclusion, learning by adoption requires a first type of dynamic capability. That includes abilities of competence, in absorptive capacity and rhetorical ability, and an ability of governance to deal with risks of spillover, dependence, reputation and psychological safety.

Learning by Collaboration

March (1991) suggested that the generation of new ideas, in exploration, follows from personnel turnover, where people from outside an organization carry fresh ideas into the organization, which may disturb the efficiency of exploitation but may contribute to exploration. That is certainly part of the process of innovation, but it is also limited due to the self-selection of entrants to fit organizational focus, and socialization into that focus, as discussed in Chapter 3.

New knowledge and competence can be generated deliberately and by design by seeking novel combinations of existing knowledge, in collaboration between different people and organizations. Nonaka and Takeuchi (1995) recognized this as innovation by 'combination', and Zollo and Winter (2002) called it 'deliberate learning', in contrast with experiential learning. While Nonaka and Takeuchi as well as Zollo and Winter claimed that such learning by combination requires articulation and codification of the knowledge involved, I disagree. While codification certainly has its advantages, it is neither necessary nor fully possible. As argued earlier, knowledge can never be fully articulated and codified, and a greater or lesser degree of tacitness necessarily remains. Furthermore, novel combinations of tacit knowledge can also arise, in close collaboration in teams.

A more fundamental point is that combination of diverse existing knowledge can also produce radical, unforeseeable novelty, and while the combination may be deliberate in the partners seeking each other out for the potential for such novelty, by definition the outcome cannot be foreseen and hence cannot be planned.

As discussed extensively in Chapter 4, in learning by collaboration one runs into both the problem and the opportunity from cognitive distance: greater distance makes mutual understanding and acceptance (absorptive capacity) more difficult, but also generates novelty value. If the first decreases, say linearly, with cognitive distance, the second increases with it, and performance of learning by interaction is the mathematical product of absorption and novelty value, an inverse U-shaped relationship results, with an optimal cognitive distance, large enough to yield novelty value but not so large as to preclude understanding and collaboration. This optimum is not fixed. For more explorative learning cognitive distance is needed. Absorptive capacity depends on the accumulation of knowledge and competence from past R&D (Cohen and Levinthal, 1990), production, marketing, organization and, in particular, experience in collaborating with others at sufficient cognitive distance. In other words, experience in dealing with others who think differently yields competitive advantage. An increase of absorptive capacity yields an increase of optimal cognitive distance.

Here also, one has to include the governance side. Inter-organizational collaboration requires cognitive coordination and governance of relational risks. A detailed discussion of the latter is given in Chapter 4. For governance, there is a toolbox of instruments such as: contracting plus requisite monitoring, insofar as feasible in view of uncertainties of environment and behaviour, a balance of mutual dependence, posting of hostages, typically in the form of competitively sensitive information, reputation mechanisms and trust building by cultural alignment of values, personal empathy and identification, and routinization of conduct.

In conclusion, a second type of dynamic capability is the ability to find partners, at optimal distance, and to effectively understand and collaborate with them, in the governance of 'relational risk'. This dynamic capability in the form of alliance capability can be developed by building absorptive capacity and experience in communicating and collaborating with partners who think differently.

Creativity and Experiential Learning

Truly, radically new ideas require creativity, in pathbreaking insights. According to the perspective of embodied cognition employed in this book that is associated, somehow, with experience, as a 'material cause', providing the 'stuff' of mental association. This experience derives from interaction with the world, particularly other people. Thus, it cannot be separated from the learning by communication and by collaboration that were discussed above. However, such learning somehow yields ideas that 'veer off' from existing ideas. How does that occur, by what 'logic of invention'? How is experience absorbed in such a way that it yields leaps of imagination by association?

In other words, how does exploration arise from exploitation? For this, I employ the ideas on a 'logic of discovery' or 'invention', proposed in Nooteboom (2000), in a cycle with different stages. This basic 'logic' is claimed to apply both to the level of individual learning, and has indeed been inspired by developmental psychology, and to the level of innovation systems. Here, it is summarized in terms of the latter.

First, to start somewhere on the cycle of innovation, there is a process in which radical novelty 'works out' into the emergence of a 'dominant design' (Abernathy and Utterback, 1978) or 'technological regime' (Teece, 1988), here called 'consolidation', which yields a basis for efficient exploitation, as recognized in the standard innovation literature. In that literature, it has been proposed that first technology converges on a technical dominant design, with competition focused on technical feasibility and market acceptance. In the convergence of a variety of prototypes on a dominant design there is 'reduction of content'. Market uncertainty decreases and demand for the emerging standard increases. The competencies involved in the new technology and product become more determinate, less tacit and more codified, thus becoming more imitable. Imitation and new market entry arise, and increased competition exerts pressure to produce more efficiently by utilizing economies of scale, enabled by growth of demand. Innovation then shifts to efficient organizational forms for efficient production (exploitation), which leads to dominant designs in organization, of firms, supply chains, and market structure. This is recognized in the emergence of 'industry recipes' (Spender, 1989) and 'dominant logics' (Bettis and Prahalad, 1995) of organization. Organizational dominant designs are embodied in rule-based procedures, such as 'performance programmes' or 'routines'.[3] Next, and here the analysis begins to add to the innovation literature, this yields a platform for transferring the practice or product to novel contexts (diffusion, here called 'generalization'), generating a 'variety of context'. Here, there is a connection with the principle of allopatric speciation, from evolutionary theory. This means that novel species arise outside or at the periphery of the parent niche. In economic systems, by applying a practice in a novel context (niche) it is removed from the grip of established dominant designs, in product, production and distribution (in the parent niche).

This yields a basis for exploration while maintaining exploitation. In novel contexts one encounters limits of viability and usefulness, of products, production, and organization, which require adaptation, in different forms. To maintain exploitation as long as possible, these adaptations first remain close to established practice (in 'differentiation'), with recalls from experience in earlier stages in the development of that practice, stored in more or less documented or tacit repertoires. What was tried before but failed then, may be tried again, in the novel context. Here, as noted by Nonaka and Takeuchi (1995), one depends on organizational memory in levels of staff between management and shop floor, and older workers, which may get lost under downsizing of the firm that eliminates staff.

Next, if such incremental change fails to satisfy needs of adaptation, one observes practices, in the novel context, which appear to perform well in aspects where one's own practice still fails. This leads to experimentation with the introduction of elements of those practices into one's own practice, in a process of hybridization (here called 'reciprocation'). This opens up a new 'variety of content'. This is a crucial move, since it allows for experimentation with novel elements, thereby testing for their usefulness, while still maintaining exploitation. When this turns out to be useful, it puts existing architectures (Henderson and Clark, 1990) of product, production, distribution and organization under strain for several reasons, but especially because the constraints that those architectures impose prevent novel elements from realizing their full potential, which is now seen to emerge.

This yields pressures to break architectures down in creative destruction, and to develop novel configurations of elements from different practices and contexts. Experience accrued from the earlier stages of generalization, differentiation and reciprocation feeds imagination, and gives indications for what elements and architectural principles to try out. In this way, experimentation with novel combinations is not blind or completely random, but there is still radical uncertainty, and much trial and error. And next we arrive back at the beginning, with a highly promising but still ambiguous and unsettled radical novelty that requires consolidation. Summing up: discovery emerges from an alternation of variety of content and variety of context. Variety of content is reduced (in consolidation), is then subjected to an opening of variety of context, which yields the basis for creating new variety of content.

The heuristic of discovery yields three points that are analytically crucial:

- It indicates how there may be continuity (intermediate steps, emergence) in the generation of discontinuity (episodic change).
- It shows why the emergence of radical novelty is slow relative to breakthroughs (punctuated equilibria).
- It shows how radical novelty may be non-random, based on learning, while still entailing much trial and error and unpredictability of outcomes.

The different stages together make up a cycle of discovery, as illustrated in Figure 5.1.

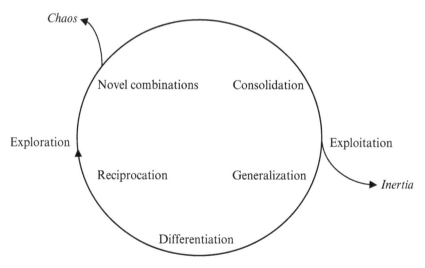

Figure 5.1   Cycle of discovery

In conclusion, the ability to implement this heuristic of invention yields a third dynamic capability. Such capability entails the ability to shift existing capabilities to new fields of application (fields of technology, products, processes, markets, institutional environments), to allow for local variation for the sake of differentiation, to allow for and enable the absorption of foreign elements for the sake of reciprocation, and the ability to engage in more radical change of both architecture and elements of the organization's system when the potential of novel elements becomes visible. This entails adaptations of organizational focus, in subsequent changes of its features, defined in Chapter 3.

Note that the logic of the heuristic is claimed to apply generally, in individual and collective generation of ideas. It applies to thinking and to innovation. Shifting existing practice to a new context, in generalization, my be actual, in shifting the application of a technology to novel fields of application, or the supply of a product to new markets, or the use of an organizational form in new institutional settings. For an organization, the process may yield a significant shift of organizational focus. The process may also be virtual, in thought experiments or computer simulations, where existing ideas or designs are tried out in new areas. As firms shift activities to novel contexts, and are subjected to new challenges, the problems encountered are typically tackled, in differentiation and reciprocation, with the aid of mental experimentation, increasingly supported by computer simulation.

Novel contexts may be sought deliberately, as part of entrepreneurship, but may also be imposed involuntarily, for example by the invasion and creative destruction in existing markets caused by innovations from abroad or from other industries. For example, publishers have been forced to go along with new opportunities from the Internet, rather than developing those themselves.

Novel contexts may also arise from collaboration with other firms, where the novel context consists of the ideas (cognitive scope) and practices of alliance partners. Thus, the present dynamic capability may be related to the dynamic capability of learning by collaboration, discussed in the previous section. Or rather, perhaps the ultimate explanation of innovation by collaboration may lie in the logic of the present heuristic of discovery. By pressures to connect one's knowledge with someone else's, in crossing cognitive distance, one is faced with the need to generalize, differentiate and reciprocate one's knowledge, which forms the basis for novel combinations and radical shifts of ideas.

In the next paragraph, the heuristic is analysed in more detail. It is also applied to the debate, in Paragraph 5.1, on different aspects of entrepreneurship and their connections. A specification is also given of the corresponding changes, in different stages, of the features of organizational focus, defined in Chapter 3.

A HEURISTIC OF INVENTION

The heuristic of invention aims, among other things, to show how there may be continuity in discontinuity, and how exploration may emerge from exploitation. The term 'heuristic' is used, rather than the term 'logic' of discovery, or invention, since it does not represent an inexorable, necessary sequencing of steps, but a procedure that will generally work, while being subject to many contingencies, and allowing for exceptions. The heuristic consists of several stages succeeding each other in an ongoing cycle. In this paragraph, these stages are discussed in some detail. Much of the text is taken from Nooteboom (2000).

Consolidation

Novelty (in knowledge, technology and organization) does not spring forward ready-made and out of the blue, like the ancient Greek goddess of war and wile Pallas Athene springing fully armed from the brow of Zeus, the chief of gods. New ideas often seem serendipitous i.e. spontaneous and apparently coming out of the blue, but upon closer inspection such revelations appear only to the prepared mind, saturated with prior experimentation, often when it relaxes from concentration and opens up to association.

Novelty (novel ideas, practices, products, technologies) at the outset tends to be incompletely determinate. It emerges as a groping around with improvisations that need to crystallize and achieve consolidation in best practice, on the basis of experience with success and failure. It is only after consolidation that geniuses can be distinguished from fools. Radical novelty tends to be ill defined, ambiguous, and messy, with encumbrances from previous practice, and lapses back into more familiar practice. Novel ways of doing things seem to suggest themselves, but it is not clear how or why precisely they should work. This happens even in areas that appear to be quite determinate and purely deductive, such as mathematics. The mathematician Gauss once exclaimed: 'I have got my result; but I do not know yet how to get it' (Popper, 1973: 16). Repeated trials and application, supported by ancillary innovations in tools, methods, and materials, are required to find out what properly belongs to the novel practice and what not. This yields increasing efficiency from a process of narrowing down, in a reduction of variety, by elimination of what step by step is found out to be redundant, inefficient or counter-productive. This is related to the notion of exploitation. It is also related to what in the economic literature is known as learning by doing, and the 'experience curve': efficiency increases as a function of cumulative experience (Yelle, 1979).

In industries, the speed of the process depends on pressures for standardization. In case of network externalities, for example, such pressure is great. The famous example is the race towards a technical standard for video recorders. The selection of one outcome from possible alternatives is influenced by current institutions and flukes of chance and coincidence: what happens to be around in the form of adequate materials, skills, instruments, organization, infrastructure, attitudes, habits of thought and other institutions. That is why a given technology may yield different practices in different countries or even in different organizations within an industry. Barley (1986) gives an example of how the use of electronic scanning devices was organized differently, with different results, in different hospitals. The outcome often is not predictable and may not be intended. Development may be locked into a path that later turns out to be sub-optimal or even counter-productive (Arthur, 1989; David, 1985).

The history of technology presents ample evidence of how science has often followed from the 'tinkering' or trial and error of technology, rather than leading technology. Mokyr (1990: 170) claimed that in the last 150 years the majority of inventions were used before people understood why they worked. This occurred in agricultural technology, mechanical machinery, metallurgy, the textile industry and shipping. However, increasingly, from the second half of the nineteenth century, scientific understanding came to feed technological development. An example is the invention of telegraphy, which required the theoretical notion of electro-magnetic waves invented by Maxwell in 1865 (Mokyr, 1990: 144). Chemistry also was to a large extent guided by science. Nevertheless, the reverse order of practical tinkering preceding understanding still occurs, as has been exemplified in the information technology revolution (Dosi, 1984).

Why does consolidation take place? It results from a drive towards efficiency and standardization of operation, application and production. At first, the drive is towards feasibility, in the form of a working model. After a novel technology or product gets consolidated, in an architecture of components or elements, it gets translated into an organizational architecture for efficient production and distribution, with specialized activities for different elements of a system. Subsequently the focus shifts from the architecture of product and organization to the optimization of elements or activities within it.

The outcome of consolidation serves not only as a basis for efficient exploitation, but also as a platform for expansion and new applications, in a new 'techno-economic paradigm' (Freeman and Perez, 1989). This provides the second rationale for consolidation. This expansion, called 'generalization', provides the basis for exploration, in the accumulation of experience in different applications, as an input for experiential learning.

In terms of organizational cognitive focus, the stage of consolidation entails the creation of focus from a diversity of fragmented elements derived from a variety of earlier foci. In terms of the features of focus proposed in Chapter 3, this entails the definition of the range of activities to which focus applies (width), specification of aspects of each that fall under the focus (reach), increased tightness with which they are controlled, and a deepening of the level of abstractness and generality of concepts by which focus exerts its control.

This stage can be identified with some of the types or aspects of entrepreneurship, discussed on pp. 174–5. First, there is a need to escape from the chaos of trial and error, to commit to a design and carry it through development, testing and entry to markets. This requires leadership and charisma to mobilize people in an uncertain and sometimes quite arbitrary looking venture, as recognized by Schumpeter. For those reasons it may be difficult to obtain outside capital, so that the entrepreneur may also have to be a capitalist, as recognized by Marshall. It requires the willingness to accept risk, and tenacity to survive the inevitable setbacks, as recognized by Knight. There is also an element of arbitrage, in matching new supply to unsatisfied demand, as recognized by Cantillon and the Austrians. However, it is not adequate, in this stage of the cycle, to conceive of this in terms of given products and demand on the basis of given preferences. New opportunities may enable and require new preferences. Here, there is still experimentation and selection among different product forms.

As a dominant design of technology and product arises, a different kind of entrepreneurship is needed, to establish a fitting organizational architecture. Here, a new entrepreneurial firm runs into obstacles in development (Greiner, 1972). As sales expand, authority and control have to be delegated, and more formalized procedures have to be designed, in a Weberian or Chandlerian type of organization. This is related to the more managerial notion of entrepreneurship, recognized by Marshall and Say. However, here management is certainly not routine. This organizational development requires a genuine kind of entrepreneurship. It entails risk and requires imagination and leadership for the development of novel forms of organization. But it is different from the earlier kind of entrepreneurship. Often, the initial entrepreneur fails to make the turnaround to this managerial type of entrepreneurship. This may result in the firm being taken over to consolidate its success.

Inertia

While consolidation is needed for efficient exploitation and for generalization, it can develop into inertia. In terms of organizational focus: the focus
can become too strong or constraining, or, more precisely, too cohesive
and too inclusive, with too much width, reach and tightness, in the terminology developed in Chapter 3, fixing too much to allow for novelty
and requisite variety.

Why this inertia? Why stick to established views and practice in the
face of failures? Clearly, inertia can be disastrous. But directly after a
novelty has settled down, and 'come into its own', one could not possibly step directly to the next novelty. Such a leap is difficult to imagine.
Entrepreneurship may consist of radical jumps into the dark, with a large
risk of failure and a small chance of successful radical innovation. On the
aggregate level of the economy such jumps are beneficial when the weight
of incidental success exceeds the weight of frequent failure. But on the level
of the firm it is generally ill advised. It is counterproductive to drop and
replace practices too soon, before one knows their limits and possibilities
for replacement. That would lead to random drift rather than improvement (Lounamaa and March, 1987).

In scientific development, Kuhn (1970) not only noted, descriptively,
that scientists tend to stick to the 'puzzle solving' of 'normal science', but
also indicated, normatively, that a certain amount of theoretical tenacity is
rational. First, there is a principle of economy: we do not and should not
surrender theory at the first occurrence of a falsifier, indicating that our
theory is not perfect. It is rational to wait until the cumulative weight of
anomalies becomes excessive in some sense. But there is more: it is only by
ongoing tests of theory that we find where its real strengths and weaknesses
lie. Even Popper (1970: 55) recognized this, in spite of his drive to keep
science open to criticism. We need to exhaust our theories to a sufficient
extent, before we give them up, not only to recoup our investment in them,
so to speak, but also to develop the motivation for a novel alternative, by
an accumulation of anomalies.

This has been recognized also in the literature on organizational learning. There is a trade-off between the need to adapt and the costs involved
in terms of uncertainty whether novelty will be successful, and uncertainty
about the organizational repercussions (March, 1991). To make the step
to novel practice one must be prepared to 'unlearn' (Hedberg, 1981), in
the sense of no longer taking established procedures for granted. Thus a
condition for innovation generally is that there is perceived need, mostly
from external pressure, a threat to continued existence or a shortfall of
performance below aspiration levels, as has been the dominant view in

the literature on organizational learning (see the survey by Cohen and Sproull, 1996).

However, there is more, which does not seem to have been recognized in the economic and organizational literatures. While necessity may be the mother of invention, that may also need a father. Above all, we need to accumulate experience to find out what elements are eligible for preservation in the exploration of 'novel combinations', and what other elements and from where, to combine them with. Before we are able to replace any practice, of theory, technology or organization, we first need to pursue its potential, in a range of applications in a variety of contexts. We need this not only to build up the motive for change, in an accumulation of misfits, but also to discover where the limits of validity of an established practice lie, and to gather indications what elements to preserve from it, and how, in a novel practice. We do not know beforehand which elements are robust under changing contexts, and hence worth preserving, before we have subjected them to a variety of trials.

This is how we might combine exploitation and exploration: while employing the practice we are at the same time exploring its limits and opportunities for its change and replacement. This puts the notion of 'inertia' of organizations into a new perspective. Inertia is not only needed for co-ordination and control, for the sake of efficiency in exploitation. It also represents the principle of tenacity: the need to preserve existing principles in order to find out where and why they fail and how they might be replaced, as a contribution to exploration. Thus a certain amount of conservatism and inertia is rational, while it can easily become excessive and block innovation.

Generalization

Let us see how exploration is likely to proceed. If the objective is to conduct exploitation in such a way that it leads on to exploration, we should seek to do it in a way that optimizes both profit from exploitation and the gathering of the elements of discovery: motive, opportunity and means. The most straightforward way to do this is to generalize application of the practice to novel contexts. The novel context needs to be sufficiently close to afford viable exploitation and sufficiently different to yield novelty of tests and novelty of insight where limitations and opportunities for improvement lie. We see this in individual development as well as in development of firms and markets: attempts are made to carry a successful practice into neighbouring areas of application.

This connects with the analysis of optimal cognitive distance, in Chapter 4. We need sufficient difference to yield novel challenges and insights, but not so much difference that there is no perspective for ongoing exploitation and for absorbing and making sense of new threats and opportunities.

As in crime, the transgression of existing principles requires motive, opportunity and means. Before the need for replacement of an existing practice arises such a move would be wasteful, and before opportunity and means arise it would be impossible. First, generalization yields an opportunity for change in the escape from the sway of dominant practice, outside the 'parent niche'. Next, it yields a motive for change, from insight in the limitations of current practice. Next, it yields the means for change, in three forms. First, it yields an identification of elements of current practice that can be preserved in novel combinations, because they do not form the cause of such limitations and are persistently effective. Second, recognition of elements from other, neighbouring practices with which they can be combined with a reasonable perspective for useful and workable novelty. Third: insight in architectural principles by which these elements can be combined with a reasonable chance of success in utilizing their potential.

In economies, the contexts across which a practice is generalized may be new applications of technologies or new markets for existing products. For example: new segments in domestic markets, or foreign markets, with new conditions of demand and competition, new distribution channels, new technological conditions of production (labour, materials, components, machinery, tools), different technical infrastructures (transportation, energy, communication), and different institutions (labour markets, education and training, legal conditions, professional organizations, intermediaries, central and local government). Exploration of novel applications across contexts can to a greater or lesser extent be done virtually rather than actually, by thought experiments, scenarios, simulation of prototypes, inspection or 'reverse engineering' of practices or products used elsewhere.

In terms of organizational focus, generalization requires a reduction of inclusiveness, that is the involvement of people who are tied up in the firm to a lesser extent, and have more outside roles and connections. It is also likely to require less reach, that is a reduction of the number of features of a given activity that are constrained by the focus. Finally, it may be helped by a deepening of focus, that is the formulation of more abstract, fundamental underlying notions that allow more variety of 'surface' arrangements (see Chapter 3 for an elaboration).

In this stage of generalization we find entrepreneurship in opening up or entering new markets, as recognized by Mangoldt and Schumpeter. However, there is also an element of arbitrage: carrying products to unsatisfied demand.

As discussed in Nooteboom (2000) the analysis may throw new light on the debate, in the management literature, on the conduct of multinationals, in processes of globalization. There, an important question is whether multinationals should engage in a 'global strategy', imposing their practices world-wide, or allow for variety, in a 'multi-national strategy'. There are many relevant considerations here. The choice depends on economic arguments, such as the need for a uniform practice to maintain economies of scale. That, in turn, depends on technological opportunities and competitive pressures on price, and on commercial considerations, such as demand for differentiated products as a function of different circumstances of use, technical differentiability of products, or, on the contrary, market considerations to maintain a uniform product worldwide (for example to reduce search costs, as in the case of McDonald's). This is not the place to reiterate the relevant literature. The point here is that even if multinationals have the power, in their offer of employment, technology, capital and access to global markets, to impose their home country practices, it may in the longer term be wiser to employ adaptation to different circumstances in different host countries, as a learning strategy (for a study of these two alternatives, in multi-national ventures in China, see Child, 2002).

Differentiation and Reciprocation

As one moves to new contexts, practice needs to be differentiated to fit to them. One may need to adjust to a different availability of material inputs and tools, competencies of people, conditions of use by customers and technical infrastructure. Here, the process of narrowing by eliminating redundancies, and the reduction of variety of practice, in the first stage of consolidation, is reversed into a process of widening into different versions and extensions of the novelty, with increasing 'variety of content'.

A proximate form of differentiation is to modify elements while preserving the architecture in which they are connected (Henderson and Clark, 1990). Next, one may re-arrange elements of an existing practice into novel architectures. For this one may tap into memory of previous applications, and experience with trials in the earlier stage of consolidation. This is a process of problem solving, defined as seeking recourse to known ways of doing things (Holland et al., 1989: 11). The potential and the success of this depend on what is available from previous experience in (organizational and personal) memory, on inventiveness in problem solving of the people involved, and on communication and co-operation between them.

A wider, more 'distant' form of structural change is to adopt elements from foreign practices encountered in the novel context, which are successful in aspects where one's own practice fails. Speculations and experiments arise concerning the adoption of elements from such neighbouring practices. It can also go the other way: elements from one's own practice are transferred to the architecture of a foreign practice. Such transfers are called 'reciprocation'. The mental equivalent of this is association between different mental schemata.

In terms of organizational focus, differentiation requires, next to a reduction of reach already allowed in the stage of generalization, a relaxation of tightness, to allow for non-standard ways of fulfilling certain activities, while maintaining the set of activities to which focus applies (width). Reciprocation requires a reduction of width, that is the allowance of activities that fall outside the grasp of focus.

In this stage of differentiation and reciprocation we see the entrepreneurship of crossing boundaries of accepted practice. Entrepreneurs need to convince others to join, or at least to permit such heterodoxy. Here, the inertia of the integrated firm may take its toll. In multinationals there are battles between central office in the home country that wants to maintain coherence and company-wide standards and practices for the sake of exploitation, and host country subsidiaries that demand room for differentiation and reciprocation. The battle gets especially fierce when for the sake of novel combinations competencies are developed that are at odds with what is perceived as core competence, or alliances are sought with outside business units that are part of competing firms. Lack of acceptance may impel the internal entrepreneur to leave the firm and start up for himself. Such exit in order to realize opportunities that are not recognized and legitimated within a firm is, of course, the well-known phenomenon of entrepreneurial 'spin-offs'.

There is also an entrepreneurial challenge at the level of top management. The paradoxical challenge is to combine the preservation of structures for exploitation with an allowance for deviations for the sake of experimentation for exploration. In terms of organizational focus, the question is how far one can go in weakening the focus, allowing for greater internal cognitive distance. The difficulty of this depends on how 'systemic' versus 'stand-alone' the architecture for exploitation is (Langlois, 1998). When highly systemic, the system has many densely connected elements, with narrow tolerances in interfaces. Here, deviations in elements, for the sake of experimentation, would entail wide repercussions for adaptation in other elements of the system. An example is a refinery. Then, there is a high cost, while the promise of results is highly uncertain. On the other hand, in stand-alone systems elements are highly autonomous in their exploitation. If, in addition, exploitation itself already requires highly differentiated products for different customers, there is more scope to combine exploitation and exploration. An example is a consultancy firm. An intermediate case is that of a modular system, where elements are many and mutually connected but self-contained and replaceable, provided that they satisfy the constraints in the system. There is genuine entrepreneurship in these issues of organizational design, to balance exploitation and exploration. There is a range of options for such design but it would go too far to discuss them here (see Nooteboom, 2000). This entrepreneurial task can, perhaps, be seen as of the 'managerial' type (Marshall), but it goes beyond any simple, optimal matching of production factors, according to a given 'production function'. The problem is especially deep if the new venture entails a shift of organizational cognitive focus, in a change of fundamental views and convictions about what 'the firm is about'.

In case exploration cannot be allowed within the system, for risk of weakening organizational focus too much, one may locate exploration outside it, or at the periphery of the organization. An example is the 'skunk works' of 3M company, where entrepreneurial units are allowed to go their own way, outside the established order of structures, procedures, rules, guiding concepts, and established meanings. However, then the question arises what sense it makes to maintain them within the organization at all. An alternative then lies in 'external corporate venturing', where the firm facilitates headstrong entrepreneurial types to spin off their own ventures. For this, the firm may act as a venture capitalist, and may offer a guarantee of return to the firm in case of failure. By having a stake in the capital of the venture, the firm may hedge its bets and keep the option open of integrating the outcome after proven success, when it is clearer what the potential revenues and repercussions in upsetting established organizational structure would be. In case of too much lack of fit even then, the firm may sell its share. Here, the firm adopts the entrepreneurial role of a venture capitalist. A problem here from the perspective of public welfare might be that the firm uses its stake to put the innovation on hold, in case it yields products that cannibalize existing products that the firm wants to maintain, in a further stretch of its 'life cycle'.

Transformation

Recombination of elements from different practices in novel architectures can lead to 'accommodation' in the form of 'novel combinations' (Schumpeter), yielding 'radical' or 'large' or 'macro' innovations. Often this is 'competence destroying' for incumbent organizations, and outsiders may be needed to make such a break.

A radically novel combination is not easy to identify as an opportunity, since it literally does not make sense; it cannot be interpreted in terms of existing practices, and therefore extends beyond established meanings and corresponding categories. It has no recognizable identity. It requires a leap of imagination. That is why it is more of a lonely, personal affair: it is difficult to have the hunch make sense even to oneself, let alone others. A handful of people stumbled upon X-rays, but only Madame Curie saw what it might mean, and what its implications and uses might be. The role of chance increases: we are in the field of serendipity, but it is the serendipity of the prepared mind. This yields the 'King Saul effect' (Mokyr, 1990: 286). Looking for a better dynamo for bicycle lights, Philips Company hit upon the development of an electric shaver. Gasoline at first was a useless by-product in the derivation of lubricants from crude oil, before it was developed into a fuel for the internal combustion motor. Bessemer invented his steel making process while trying to solve problems of a spinning cannon shell (Mokyr, 1990: 116).

How, then, do radically novel combinations arise, in new architectures of elements from a variety of previously unconnected practices? Here, it is proposed that the process may run as follows. Problems accumulate in the preceding process of reciprocation, in hybrid structures of elements form different architectures. Ad hoc additions and modifications mess up the clarity ('spaghetti'), consistency and efficiency of the practice, and increase complexity, resulting in loss of efficiency and diminishing returns: it becomes increasingly difficult to make further additions or modifications while maintaining coherence. Elements are duplicated, in different parts of the architecture, with forgone opportunities for economy of scale. Unsolved failures to perform are accumulated. This provides an incentive to consider a clean-up by dropping rather than by only re-arranging elements, in novel architectures. Above all: existing architecture imposes limits on the novel elements brought in, preventing realization of their true potential. Thus pressures build up to break down the architecture to realize the potential of novelty. Experience has accumulated to suggest which novel combinations of elements, gathered in reciprocation from a variety of old practices, might be successfully combined, and by which architectural principles. There is a basis for reasonable hunches.

In terms of organizational focus, here we find its breakdown, in casting about for novel elements to fall under its scope (width), questioning how far they should be controlled, and how tightly, and often a fundamental re-conceptualization at the deep level of focus, in fundamental conceptions about what an appropriate firm would 'be about'.

Here, in the imagination and trial of novel combinations the Schumpeterian entrepreneur comes into his own, as the creator of ideas not only concerning technology, product and market, but also concerning organization and its cultural identity. And when success emerges we are back at the beginning, with a need for consolidation.

In Chapter 4 it was indicated how external relationships of firms can have implications for internal focus, which may need to weaken to allow focus between organizations to strengthen. In particular in the stage of reciprocation parts of the firm must be allowed the freedom to explore novel combinations with other organizations. This may require a reduction of the width, reach, or strictness of organizational focus. As exploration moves into exploitation, in the emergence of a new dominant design and consolidation, focus needs to be strengthened again to leverage the results. Width of focus includes new activities, or shifts from old to new ones, there is coordination of more aspects of practice (increased reach), coordination becomes tighter, and variety of fundamental principles may again be curtailed. In a larger firm, a complication arises when different parts of the firm (for example subsidiaries in a multinational corporation) are in different stages of exploration and exploitation. Focus may need to be weakened for those in exploration and strengthened for those in exploitation. This is the challenge of combining exploration and exploitation in an 'ambidextrous organization'.

A problem then is that one does not know in advance whether the uncertain outcome of exploration can indeed be usefully, feasibly and efficiently be integrated in a novel focus, with sufficient coherence with exploitation elsewhere in the firm. And here the logic of spin-offs and external corporate venturing comes up again. Why not spin off the subsidiary when it enters upon external exploration, giving it all the freedom needed, and then re-integrate again only if it turns out that the outcome can usefully and feasibly be integrated in exploitation? Of course, this consideration has to be balanced with other considerations, concerning strategic positioning (after letting go, is one still in a strategic position to re-integrate later?) and the transaction costs of spin-off and re-integration.

Network Dynamics

Now we can also specify network dynamics: the change of the structure and strength of ties. For this, a connection is made between the analysis of the structure and density of ties in Chapter 4 and the cycle of discovery that was indicated above (see Figure 5.1) (see Nooteboom and Klein Woolthuis, 2005).

First, if we start at the early stage of exploration, in the experimentation with novel combinations of elements from different pre-existing practices (reciprocation), with requisite transformations of those elements as the process proceeds, according to novel architectural principles or basic logics or design logics, we would expect the following. Concerning network structure, compared to other stages we would expect a relatively volatile structure, with frequent exit and entry of participants to allow for frequent and fast re-configuration of ties, a dense structure to allow for the hedging of relational bets that such volatility requires and the availability of high shared absorptive capacity, in pooling ability to understand and to engage in the triangulation needed to cope with knowledge that is still highly novel, fluid and ambiguous. Here competition is on technical and commercial viability rather than efficiency and attendant large-scale production and distribution, which limits the direct cost and opportunity cost of redundant ties. Density of ties also supports gossip as a basis for a reputation system, needed for governance especially in the face of uncertainty and fluid knowledge, with consequent limits to governance by contract or hierarchy. Next to reputation, governance is likely to be based on mutual balance of dependence. Direct ties are sought at optimal cognitive distance, and indirect ties help in playing roles of go-betweens for governance as well as for crossing cognitive distance that is too large to deal with by oneself. Participants with high betweenness centrality offer bridging of structural holes, in ties with distant clusters as sources of new knowledge. Concerning the strength of ties we would expect wide scope (large multiplexity) to deal with the large range of uncertainty (concerning both technical and commercial knowledge, network structure and membership, reputation concerning both competence and intentional reliability of potential partners). Also, we would expect high frequency of interaction, in view of fast change of conditions, a great deal of trust building to compensate for difficulties of contract and monitoring, on the basis of shared (often professional) ethics, empathy or identification. Ties should not be rigid, lasting too long, unless long term ties are complemented with access to non-overlapping links with other parties (the tie crossing a structural hole). Here network focus should have limited width, reach and tightness, with perhaps only some coordination on the deep level of fundamental principles and ethics.

Towards consolidation knowledge settles and becomes less ambiguous and more codified, absorptive capacity develops and knowledge diffuses. More division of labour and specialization arise. Competition shifts from technical and commercial viability to efficiency of production and price of products, and low costs of redundancy. Redundancy of ties is less needed because of less uncertainty. Less uncertainty enables more governance by contracting, reducing the need for reputation mechanisms, and its attendant density of ties, and of personal trust on the basis of shared ethics, empathy and identification. Ties become less personal. In competition for efficiency and the use of economies of scale to achieve them, there is a shake-out of firms and concentration increases. Density decreases and some participants assume coordination roles, as hubs, in positions with high degree centrality. Which participants take up such central positions depends on their initial positions, their build-up of absorptive capacity, and their transition from exploration to exploitation, with abilities to achieve organizational innovation for more efficient production and distribution, and to build up volume. More peripherally situated participants literally and figuratively take up marginal positions, and drop out more easily in the shake-out process. We expect ties to become weaker in scope, because ties become more specialized in certain areas of specialization of participants, and weaker in frequency of knowledge exchange, since knowledge has stabilized. Ties are expected to become stronger in duration, with attendant reduction of network volatility, in specific investments for the sake of scaling-up, and for efficient systems of production and distribution, and in formal contracting, enabled by less uncertainty and needed because of loss of personal bases for trust. Here, either network focus breaks up into different foci for individual relationships, or focus becomes more cohesive, typically around a central hub.

In consolidation, there are tendencies towards rigidity by lock-in. Central participants become more central by the process of 'preferential attachment': being central they become more attractive for additional partners. It becomes more difficult for outsiders to come in and occupy positions of centrality. Increasingly, internal standards of technology, safety, certification, training and structures of distribution emerge that bind participants. For an example of the emergence of a stable core-periphery structure see the study of alliances in biotechnology by Orsenigo et al. (1998) and Gilsing and Nooteboom (2006).

To embark on a novel path of exploration, either network structure has to be broken up by an exogenous shock, such as by an external innovation, or there have to be 'spin-offs' of activity from the existing network into new selection environments, that is novel niches of exploitation, in the stage of generalization. The trigger for this may lie in the drive of expansion from saturated nearby markets. Here, peripheral participants may see and take the opportunity better than central ones, and in view of their more marginal position they have a greater incentive to do so. As they move into new territories, they are confronted with the need to adapt existing practice to new conditions of demand, supply, production, organization, distribution or service. For this they need the space to do so, in the case of subsidiaries of multinational companies an authorization from the head office or more slack in regulations, procedures and monitoring, which puts relations with head office under stress. Independent companies need similar relaxation from the networks they were embedded in, and again the advantage lies with more peripheral participants, in view of their fewer direct ties that may constrain their deviance. It may happen that such peripheral participants develop into channels between the network and distant clusters, to revitalize the network. Here network focus weakens or breaks up.

If in the new context of application mere differentiation of existing practice does not suffice to survive and flourish, more radical departures may
be triggered, in 'reciprocation' of elements for foreign practices into one's
own familiar practice, in experimentation with hybrids. This puts further
stress on relations with the head office or network. When reciprocation
leads to the next stage of more radical reconfiguration with novel architectural principles, or basic logics or design principles, local networks start to
develop in the new context, with the features of structure and strength of
ties for exploration networks that was described before. A complete break
may arise with the head office or home network. Alternatively, if the new
innovation develops into a success it may invade the home niche, and the
explorers may seek each other out in the emergence of a new network,
along the periphery of the old one, and they may develop into the central
agents in the new network as it, in turn, develops towards consolidation.

For dynamic capabilities, the implication is that one should understand
network dynamics to assess consequences and perspectives of network structure and one's position in it, and the ability to apply such insight in seeking
or developing networks and one's positioning in them, including opportunities to escape from a network and set out on a path of discovery, where
peripherality may be transformed from a disadvantage to an advantage.

CONCLUSIONS AND RESEARCH AGENDA

Starting with a survey of notions and aspects of entrepreneurship, in this
chapter I analysed dynamic capabilities, to answer Question 9 from the
questions listed in the introductory chapter, as follows:

Question 9: What are dynamic capabilities?
Answer: On the level of individuals, one dynamic capability is to adopt
knowledge from others, on the basis of absorptive capacity and to help
them to absorb your knowledge, with rhetorical capabilities to trigger
understanding, and governance capabilities, particularly the ability to
identify and solve possible problems of spillover, mutual dependence,
reputation and psychological safety.

On the level of organizations, a second dynamic capability, discussed
in more detail in Chapter 4, is the intellectual and behavioural ability to
collaborate with other organizations, at optimal cognitive distance, with
governance capabilities to deal with relational risks of dependence and
spillover.

A third dynamic capability, discussed in some detail in the present
chapter, is the ability to employ a heuristic of invention for developing

exploitation into exploration, by shifting activity to appropriate novel contexts that offer an opportunity of ongoing exploitation but also novel challenges to survival, insights into limitations of current practice, opportunities for experimenting with novel local elements, and the ability to shift to more radical architectural reconfigurations of old and new elements to realize the potential of emerging success of novelty. This requires great governance capabilities to deal with internal variety and to integrate it into a new organizational focus.

Question 14: How to explain cluster dynamics?
Answer: Networks dynamics can be explained in terms of changes in features of structure and strength of ties along the cycle of discovery, and a change of network focus. In the early stage of exploration, in novel combinations, ties tend to be volatile and dense, with frequent interaction, large cognitive distance, limited duration, limited specific investments, large scope (multiplexity) of ties, governance to a large extent by reputation and personal bonding, complemented by more sparse and weak linkages to distant communities, and advantages for players with high betweenness centrality. Network focus is cohesive relative to other stages, though still less so than within organizations. Towards consolidation density decreases, frequency of knowledge exchange decreases, scope of ties decreases, ties last longer, specific investments increase, governance shifts from trust to contracts, ties become more impersonal, and advantage arises for players with high degree centrality. Peripheral players are at a disadvantage and new entry becomes increasingly difficult. Network focus becomes less cohesive. In following stages of generalization, differentiation and reciprocation, new outside ties arise, set up by some, especially peripheral players who may subsequently spin off from the network and start to develop their own network. This may lead on to the situation described at the start.

It may well be that the dynamic capability of learning by collaboration is to be explained as a special case of the dynamic capability of employing the heuristic of invention, where different alliance partners present, to each other, novel contexts of action, yielding opportunities and mutual help for reciprocation (in the technical sense employed in the logic of the heuristic).

Nooteboom (2000) proposed that the cycle of discovery is accompanied by a cycle of organizational integration and disintegration. Integration occurs in the stage of consolidation, to achieve increasing scale, often accompanied with mergers and acquisitions of firms in the same industry. Generalization requires a certain amount of decentralization, with a certain autonomy for foreign subsidiaries, reciprocation is typically

Table 5.1   Organizational focus along the cycle of discovery

Stage	Focus features
Consolidation	Focus formation: increasing width, reach and tightness of focus
Generalization	Less inclusiveness of focus, reduced reach, possibly increased depth
Differentiation	Reduced tightness
Reciprocation	Reduced width
Transformation	Breakdown and reconstitution of focus

accompanied by alliances with other firms, and transformation is typically accompanied by disintegration.

It requires great organizational capability of governance to implement the heuristic of invention. In terms of organizational focus, different stages require different steps, as discussed above and summarized in Table 5.1.

There is much more to say on details of organizational arrangements for combining exploitation and exploration, as a function of contingencies concerning e.g. technology, markets, and institutions, but that has been discussed in some detail elsewhere, in Nooteboom (2000).

The main priority for further research is to develop the analysis into empirical tests.

NOTES

1. The term 'discovery' has the connotation of literally removing the cover from something that already exists. I do not intend that meaning here. Here, discovery is synonymous with 'invention'.
2. As the notion of 'tacit knowledge', the notion of 'indwelling' also derives from Michael Polanyi.
3. In cognitive science we encounter 'paradigms' (in the sense of exemplars to be emulated), 'mental models' (Johnson-Laird, 1983), 'scripts' (Abelson, 1976; Shank and Abelson, 1977), mental 'prototypes' (Rosch, 1977) and 'stereotypes' (Putnam, 1975). Across all these fields of technology, organization, knowledge and language we see the notion of novelty becoming consolidated in a standard practice, which provides the basis for efficient exploitation.

6. Evolution

INTRODUCTION

This chapter concerns evolutionary theory of the firm. Does evolutionary theory help, with its core processes of variety generation, selection and transmission, for a cognitive theory of the firm? It does, to some but also limited extent. Evolutionary theories of economies, and of culture, have acquired considerable following, but have also been subject to considerable criticism. Most criticism has been aimed at inappropriate biological analogies, but recently it has been claimed that a 'universal Darwinism', purged of all such mistaken analogy, is both useful and viable. Why should we try to preserve evolutionary theory, and will such theory stand up to sustained critical analysis? How useful is it for the theory of the firm? Evolutionary theory appears to be the most adequate theory around for solving the problem of agency and structure, avoiding both an overly rational, managerial 'strategic choice' view of organizations and a 'contingency' view of organizations as fully determined by their environment. Whether universal Darwinism stands up to critical analysis remains to be seen. Here, the focus is on evolutionary theory of organization and of knowledge. Two of the subjects that will not be considered here are evolution of institutions more generally, beyond organizations, and evolutionary game theory.

In evolutionary theory there is a distinction between the ontogenetic development of an individual and the phylogenetic development of a species or population of individuals. In Chapter 3 I paid considerable attention to the ontogenetic development of firms, and in the present chapter attention also turns to the phylogenetic development of forms of organization.

Using insights from 'embodied cognition' and the resulting 'cognitive theory of the firm', set out in Chapters 2 and 3, I aim to contribute to the critical analysis of evolutionary theory, and perhaps its further development, or its replacement, in economics and the study of culture. In particular, the question will be in what way, and to what extent, organizations, including both firms and scientific organizations and societies, can be understood as 'interactors' that carry capabilities or knowledge as 'replicators' within industries or scientific disciplines as 'populations'. Using the results from Chapter 3, I analyse how organizations, seen as carriers of a cognitive focus, may act as interactors. Using results from Chapter 4 I analyse differences between firms and mechanisms of transmission (in the evolutionary sense) between them within and between industries. Using results from Chapter 5 I analyse how, if at all, 'dynamic capabilities' can be fitted into evolutionary theory. In particular, I discuss in what sense, and to what extent, these sources of 'variation' are 'blind' or random, as postulated in evolutionary theory. While the focus is on the analysis of organizations, I also consider the evolution of culture more generally, in particular the evolution of knowledge. If organizations are fruitfully seen as being characterized by a cognitive focus, as argued in this book, then the evolution of organizations and cognition are connected, and we should have a theory of both.

ISSUES IN EVOLUTIONARY THEORY

In this paragraph I discuss key issues in evolutionary theory for behavioural science, in order to specify the questions to be answered in this chapter. The first issue concerns the need to abstract evolution from evolution in biology, in a more general 'universal' Darwinism. The second issue concerns the notions of replicators and interactors, and their meaning and relevance for organizations and knowledge. The third issue concerns the influence that interactors may have on selection conditions. The fourth issue concerns replication by means of imitation and communication, and its relation with the generation of variety. The fourth issue concerns the extent to which, and in what sense, variety generation is 'blind' and how it may be guided by experience in selection.

Universal Darwinism

Beyond biology, a generalized evolutionary framework, with its basic principles of variety generation, selection and transmission, has been applied to a wide range of socio-economic phenomena, such as organizations (Aldrich, 1999; Baum and Singh, 1994; McKelvey, 1982), industries (Hannan and Freeman, 1977, 1984, 1989), economies (Hodgson, 1993, 2002b; Hodgson and Knudsen, 2006; Metcalfe, 1998; Nelson and Winter, 1982; Veblen, 1919; Witt, 1993, 2004), knowledge (Campbell, 1974), neural structures (Edelman, 1987) and culture (Boyd and Richerson, 1985; Hull, 1988).

In behavioural science, the evolutionary perspective has a number of attractions. It accounts for development of forms (here forms of organization and of cognition) under limited foresight. Wittgenstein (1976) spoke of language as a 'form of life', and perhaps evolutionary theory applies to all forms of life, in biology and culture. In economics and management evolutionary theory keeps us from the error of an unrealistically rational, magical view of development as the design by somehow prescient, or even clairvoyant, managers, entrepreneurs and scientists, as well as from the opposite error of institutional or technological determinism, whereby forms of organization are dictated by external conditions of technology and market (McKelvey, 1982). In the first, managerial actors are omnipotent, and in the latter actors are absent. Evolutionary theory helps to deal with what in sociology is called the problem of agency and structure. It forces us to recognize both the role of actors, with their individual preferences and endowments, in the processes of variety generation and transmission, and the enabling and constraining conditions for action, in structures of markets and institutions, in the process of selection. While characteristics of entrepreneurs and organizations have a causal effect on survival and growth of firms, causality can also go the other way, with characteristics being the result of processes of selection and retention (Aldrich, 1999: 336). It forces us to recognize causes of change both within organizations ('autogenic') and outside them ('allogenic') (McKelvey, 1982). It makes allowance for the radical uncertainty of innovation (Shackle, 1961), and for evident and ubiquitous error and failure in human endeavour.

Of great intellectual but also moral importance, evolutionary theory also forces us to accept diversity as an essential element of development and of societies. The old practice, in economic analysis, of dealing with an industry on the basis of a 'representative firm' is a fundamental mistake. As Hayek recognized, knowledge is dispersed and differentiated.

Competition in markets and fields of knowledge, with constraining and enabling effects of institutions, are straightforwardly seen as yielding a process of differential survival and retention of products, practices and ideas. There is plausibility in seeing entrepreneurship and invention as sources of variety generation, and to see personnel turnover, training, personnel transfer, imitation, consultancy and growth as mechanisms for the transmission of proven success.

Anyone who has studied socio-economic evolution recognizes that in many respects it differs radically from biological evolution. While earlier literature was often based on analogies from biological evolution, in more recent literature (Hodgson, 2002b; Hodgson and Knudsen, 2004, 2006) a radical abstraction has been made, in the definition of 'universal Darwinism' (Dawkins, 1983) in terms of only the overall, 'meta-theoretical framework' (Hodgson and Knudsen, 2006: 16) of variety generation, selection and transmission, regardless of the very different ways in which they operate in different areas of application. Hodgson and Knudsen claim that this overall framework applies universally to biological as well as economic, cultural, and cognitive systems. It is needed to explain why some organizations last longer or grow more than others, and why some are imitated more than others. While universal Darwinism gives a useful conceptual orientation of research, it leaves most of the explanatory work still to be done, in a specification of the processes of variety generation, selection and transmission, in terms of people, cognition, work, management, invention, innovation, organizations, industries, markets and institutions.

However, universal Darwinism goes further and specifies the principles of variety generation, selection and transmission in terms of the notions of replicators and interactors (Campbell, 1974; McKelvey, 1982; Hull, 1988) or *vehicles* (Dawkins, 1983), and the notion of *populations*. Interactors/vehicles (in biology: organisms) interact with their selection environment, and are members of *populations* of similar but differentiated interactors (in biology: species). The suggestion is that these are essential elements of evolution, without which the notion of evolution becomes loose and indeterminate. They distinguish, it seems, Darwinism from a more general, looser, less determinate notion of evolution in the sense of 'development'. However, as argued recently by Nelson (2006), this is also where the problems begin. The question then is how meaningful evolutionary theory is if the notions of interactors and replicators fail to apply.

To function as an interactor, an entity must have a reasonably cohesive and stable set of components. This is the ecological side of evolution (Baum and Singh, 1994). Interactors carry replicators (in biology: genes) that in the ontogenetic development of interactors generate characteristics of interactors that affect their survival and the replication of their replicators. This generation of characteristics (in biology: gene expression) takes place in interaction, within the interactor, between replicators and other features of the interactor, as well as with the environment of the interactor. Replicators may lie dormant until triggered by conditions. Note that it is not the replicators themselves that determine survival but the characteristics that they produce. Replicators may generate characteristics on different levels, including abilities to generate characteristics, depending on the circumstances.[1]

Replicators from surviving interactors are replicated and re-combined, mostly within populations of interactors that partake of a common pool of replicators. This is the genealogical side of evolution, in the phylogenetics of a species.

In economics, firms, in particular, are seen as interactors in their environments of markets and institutions in which they may go bankrupt, as members of industries that are seen as populations, and their competencies

(McKelvey, 1982) are seen as the corresponding replicators, with industries sharing a common pool of such competencies. In science, interactors presumably are most of all scientists, with survival here denoting career success, but what their replicators are is not so clear.

The contribution of this chapter lies in the analysis of the three least researched aspects of evolution in social science (Baum and Singh, 1994): the identity of interactors, the nature and characteristics of replication, and the process of variety generation. The structure of the chapter is as follows. First I give a discussion of key issues in evolution in social science, in order to specify the questions addressed in this chapter. Second I summarize the theory of cognition used here, as set out in Chapter 2, and the cognitive view of organizations to which it leads, as set out in Chapter 3. This yields a view on the possible nature of their replicators, their identity as interactors, and on intra- and inter-population differences between them. Third, I give an analysis of the sources of variation. The chapter ends with a summary of conclusions.

In the literature on organizations, the present discussion falls squarely in what Aldrich (1999) called the 'knowledge development' stream of organization theory. Here, use of insights from cognitive science is inspired by the fact that in socio-economics both replication and variety generation are fundamentally cognitive and linguistic processes (Nooteboom, 2001). That is entirely in line with the cognitive theory of the firm developed here.

Interactors and Replicators

The literature on evolutionary theory of organizations allows for connected evolutionary processes on multiple levels: of skills and jobs; of workgroups or communities of practice (Brown and Duguid, 1996) within organizations (Burgelman, 1983); of organizations within industries; and of industries in wider socio-economic systems (Baum and Singh, 1994). However, it is not always clear what, precisely, the interactors and replicators are, on different levels. Here I focus on organizations as interactors in industries, and on scholars as interactors in disciplines or scholarly 'forums' (de Groot, 1969). The following questions arise.

The most fundamental question, perhaps, is to what extent in socio-economics the notions of interactors and replicators make sense at all (see Nelson, 2006). Unlike biology, in the evolution of organizations and knowledge replicators in the form of organizational competencies and scientific ideas do not depend on the survival under selection of the interactors that carry them, as noted for example by Nelson (2006). It is not even completely clear what 'failure' or 'being selected out' entails, and I will return to this point later. Whatever it means, competencies and ideas from organizations and scholars may be adopted by other organizations and scholars long after the latter have 'failed'. Often geniuses are not recognized, and their ideas are not adopted, until long after their death. Ideas can subside into obscurity, lurking in libraries, to be rediscovered or re-evaluated much later, without the need for intervening survival of its carrier. When organizations or scholars fail, whatever that means, some of their capabilities or ideas may still be seen as useful and adopted accordingly. Thus, purported replicators may float around, so to speak, disembodied from their carriers, possibly buried in unpublished documents, before they are replicated. If replicators may be disembodied from interactors, does the notion still make sense?

In biology, replicators generate, in ontogenesis, the characteristics of interactors that carry them. In organization and scholarship, actors are not only active in interacting with their environment but also in cognitive construction, which entails that they develop their replicators, on the basis of experience (Witt, 2005). As is widely recognized, ontogenetically produced replicators may be adopted by others, so that here evolution is, at least in part, Lamarckian, with 'inheritance of acquired characteristics'. Thus, while interactors may be generated by replicators they also generate them. Furthermore, according to the perspective of 'embodied cognition' from Chapter 2, interactors develop in interaction with a variety of other people, adopting and transforming some of their ideas and skills. Thus they are generated by the replicators not only of any well-defined parent, but from a host of other interactors with greater or lesser 'parenthood'. The notions of 'parents' and 'offspring' become diffuse. While in biology there is a clear separation between ontogenetic and phylogenetic development, in society there is not (Witt, 2005).

It is widely recognized that in social science interactors to some extent shape their replicators. For any remaining validity or usefulness of universal Darwinism, a key question is how far such shaping goes, and to what extent it reliably reflects selection conditions. Hodgson and Knudsen (2006) recognize that if direct shaping of replicators by their carriers were complete and fast, and would reliably reflect any shift or variety of the selection environment, evolution would break down. Survival would no longer be an indicator of success, and many unproven, worthless or deleterious traits would be imitated along with favourable ones. In other words, as recognized by most authors, for evolution to work there must be some isolation of replicators from influence by interactors, or, in other words, some inertia of interactors (Hannan and Freeman, 1984). My worry here is that the shaping of replicators may indeed to a considerable extent reflect often more or less erroneously perceived or inferred changes in the selection environment, in ways unproven by selection, and that indeed 'many unproven, worthless or deleterious traits (are) imitated along with favourable ones'. Here, evolution perhaps does indeed break down.

For groups of people, such as organizations, to operate as interactors, in evolutionary terms there must be group selection. For that to work, individual interests must somehow be subjugated, to a sufficient extent, to collective interest. Organizational identity, cohesiveness and stability may be prevented by the dominance of centrifugal individual or group interests within the firm (Campbell, 1994). So, what provides organizational cohesion and stability? As indicated in Chapter 3, scholarly societies are also organizations, and a similar question arises there. I propose that organizational cognitive focus indeed yields an organizational identity that has some stability, as argued in Chapter 3. Here the notion of cognitive focus aids evolutionary theory of the firm. Organizational focus enables but also constrains absorption of novelty that feeds organizational change. It serves as a filter for admitting and accepting outside ideas and people. In scholarly societies, established paradigms to some extent encapsulate the society from its environment. In other words, organizations are indeed subject to greater or lesser 'inertia' (Hannan and Freeman, 1989). However, it still remains to be seen to what extent organizations may still escape from inertia. Indeed, the very notion of radical innovation seems to entail such an escape.

If organizations and scholars are interactors, what are their replicators? As indicated earlier, the meaning of the notion of 'replicators' has several dimensions: (a) things that are carried by an interactor; (b), generate the interactor's characteristics relevant for success in its interaction with its selection environment; and (c) are transmitted to generate new interactors. McKelvey (1982) proposed that organizations are characterized by 'dominant competencies'. Nelson and Winter (1982) used the term 'routines', but there is some ambiguity and confusion around that term, and I prefer McKelvey's terminology. What, precisely, are these organization-level competencies? From the perspective of Chapter 3, I would say that elements of organizational cognitive focus might qualify, plus technologies and skills. If scholars are interactors, are their replicators ideas, hypotheses, or theories? These entities can indeed be seen as being carried by organizations and scholars, to generate their organizational and cognitive identities, and to be subject to transmission to others. However, as already noted, those entities may also be transmitted as disembodied from their carriers, to adopters whose identities are formed from multiple sources.

To what extent can we meaningfully speak of 'replication' at all? Replication entails the maintenance, as a rule, of the content or properties of a replicator, with only occasional or limited 'copying errors', and without significant transformation of form, content or function. Is transmission of organizational competencies and of ideas sufficiently like that? According to the view of cognition and meaning set out in Chapter 2, in communication significant transformation of meaning generally occurs, in the process of absorption or assimilation into existing mental frames. Such assimilation is not a passive practice of copying but an active process of structuration and transformation.

For industries to make sense as populations of organizations, there must be both differences and similarities between firms within an industry, and possibilities for replication that are greater within than between industries. Due to imitation and personnel mobility between organizations in an industry, or even between industries, organizational identities may not be sufficiently differentiated and isolated for selection to work (Boyd and Richerson, 1985). How do we account for intra- and inter-industry differentiation? In science, do disciplines make sense as populations? Or are the populations here scientific societies within or across disciplines, or are those to be seen as niches within disciplines?

In sum, the questions in this section are: what constitutes the replicators of organizations, in the form of organization-level competencies, how do these yield a cohesive and stable organizational identity, how does this yield differences as well as similarities within industries, more opportunities for replication within than between industries, and some but limited shaping of competencies as a function of experience in environments of markets and institutions. Partial answers have already been given. I will later analyse the questions in more detail, on the basis of the cognitive theory of organizations set out in Chapters 3 and 4.

Selection

In socio-economics, what is failure of interactors under selection? Is it the death of the interactor (organization, scholar), or some other manifestation of failure? In the context of firms selection arises from competition in markets, which may lead to their bankruptcy, take-over, break-up or management buy-out. As noted earlier, even in case of complete failure, in bankruptcy, some of its capabilities may be adopted as useful by others. In science, selection takes the form of refutation, ideally on the basis of empirical falsification (Popper, 1959), or other critical debate in scientific 'forums', rejection of papers by journals and rejection of proposals for funding research. This may kill, but only one idea or publication, which may subsequently be revised or improved to survive later in a different form.

Also, as noted by Witt (2005) and Nelson (2006), particularly in economics and science there is much 'pre-practice' testing, in mental thought

experiments, debate, computer simulations, the testing of physical prototypes, market testing and consumer focus groups. Human beings learn
testing and experimentation before practice at an early age, in child's play,
and proceed to refine their mental experimentation in later education.
Such outside-practice testing would have to be included in the notion of
selection. However, that means that some selection is not in the selection
'environment' but internal to an individual actor or organization.

A key issue in evolutionary theory of organizations and scholars is
that singly or collectively they can to a greater or lesser extent affect or
even mould the external selection environment of markets and institutions to favour their survival and reproduction, in 'co-evolution' or
'niche-construction' (Aldrich, 1999). Selection is political, and is shaped
or avoided by debate, rhetorics, indoctrination, coalition formation and
positions of power and influence (or the lack of it). Are these to be seen as
part of selection or as avoidance of it? While influence of interactors on the
selection environment, in co-evolution, is not unique for socio-economics,
and also occurs to a considerable extent in biology, in economic systems
the scope for it seems to be of a different order of magnitude, on the basis
of some intelligent inference of selection forces and the ability, power and
political influence of some organizations to shape such forces, in setting
standards of technology, conditions of legitimacy, shaping market structure (for example distribution channels), and erecting entry barriers.

An example of the setting of selection conditions from Garud and Rappa
(1996) concerns the rivalry between competing technologies for hearing
aids in the form of implants in the cochlea, in the inner ear. There were
two rival systems: a single channel and a multiple channel device. The first
carried less risk than the second did, but the second yielded a greater and
easier improvement of hearing. The problem was that objective, independent measures of these dimensions of performance were not available, and
the balancing between them is subjective. The same ideas that informed
the choice of device also informed the methodologies for selecting between
them, so that there were rival evaluation methods. The rival methods were
championed by rival commercial interest groups, and the stakes were high.
The single channel group argued that the obvious choice was to begin with
the low risk device, and step up to the other after its risks were clearer
and could be reduced. The multiple channel group argued that this would
not reduce risk but add to it in the process of taking out one device and
replacing it with the other. No objective experience was available to back
up either claim.

Let me give another illustration. In the innovation of a cotton carpet
(instead of wool), it was first introduced for bedrooms, in view of the moist-
ure regulating properties of cotton and its nice feel to bare feet. However,

cotton fibre does not have the natural resilience of wool, so that in use the pile of a cotton carpet rapidly flattens, but after vacuuming regains its fresh look. Now, resistance of carpets to such pile flattening was a key feature in the existing certification of quality, thus favouring wool over cotton, and the new carpet could effectively enter the market only after the innovator, sufficiently large and influential, managed to wield its influence to have the certification procedure modified to accept vacuuming prior to inspection. Such actions to mould the selection environment are also amply illustrated by Aldrich (1999: 334).

In science, when scholars face a lack of survival and replication of their ideas, in failed access to journals, or in their papers remaining ignored or uncited, they can, and often do, create their own selection environment by founding their own scholarly societies with their more or less proprietary journals. Their ideas survive not only, and perhaps not even primarily, from their scientific as from their organizational and rhetorical skills.

One may argue that even though for these reasons selection may be limited or inefficient, not even the most visionary entrepreneur, nor the most powerful of corporations, nor the most able organizer or rhetorician can completely mould his environment to guarantee success, survival and dominance, and some selective pressure will remain. The limits are not only limits of power, but also cognitive limits. One is not infallible in inferring what structure of selection favours differential survival and growth, for lack of insight in causalities of selection and in opportunities that any change might yield to unforeseeable new innovations that may constitute a threat to incumbent organizations. Returning to the example of the cotton carpet, the most salient thing is perhaps that it took effort to alter the selection conditions, even in only one though crucial respect, which might have failed, in which case the innovation would likely not have survived. While there is much more to be said about this issue, it is not a subject for the present chapter, since although selection seems very imperfect it still seems sufficient to let this issue pass. In sum, for the sake of argument here I will accept that selection by competition still makes sufficient sense, in markets and scientific rivalry.

Replication

A third issue concerns processes of replication, and the relation between replication and variety generation. In socio-economic evolution, replication entails reproduction and imitation of knowledge and competencies, on different levels. This occurs on the basis of observation, communication and apprenticeship. Successful products and practices are copied or imitated on the basis of observation and inference, reverse engineering, publications and documents, oral presentations, courses, reports and explanations by consultants, and the like. Apprenticeship may merit special notice. Knowledge is externalized not only in speech, documents, software and ostensive activity, or role models, but is also embodied in tools, in a general sense including machines, procedures and forms of organization. In learning to use tools, an apprentice may reconstruct some of the mental schemas that lay behind the design and production of the tool.

In socio-economics, these forms of replication entail linguistic processes of expression, sense and reference, and cognitive processes of assimilation into mental schemata (Aldrich, 1999; Piaget, 1970, 1974) or mental models (Johnson-Laird, 1983) that constitute absorptive capacity (Cohen and Levinthal, 1990). Fundamentally different from replication of genes in biology, replication of knowledge and competencies is:

- at least partly voluntary and subject to choice: one adopts what is perceived to be successful;
- partial: one may, within restrictions of systemic coherence, adopt only part of a bundle of replicators carried by a given interactor; and
- subject to decay, distortion, reduction, extension and transformation (going far beyond the copying errors, deletions and duplications of genes in biology). In other words, replication at the same time entails a kind and a degree of variety generation.

This issue will be analysed with the use of insights from the embodied cognition branch of cognitive science that was discussed in Chapter 2.

Variation

A fourth issue, in evolutionary theory, and this is the third subject for the present chapter, concerns the sources of variation, in particular the question how blind, or random, and how independent from selection variety generation is.

According to most evolutionary accounts, the main trigger of radical innovation is a shock in the form of a break or shift of the selection environment, which may increase competition for scarce resources, disadvantage incumbent species, and create new opportunities for new variety. Such a shift or shock may be due to natural disaster, political upheaval and war, a shift in demand, a shift in institutions (for example regulations for protecting the environment), or a shift due to developments in related industries or markets. However, this tells us only of new opportunities, of how radical innovation is enabled or triggered, not of how it is generated.

In evolutionary theory, generation of new variety, in new interpretations or new ideas, is generally ascribed to errors in replication, and random, uninformed trials as steps into the dark ('mutations'). In the methodology of complex adaptive systems (Holland, 1996), the conduct of agents is modelled in terms of if-then rules, which are sometimes modelled, in analogy to chromosomes, as bit-strings of messages sent in response to bit-strings of messages received, and the discovery of rules is modelled as random mutations of values at positions in the string plus random crossover of strings, in analogy to sexual reproduction. How valid or adequate is this, as a model of human learning and communication?

In socio-economic evolution there is no doubt much trial and error in entrepreneurial venturing, and more so to the extent that the innovation is radical, that is it entails destruction of existing competencies (Anderson and Tushman, 1990; Tushman and Anderson, 1986), technologies, and forms of organization, limiting the opportunity to build on existing knowledge and competence. However, evidently in socio-economic evolution there is invention and knowledge development that is informed, somehow, by experience from failures and resulting inferences about where sources of failure may lie and where to look for improvements. This is too obvious to ignore or deny, and Aldrich (1999), Foster and Metcalfe (2001) and Nelson and Winter (1982), to name only a few, all recognized that next to blindness there is also intentional, deliberate, and somehow directed variety generation.

Thus, according to Foster and Metcalfe (2001: 10): 'The rate of economic progress that we observe reflects guided variation within conceptual schemes that channel explorative, creative enquiry in particular directions'. However, they immediately add: 'Of course, all variation is, in effect, blind variation, since it necessarily deals with the unknowable consequences of a present decision.'

What does it mean that variation is both guided and blind? Little, if anything, in the evolutionary literature, is said about how the 'guidance' or 'direction' of variation works in 'explorative, creative enquiry'. More generally, the generation of variety is the least developed side of evolution in socio-economic systems (Baum and Singh, 1994: 18).

According to Hodgson and Knudsen (2006: 11) evolution is blind in two senses. First: 'particular outcomes are not necessarily prefigured or predicted in advance'.

I agree with that. However, this leaves open the possibility of an intelligent design of a heuristic path of discovery, guided by experience from selection, that is likely to yield radical novelty, even though it cannot be predicted what that will be. That is precisely what I will argue.

According to Campbell (1987):

any capacity for foresight or prescience must be based on tried and tested knowledge, otherwise we have no grounds to presume its effectiveness. Accordingly, when genuine innovations are launched, we are unable to assess the probability of their success or failure (Hodgson and Knudsen, 2006: 11).

I agree with the first part (experience is needed to presume effectiveness) but I disagree with the second part. Because we can make inferences from experience we can 'presume effectiveness', that is increase likelihood of success beyond blind trials, even if perhaps that cannot be rendered in terms of probability theory (see Shackle, 1962).

Campbell (1974) specified blindness as entailing variations that are: (a) independent of each other; (b) separate from the environment; (c) uncorrelated with the solution; and (d) later variations are not corrections of former ones. Applying these criteria, I will argue that there is non-blind variation.

The often-heard claim that a theory of invention would be self-defeating or even self-contradictory, because by definition invention cannot be predicted, is based on confusion between prediction and explanation. One can claim to have some understanding of processes of invention without thereby claiming to be able to predict its outcomes. That applies to evolutionary theory more broadly: it explains principles of process without claiming to predict its outcomes.

In the evolutionary literature, some authors have allowed for variations that are guided from higher level, variety generating 'search' routines (Nelson and Winter, 1982). Other literature also suggests that there are higher level 'dynamic capabilities' that direct the change of lower level capabilities (Teece et al., 1997). Dynamic capabilities include rational inference of cause-effect relations, rules for experimentation, and ability to utilize organizational memory. They also include exchange of codified knowledge with others, in what (Nonaka and Takeuchi, 1995) called 'knowledge combination'. So, the question now is to what extent, and how, organizations can develop dynamic capabilities to escape from inertia. In what sense, and to what extent is this blind? How is it related to selection, and to what extent can it anticipate success in selection? In this chapter only a partial answer will be given. Dynamic capabilities were analysed in Chapter 5, and the results will be used to form a judgement on these issues.

ORGANIZATIONS, INDUSTRIES AND SCIENTIFIC COMMUNITIES

In this section I analyse the identity of organizations as interactors in terms of the notion of organizational cognitive focus and its cultural expression, differences between organizations within and between industries, seen as populations, and the 'isolating mechanisms' between populations.

Organizational Identity

Hodgson and Knudsen (2004) usefully argued that the cohesiveness of the interactor, needed for evolution to work, requires at least a core of components that stand or fall together with each other and with the interactor as a whole. More precisely, the probability of survival of one component is connected with the survival of other components in that core. The question now is how organizations achieve the cohesion and stability required for interactors.

The answer proposed here lies in the notion of an organization as a cognitive focusing device, developed in Chapter 3. To function as a coordinated system of actions, organizations need some more or less specialized shared language or jargon, perceptions, understanding and morality, as part of organizational culture (Schein, 1985). Without such focus of shared perceptions, meanings, understandings and values, too much effort, time and aggravation would have to be spent to disambiguate meanings, eliminate misunderstanding, set priorities, establish directions, coordinate activities, align incentives and negotiate the terms of collaboration. This is the view of organization as a system for 'sense-making' (Weick, 1995), 'collective mind' (Weick and Roberts, 1993), system of 'shared meanings' (Smircich, 1983). Witt (2005) later offered a related view of entrepreneurs as providing 'cognitive leadership'.

The main point here, for the present chapter, is that organizational cognitive focus, produced and reproduced by organizational culture, and by people socialized into that culture, forms the core of organization-level competence, to achieve coordinated bundles of competencies or capabilities. As discussed in Chapter 3, organizational focus constitutes a cohesive (but not necessarily consistent) whole of perceptions, meanings and values that define roles, relations and procedures of interaction, and thereby yield the requisite cohesion and stability of organizations as interactors. Now, is it this focus or the set of capabilities that are coordinated by it that constitutes the set of replicators of an organization? Clearly it is the focus, since that is unique and specific to the organization, while the capabilities that it coordinates are on the individual rather than the organizational level, and are more universal, ranging across organizations, in professions.

How does this compare with McKelvey's view of replicators as 'dominant competencies'? There is no conflict if we see the latter as organizational rather than individual, and the cultural and cognitive elements of focus may be seen as a further specification of those organizational dominant competencies. Here, 'dominant' means that they are shared by at least a 'dominant coalition', and that they condition, that is structure, enable and constrain, actions, and have normative content or import. In other words: they are institutions, as defined in Chapter 1. Thus I prefer to see the replicators as institutions rather than competencies, though they do constitute organizational competence. Nelson and Winter (1982) speak of 'routines'. But, again, in view of their regulatory, constitutive and normative nature I prefer to see them as institutions. However, they are a specific kind of (organizational) institution, and I prefer to simply call them elements of organizational focus.

While the *raison d'être* of organization as a focusing device is that it enables cognitive and moral coordination, for the sake of efficient goal achievement, and is therefore selected for in market competition, it also helps to create the stable and differentiated organizational identities needed for evolutionary selection of organizations to work.

As noted before, in Chapter 3, organizational focus emerges from the imprint from the entrepreneur who started the organization, is subject to some drift due to turnover of staff, and to shifts due to crises, caused, in particular, by shifts in the environment, or by new, challenging interpretations of the environment, and by the weeding out by selection, in population effects. When resources are scarce and competition is tight, selection is likely, in the long run, to yield organizational cognitions and structures that reflect the exigencies of the environment of markets and institutions. Consider, for example, the view that stable environments tend to favour 'mechanistic' organizations while turbulent environments tend to favour 'organic' ones (Burns and Stalker, 1961), or more specialist versus more generalist organizations (Hannan and Freeman, 1977). However, focus is stable because it is reproduced in action by people who are selected, partially self-selected, in recruitment, according to their affinity to the focus, are socialized into the organization, and further construct their cognition from the input from interaction in the organizational institutional environment. Recall, here, that according to the idea of intelligence as internalized action, discussed in Chapter 2, the further development of cognition reflects the environment, in this case the organization, in which cognitive construction takes place.

Organizational focus cannot be integrally and instantly re-shaped as a function of experience in selection, and this limits Lamarckian adaptation, and yields some organizational inertia. The limits to such change lie in the systemic cohesion of elements of cognitive focus and in the fact that cognitive focus serves as an absorptive capacity that tends to mostly confirm itself in its functioning (imprinting). However, and this will be discussed later, in the discussion of the 'cycle of discovery', there is a process by which absorptive capacity does transform itself in its functioning, so that there is some Lamarckian mechanism, and an escape from inertia, but in a series of conditioned steps that require time. It is an empirical question to what extent the speed of that is sufficient to escape from selective pressures.

Organizational Boundaries

As discussed in more detail in Chapter 4, the cognitive perspective of organization gives a new slant on organizational boundaries and on inter-firm alliances. Aldrich's (1999) definition of organization as goal-directed, coordinated activity systems (which I adopt) also includes the maintenance of more or less clear, stable boundaries (which I reject). Of course, bound-aries of legal identity remain fairly clear, as they should (Hodgson, 2002a), but organizationally there may be durable relationships between organiz-ations, supported by some cognitive focus of shared perceptions, language and norms, even though that focus is less cohesive, and probably also less inclusive, as defined in Chapter 3, than within organizations. In that sense, counter to Hodgson (2002a, 2006), it is quite legitimate to speak of 'fuzzy boundaries', in terms of elements of organizational focus that are shared between organizations, and of common institutions, even while clarity of legal boundaries and legal identity is preserved.

While clear and stable boundaries may apply to most traditional organ-izations, it is much less the case for modern web-based, 'virtual' enterprises and network forms of organization. Apparently, the assumption of clear and stable boundaries is deemed necessary to yield the organizational cohesion needed to make evolutionary selection work. But why would entrepreneurs or managers want that selection to work? If with fuzzy and/ or variable boundaries, imitation, and buy-out of personnel from other firms they can escape selective forces, why shouldn't they? The following conundrum then arises. If organizations are selected, in evolution, for their ability not to have clear and stable boundaries, while those are necessary for selection to work, how can this be?

My view is that the notion of cognitive focus is sufficient for a stable and cohesive identity of organizations while it does not require clear and stable boundaries of activity, and allows for parts of focus being shared with other organizations, as long as organizational focus is still distinctive. It may be that organizations make their focus so lacking in cohesiveness, with a small width, little or no reach, and little or no tightness, that boundaries are hard to establish, apart from the legal ones, and the firm becomes like a market. But then the organization would have hardly any identity left, and one could hardly speak of an organization any longer. Likewise, Penrose (1959) did not recognize mere holding companies as proper firms.

Organizational focus creates organizational myopia, more so to the extent that it is cohesive and inclusive, and in addition to all the other motives for inter-firm alliances, familiar from the extensive alliance literature, this gives an additional, cognitive reason, to prevent myopia by means of complementary outside cognition from alliance partners (in 'external economy of cognitive scope', Nooteboom, 1992, 1999), as elaborated in Chapter 4. Here, the notion of cognitive distance applies to organizations, as differences in shared language, meanings, perceptions, understandings and values and norms of behaviour. As shown in Chapter 4, in empirical work measures of the cognitive distance between firms have been constructed on the basis of indicators from organizational data and technological profiles derived from patent data (Wuyts et al., 2005; Nooteboom et al., 2007).

Note here the condition, familiar from the alliance literature, that when organizations outsource activities they must often still retain absorptive capacity with respect to those activities to properly collaborate and coordinate with outside sources (Granstrand et al., 1997). And I reaffirm, to make sure, that while organizations may not have clear boundaries of activities, in sharing activities with other organizations, and may have shifting boundaries, in outsourcing and integrating activities, and may share elements of organizational focus with other organizations, firms do and should have a clear legal identity, as pointed out by Hodgson (2002a). Unclear boundaries of legal ownership and liability would create institutional havoc.

Intra-Population Differentiation

Within industries, cognitive distance, thus difference in organizational focus, is limited, particularly concerning the competence side of technologies and competencies, in shared technologies, market demand, market structures, technical and professional standards and so on, yielding what may be seen as a common pool of competencies (McKelvey, 1982). As a result, staff exchange between organizations is feasible and can create and confirm the identity of an industry (McKelvey, 1982: 197), yielding 'industry recipes' (Spender, 1989). This is also enhanced by pressures towards conformity to dominant designs and practices from needs of efficiency and of social, political or financial legitimation ('mimetic forces') (DiMaggio and Powell, 1983). However, while firms may share component skills and technologies, particularly within an industry, their overall composition of capabilities and activities, in a coherent system, may differ substantially. But above all, organizations have their distinctive identities of cognitive focus.

As noted before, to the extent that an organizational system is systemic or complex, as defined earlier, piecemeal, local variation of single elements is problematic since it soon affects the integrity of the system as a whole. Then, when there is one difference between firms there tend to be many, in distinctive systemic wholes (Levinthal, 2000).[2] In sum, when operational structure is complex, even with similar components integrated systems may differ greatly.

For an illustration of this, I return to the comparison, in the automobile industry, between the older 'Fordist' production system, and the newer 'Toyota' system that I used before, in Chapter 3, on the basis of Coriat (2002). Earlier, I indicated how the two systems differ on the deep level of fundamental cognitive categories and on the middle level of general principles of organization, with connections between the two levels. Here, I want to point out the systemic nature of the differences, focusing on the Toyota system. That has a tight connection of mutual conditioning between the goal of small series of differentiated products, the organizational principles required by the 'pull' principle, such as integrated team responsibility for quality and scheduling, lack of hierarchical planning, zero stocks, and just in time production, human resource principles of multi-skilled workers, job rotation, and career prospects, and the physical configuration of machinery according to the sequence of value adding activities. One cannot change any of these components without changing others, and ending up in an entirely different system.

Also, even within industries organizational focus is more varied, and organizational cognitive distance is correspondingly greater, on the governance side of the moral, intentional, institutional order, in different styles or cultures of management. Deep differences in fundamental perceptions, views and (largely tacit) assumptions concerning man, his knowledge (for example objective or constructed), his relation with his environment (passive or active), his morality (basically good or bad), and relations with other people (egotistic or altruistic) (Schein, 1985), yield differences in risk perception and acceptance, pro-activeness ('locus of control'), formality or informality, rivalry or cooperation, intrinsic or extrinsic motivation, instruments and styles of governance and conflict resolution. From an evolutionary perspective, the persistence of such differences, in spite of selection pressures, suggests that on the moral, intentional side there are different ways to be successful, within an industry.

As indicated in earlier chapters, a central issue is how to combine exploitation and exploration (March, 1991). While earlier some industries were relatively stable, allowing for a focus on exploitation, and others were in a state of flux, yielding a focus on exploration, now the combination of the two is needed in most if not all industries, although the priority of exploitation or exploration varies, depending on the volatility of technologies and markets involved. Combination of the two is particularly difficult when exploitation is highly systemic, as defined earlier. Then, by definition, units within the system hardly have any room for the experimentation and deviation needed for exploration, since they would jeopardize systemic integrity. In that situation, exploration needs to be relegated to a different time or place. The classic case is the division between departments for production and for R&D. This yields the classic problem of divergent mentalities and priorities between them, with resulting misunderstandings, conflicts and recriminations. It is difficult, though not hopeless, to find an organizational focus that accommodates both. One method is to engage in cross-functional teams, and another is frequent staff rotation, with an organizational focus to support that, mostly on the governance side, in values and norms of conduct that favour acceptance of differences in competence, work conditions, styles of thought and action, time framing, and tolerance of ambiguity and uncertainty. Another would be to create more flexibility by decomposing the exploitation system into more autonomous parts, accepting loss of exploitative efficiency for the sake of exploration. Such choices may be made differently by different firms, even within an industry, with corresponding differences in organizational cognitive focus.

As noted before, cultural differentiation between organizations is maintained, in spite of turnover and exchange of staff, because in the entry into an organization there is (self)selection according to expected fit to organizational culture, adaptation by socialization into organizational culture, and organization-specific cognitive construction.

Finally, there are differences in the content of focus. Some firms may emphasize surface level elements of focus, in more ad hoc specific rules and procedures, leaving wider variety in underlying thinking and values, while others may emphasize more generic deep level elements, with a larger degree of ideological indoctrination, in a stronger culture. The first has the advantage of greater liberty and scope for idiosyncracy, the latter has the advantage of faster response in new configurations of activity, and more intrinsic motivation.

Inter-Population Differences

Between firms in different industries there are greater differences, not only on the governance side but also on the competence side of cognitive focus. There are, for example, deep differences in professional skill. As McKelvey (1982: 202) phrased it 'Would you fly on an airplane that had recently been staffed with non-airline employees? Would you enter a coal mine operated by hotel employees? Would you eat in a restaurant staffed by truckers?' However, even between industries isolation is far from complete, and replication across industries does take place. McKelvey (1982: 206) suggested that to the extent that organizations are simpler, characteristics are more easily exchanged, also between industries.

For an illustration, consider the emergence of self-service. It emerged in retailing, largely outside large firms, initiated by independents but swiftly adopted by large chain store firms after it proved a success. Self-service retailing constitutes a distinct 'species' from service retailing, with a different structural logic, in that a fundamental reversal of roles occurred between shop attendant and customer. In service, the attendant moves about to collect items for a shopper's basket, while the customer remains stationary at a counter, and in self-service these roles are switched, with the customer picking out its own goods, and a stationary attendant at a checkout, in a correspondingly different lay-out of the shop. This eliminated a limit to shop size. In a large shop, with many products, in the service mode the attendant would have to move about too far, with an unacceptable increase of waiting time for the customer. The emergence of self-service, with its consequent opportunity for larger shop size, was favoured by a shift of the selection environment towards knowledgeable customers who no longer needed advice from shop attendants, an increased demand for less frequent, 'one-stop' bulk shopping, due to greater scarcity of time, enabled by transport capacity from car ownership and by refrigerated home storage capacity. In its turn, self-service affected selection conditions, in co-evolution, in that it enabled economies of scale that pushed out small shops. With its demand for pre-packaged goods, it also had wide repercussions for the selection conditions in packaging and food industries. In replication, however, isolation with respect to other industries was very limited. The principle of self-service was quickly and widely adopted in other industries, such as restaurants and even hotels.

It is doubtful whether organizational focus could survive a merger or acquisition, and this contributes to their frequent failure. In view of greater difference in focus between than within industries, mergers and acquisitions are more likely to succeed within industries than between industries (Nooteboom, 1999), and this is confirmed empirically by Bleeke and Ernst (1991).

Absorptive Capacity and Isolation

The notion of a population requires 'isolating mechanisms' between them. Baum and Singh (1994: 12) listed a number of such isolating mechanisms: technological interdependencies (restricting the replication of single, isolated elements from bundles), institutional pressures of iso-morphism (DiMaggio and Powell, 1983), complexity of learning (difficulty of absorption), resistance to learning, imprinting, and 'network closure' (with in dense networks members looking inward and locking each other into established patterns). This section further develops the more cognitive aspects of complexity and lock-in.

As discussed in Chapter 2, interactively constructed mental categories constitute our absorptive capacity: we assimilate input through our senses into those categories (Piaget) and in so doing make sense of them, interpret them, and make inferences on the basis of them. Thus it is better to speak of the 'reproduction' or even 'transformation' rather than the 'sharing' or 'copying' of knowledge. At greater cognitive distance assimilation is more difficult, replication is less complete and faithful, and more knowledge and interpretation will be 'added'. In other words, at larger cognitive distance replication is more limited and entails more variety generation.

Knowledge, in the form of mental schema's or frames corresponding with competencies, is often largely tacit and stored in 'procedural memory', as 'know-how', and can only imperfectly be codified into declarative knowledge of facts, logic and causal relations, as 'know-that' and 'know-why' (Cohen and Bacdayan, 1996). Knowledge 'sharing', with minimal change of knowledge in communication, requires a certain commonality of absorption, or limited cognitive distance, as between practitioners of the same jobs (Miner, 1991). There, mutual understanding is quick and largely implicit, with few words needed, in jargon. Communication will be less faithful and fast but next best inside work groups of people doing different jobs (Gersick, 1988) or communities of practice (Brown and Duguid, 1996).

Recall, from Chapter 2, that mental schemas and cognitive distance include not only cognition in the narrow sense of intellect, but also more emotion-laden moral categories of how to deal with relational risks from mutual dependence and rivalry. Recall from Chapter 3 that different ways of dealing with such risks are legal or hierarchical coercion, balance of mutual dependence, reputation, and less self-interested motives of ethical conduct, empathy, identification and routinized conduct (Nooteboom, 1999). However, note also that mutual understanding does not by itself entail lack of rivalry. Indeed, rivalry may increase with similarity, if simi-larity entails competition, and between professionals in the same field, or in the same organization, rivalry may be greater than between professionals in different fields or organizations.

While cognitive distance yields some 'reproductive isolation', with limited replication, maintaining distinctive identities of organizations and industries, that isolation is far from perfect, for two reasons. First, on the level of communities of practice, outsiders from different communities can enter and become members, after some time needed for initiation and socialization, in legitimate peripheral participation (Lave and Wenger, 1991). Second, even at large cognitive distance one may still be able to selectively assimilate single but crucial elements of externalized knowledge, even from distinct industries. The case of self-service, emerging in retailing but copied by restaurants, discussed earlier, gives an illustration.

Scientific Communities

Scientific communities may also be seen as populations to the extent that there are adequate isolating mechanisms between them. That would entail obstacles to inter-group and interdisciplinary research, and such obstacles indeed exist, though perhaps more for the behavioural than for the natural sciences. To a greater or lesser extent, sciences are prone to the following social dynamics. Novelty is often shielded off by an established 'mainstream', for reasons that will become apparent in the following. Innovators then often create a following of their own, develop their prominence in it, push it or are dragged along by vested interest in reputation and serve, or are high-jacked, as role-models, with their achievements as exemplars to be emulated by their following. Exemplars settle into paradigms that sometimes harden into dogma. Typically, the founding fathers figure as editors or prominent members of editorial boards for journals that form the platform for the society's goals and ideas and constitute a niche with its dedicated selection environment.

An example in economics is the International Joseph A. Schumpeter Society (ISS), as a haven for Schumpetarian and evolutionary economists, with its proprietary *Journal of Evolutionary Economics*. Another is the European Association for Evolutionary Political Economy (EAEPE), as a haven for unorthodox institutionalist economists, with its recently instituted *Journal of Institutional Economics*. In management science, a recent example is the European Academy of Management (EURAM) with its journal *European Management Review*, instituted to provide a countervailing power to the US-dominated Academy of Management.

To promote their careers, junior scholars are well advised to focus on one such community, establish personal connections with the gatekeeping editors or members of editorial boards, at the requisite conferences or PhD schools, carefully cite their work, and submit work that is marginally innovative but not too deviant from established doctrine. Once they have built up a position of prestige, they may be able to afford larger departures from the newly developed mainstream, but the question is whether they still have the originality of mind to do so, and whether they may be motivated to deviate from the foundations of the prestige that they have so painstakingly built up.

This social dynamic indeed yields isolating mechanisms between communities, raising strong obstacles to interdisciplinary research. Connecting A and B, and saying A things to B and B things to A, one finds that for both part of what one is saying falls outside absorptive capacity and is at best fiercely criticized for its unorthodoxy or is at its worst, and most likely, simply ignored. If senior scholars do deviate from doctrine, and bridge holes between disciplines, and starting young scholars come to them for guidance, a moral dilemma arises. Should they lead such young scholars astray, into the no-man's land of interdisciplinary research, and have them pay the price of lack of visibility and attention that impedes their career? One should clearly warn them of this risk, dissuade them to take it, and coach them only if they decide to accept it anyway and live dangerously.

The strength of selection and isolation between disciplines varies. To the extent that hypotheses are more clearly and rigorously falsifiable, as is the case to a larger extent in natural science than in behavioural science, selection is more stringent, and cross-disciplinary research can more easily be vindicated by empirical success. Then, the selection mechanism is more rigorous, and in that sense in line with Darwinian evolutionary theory, but inter-group isolation is less, in contrast with such theory.

SOURCES OF VARIATION

In this paragraph I analyse sources of variation, that is the generation of new knowledge and competencies, or, in other words, dynamic capabilities (Teece et al., 1997). The question is how invention takes place, and how blind or directed it is. In Chapter 5, three sources are indicated: transformation of meaning in communication, transformation by novel combinations of existing knowledge, in learning by interaction, and experience-based learning on a path of exploitation that leads up to exploration. While the first of these is largely blind and accidental, the second can be deliberate and designed (Nonaka and Takeuchi, 1995; Zollo and Winter, 2002), and the third is directed by selection and can also to some extent be designed (Nooteboom, 2000).

Variation by Communication and Collaboration

As indicated earlier, in Chapter 2, absorption or assimilation is to a greater or lesser extent accompanied by expansion and transformation of the knowledge absorbed, and it can lead to a break and transformation of the interpretative structures that constitute absorptive capacity. In that sense, communication not only yields 'replication', but also contributes to the generation of variety. In communication, in expression by the 'sender' tacit knowledge can never be fully codified and externalized so that expressed knowledge is always incomplete, and in absorption, or assimilation, knowledge is complemented and supplemented from the existing cognitive framework of the 'recipient'. Furthermore, what is 'left out' by the sender and what is 'added' by the receiver, and how this is done, depends on clues from the context. Thus, meaning is always context dependent (though not completely context determined).

As discussed in Chapter 2, a relevant concept here is that of 'scaffolding' (Hendriks-Jansen, 1996; Shanon, 1990). The context of practice and learning, including the people involved, and the instruments or tools used, disambiguates meaning (a universal becomes specific by its place in a sentence, in a context of action), triggers relevant associations and cuts irrelevant ones, from a 'seamless web of belief' (Quine and Ullian, 1970). Classic examples are mothers that stimulate appropriate responses from infants (Hendriks-Jansen, 1996) and teachers who draw out pupils beyond their current level of performance (see Vygotsky, 1962: 'zone of proximal development'). Another example is the role of tools in apprenticeship, indicated before, in the reconstruction of corresponding mental schemas.

This source of variation is indeed, as expected from an evolutionary perspective, blind, accidental, and not deliberate, planned or designed. Using the four criteria of blindness suggested by Campbell (1974), indicated earlier, it is blind in all but one aspect: they do not seem to be independent from each other, but to cohere in a 'seamless web' of cognition. However, while the process itself is blind, it can be influenced by the selection of interactors and the context of interaction.

March (1991) suggested that the generation of new ideas, in exploration, follows from personnel turnover, where people from outside an organization carry fresh ideas into the organization that may disturb the efficiency of exploitation but contribute to exploration. That is certainly part of the process of variation, but it is also limited due to the isolating mechanisms indicated before, especially between industries, self-selection of entrants to fit organizational focus, and socialization into that focus.

More generally, new knowledge and competence can be generated deliberately and by design by seeking novel combinations of existing knowledge, in collaboration between different people and organizations. Nonaka and Takeuchi (1995) recognized this as innovation by 'combination', and Zollo and Winter called it 'deliberate learning', in contrast with experiential learning. While Nonaka and Takeuchi as well as Zollo and Winter claimed that such learning by combination requires articulation and codification of the knowledge involved, I disagree. While codification certainly has its advantages, it is neither necessary nor fully possible. As argued earlier, in Chapter 2, knowledge can never be fully articulated and codified, and a greater or lesser degree of tacitness necessarily remains. Novel combinations of tacit knowledge can also arise without articulation, in close collaboration in teams.

As analysed before, in Chapter 3, and supplied with empirical evidence, in Chapter 4, in learning by interaction one runs into both the problem and the opportunity from cognitive distance: greater distance makes mutual understanding and acceptance (absorptive capacity, ability to collaborate) more difficult, but also generates novelty value. If the first decreases, say linearly, with cognitive distance, and the second increases with it, and performance of learning by interaction is the mathematical product of absorption and novelty value, an inverse U-shaped relationship results, with an optimal cognitive distance, large enough to yield novelty value but not so large as to preclude understanding and collaboration. As analysed in Chapter 4, this optimum is not fixed. In particular, absorptive capacity depends on the accumulation of knowledge and competence from past R&D, production, marketing, organization, and, in particular, experience in collaborating with others at sufficient cognitive distance. In other words, experience in dealing with others who think differently yields competitive advantage. An increase of absorptive capacity yields an increase of optimal cognitive distance.

Inter-organizational collaboration requires cognitive coordination and governance of relational risks. As discussed in Chapter 3, for governance there is a toolbox of instruments such as: contracting plus requisite monitoring, insofar as feasible in view of uncertainties of environment and behaviour, a balance of mutual dependence, posting of hostages, typically in the form of competitively sensitive information, reputation mechanisms and trust building, by cultural alignment of values, personal empathy and identification and routinization of conduct.

In conclusion, one type of dynamic capability is the ability to find partners, at optimal distance, and to effectively understand and collaborate with them, in the governance of 'relational risk'. This dynamic capability in the form of alliance capability can be developed by building absorptive capacity and experience in communicating and collaborating with partners who think differently.

Now, in view of all this, how blind is variation by collaboration? Collaboration requires communication and as indicated this is always imperfect, and can yield unintended and unnoticed variation. That is one reason why collaboration is blind in the sense that it is subject to more or less random disturbance and fluctuation of interpretation and meaning.

It is also blind in the sense that one cannot predict the precise outcome of learning by interaction, since it is not based on experience, unless collaboration is embedded in some experiential process, to be discussed later. However, it is not blind in that it is informed by selective success: one selects partners in learning who have demonstrated to be competent in some respect. It is designed: one may have a fair guess of cognitive distance and select partners at optimal distance. Applying Campbell's (1974) criteria of blindness, variations from planned collaboration are not independent, are not separate from the environment, and later variations can be corrections of former ones. They are not, however, correlated with the solution, in the strong sense that the outcome can be predicted.

A Heuristic of Invention

In Chapter 5 I summarized and discussed a 'heuristic of invention' or 'cycle of discovery', according to which exploration of novel ideas may arise along different stages of exploitation of existing practices under novel conditions (generalization) that pose new challenges, with resulting failures that generate pressure, motivation and fresh insight for change. First with minor modifications tapped from a fund of earlier experience (differentiation). Subsequently, if failure persists, other practices in the novel environment that seem to perform well where one's own practice seems to fail suggest elements that may be imported into one's practice to improve performance (reciprocation), without yet surrendering the basic design, architecture or logic of existing practice. This is a stage of experimenting with hybrids, of one's own and foreign practice, that enables one to try out and discover the potential of novel elements. When such potential materializes, evidence is also accumulated as to where current basic design or logic inhibits the realization of full potential, and indications are gathered as to where and in what ways design might be altered to better realize potential. This may yield the basis for more radical transformation, in novel architectures of old and new elements according to old and/or new design principles (transformation). That may yield an invention, which next has to be carried into application, in a process of development towards a 'dominant design', and subsequent consolidation in appropriate forms of organization and institutions to further accommodate proven success, as amply described in the innovation literature.

This heuristic is proposed as a general 'logic' that may manifest itself in several ways. It may govern how novel mental structures arise, in reciprocation of formerly distinct parallel neural groupings in the brain (Edelman, 1987). The stage of generalization, in an exit into a novel context, appears to correspond with the well-known phenomenon of 'spin-off' in the innovation literature. The process is recognizable in the literature on innovation by internationalization of firms. While formerly internationalization was primarily a strategy to maintain growth after saturation of home markets, it un-intendedly set in motion the process of discovery, which companies then started to identify and understand as such, and subsequently have started to employ as a deliberate strategy of innovation. Above all, perhaps, the 'logic' explains why innovation by collaboration, at appropriate cognitive distance, as analysed in Chapter 4, is effective. Having to explain one's knowledge and practice to a partner in collaboration entails a step of generalization, where one obtains new insights into the limits of one's views and practice, yielding a need to adjust, first on the basis of reframing it on the basis of previous experience. Next when that does not work, partners in collaboration offer each other sources of reciprocation, in an exchange of novel elements to try out, and in exchanging design principles in search of solving the constraints and problems that arise from the resulting hybrids. It is much easier to have a partner to stimulate and assist the process than having to do everything by one's own inference.

This may contribute to a deeper understanding of the familiar notion of 'absorptive capacity': having more experience, one is better able to reframe, in cognition and competence, what a partner offers in the process of reciprocation. Earlier, I indicated that the other side of the coin of learning by interaction is rhetorical ability, to help a partner absorb what one offers to him, notably by the use of apt metaphors. The more experience one has, the greater is the fund of one's metaphors.

Here the question is: what are the implications for evolutionary theory?

In Chapter 5 I noted the empirical literature on punctuated equilibria in technological development (Tushman and Romanelli, 1985; Tushman and Anderson, 1986; Romanelli and Tushman, 1994; Gersick, 1991). While detecting that phenomenon empirically, this literature has not offered an adequate theoretical explanation. As noted in Nooteboom (2000) in evolutionary biology Eldredge and Gould (1972) and Gould (1989) offered at least the beginning of an explanation of punctuated equilibria, on the basis of 'allopatric speciation'. There, the origin of new species is attributed to a long process outside of, or at the margin of, parent niches, where there are opportunities for experimentation with novel forms without their being swamped by the dominant species in the parent niche. Punctuation is rare, relative to long periods of stability, because it takes a long process of outside trial and error to establish a new form that is strong enough to turn around and successfully invade the parent niche.

This point of evolutionary 'logic' resembles the principle of generalization in the 'cycle of discovery' set out here, with its exit to a novel context of application. However, upon scrutiny the underlying logic is different. In evolutionary theory it is only the criteria of selection that change, offering new challenges and opportunities for survival and reproduction that cause a phylogenetic drift away from the parent population since interbreeding is blocked by some physical obstacle to interaction. Here, by contrast, the novel environment is a source of novel insights into limitations of existing practice, a build-up of motivation to change, and, most importantly, suggestions for novel elements that might be tried out, in hybridization, and novel architectural principles to eliminate problems caused by hybrids. Also, while the shift of environment may be imposed unexpectedly from the outside, when disaster strikes or an invading competence destroying innovation forces one to adapt, it may also be undertaken voluntarily and by design, in a deliberate step into a novel context of application, seeking optimal cognitive distance.

A key question now is: how blind is this source of 'variation'? It is blind in the sense that the innovative outcome of the process cannot be predicted. However, it is not blind in that novel selection environments can be selected purposely, as likely to generate opportunities to continue exploitation while yielding novel challenges and indications of elements and directions for exploration. The process is informed by success and failure in selection. Applying Campbell's (1974) criteria of blindness, variations from the process are not independent, are not separate from the environment, and later variations can be corrections of former ones. They are correlated with the solution, in the sense that experience with failure and indications of solutions inform the process. However, the outcome still cannot be predicted.

CONCLUSIONS

When evolution is abstracted from biological evolution, in 'Universal Darwinism', with only the bare notions of variety generation, selection and replication, without specification of how those processes work, it can to some extent be made to fit socio-economic evolution. The attempt to maintain an evolutionary perspective is useful for developing a coherent combination of internal and external causes of change, and of agency and structure, avoiding both an overly rational view of managerial design and a view of environmental determinism without actors. However, with such a bare, abstracted framework, most of the explanatory work still has to be done. A key question is whether a further elaboration of the framework in terms of interactors and replicators can meaningfully be sustained, and here my doubts are more severe. To the extent that this is a requirement for universal Darwinism, I share the doubts and criticisms of the latter that were voiced before by Witt (2005) and Nelson (2006). In this chapter I aim to make a further contribution, building on the organizational literature, focusing on issues that have been most neglected or incompletely developed in previous literature. First I focus on organizations, and subsequently I consider science.

Organizations

I specified four issues, concerning:

- the nature of the replicators carried by organizations interpreted as interactors, the sources of cohesion and stability of organizations as interactors, and the causes and extent of their differences within and between industries interpreted as populations;
- the extent to which the selection environment of markets and institutions can be moulded by organizations;
- the nature of replication, and its relation to variety generation; and
- how blind variety generation is, and the extent to which it may be guided by design and by learning from selection.

In an attempt to deal with these issues, I offered an analysis on the basis of a cognitive theory of organization, which is in turn based on an 'embodied cognition' branch of cognitive science that yields, among other things, the notion of cognitive distance between people to the extent that they have developed their cognition along different life paths.

Concerning the first issue I offer the notion of an organization as a 'focusing device', to limit cognitive distance for the sake of efficient achievement of collective organizational goals. It consists of a culturally constituted, socially generated and maintained bundle of replicators, if one wants to try that term, in the form of basic perceptions, interpretations, meanings and value judgements concerning goals, priorities, knowledge, strategy, work, technology, jobs and roles, on the competence side, and norms and values of conduct and conflict resolution, on the governance side. These yield requisite cohesion and stability of organizations, intra-industry differences mostly on the governance side, inter-industry differences on both the competence and the governance side, and limited possibilities for integral and instantaneous revision of replicators (organizational cognitive focus) by the interactor (organization), thus implying a certain amount of inertia. The analysis also allows us to drop clear and stable boundaries of activities as part of the definition of organizations.

This may be sufficient to maintain the notion of organizations as interactors. However, the notion of replicators is more problematic, if the notion entails that the replicators:

1. are carried by interactors;
2. generate characteristics of interactors relevant for success and replication;
3. are embodied in interactors, that is cannot exist apart from them; and
4. are not shaped by interactors in ways that reliably reflect exigencies of the selection environment.

If for organizational replicators we take organizational capabilities, the first two conditions are reasonably satisfied, the third is clearly violated, and the fourth is subject to debate. Insofar as all conditions are necessary, the notion of replicators does not apply, and if that is the case the notion of evolution becomes dubious. Insofar as the notions of both interactors and replicators are needed for Darwinism it is difficult to sustain. This still leaves the possibility that a wider interpretation of evolutionary theory can be sustained, as based on generalized notions of selection, transmission and variety generation.

Concerning the second issue, of selection, without detailed analysis I granted that while indeed markets and institutions can to a greater or lesser extent be moulded by organizations, singly or collectively, and in that sense evolutionary selection can be inefficient, significant selection pressures generally remain. Hence this aspect of evolutionary theory can reasonably be maintained.

Concerning the third issue, of transmission, I gave an analysis of replication on the basis of communication, and of how next to very imperfect replication this also yields variety generation. However, while in communication there is much decay, reduction, expansion and transformation of knowledge and competencies, some similarity in transmission remains. The question is whether such similarity is 'sufficient' to count as replication. I am afraid that treating communication as replication puts the analysis on the wrong foot, and it would be better to fully recognize communication and language as categories on their own that merit a *sui generis* analysis, using theories of language and meaning (Nooteboom, 2001).

Concerning the fourth issue, of variety generation, I argued for the intelligent design of innovation by collaboration, and of a path of cumulative insight and experience guided by selection in a variety of chosen selection environments that is conducive to outcomes that are unpredictable but have an enhanced chance of success. The heuristic of invention, or cycle of discovery, proposed by Nooteboom (2000), yields a form of inference and learning from experience concerning selection conditions that leads to the shaping of new selection conditions, which can hardly be called blind and is correlated with selection processes. While its specific outcomes are indeed unpredictable, overall performance is predictable, and the process is subject to rational design to some extent. Here also, to see it as 'variety generation' may put the analysis of the wrong foot, and it would be better to fully recognize learning processes as meriting a *sui generis* analysis, using theories of cognition and learning (Nooteboom, 2001).

Overall, the component evolutionary processes of variety generation, selection and transmission are far more interrelated than in biology, with units of selection being more able to mould selection conditions, interactors being able, to some extent, to change their replicators, replication entailing the generation of variety, and ways in which experience in selection can direct variety generation.

In sum, as I did earlier (Nooteboom, 2001), I am again inclined to rate evolutionary theory as only partially valid in socio-economics, possibly misleading, and hence insufficiently acceptable at least in principle, and adequate only as a stage of development towards a more adequate theory of socio-economic development. As indicated at the beginning, the merit of evolutionary theory lies in offering a view of both agency and structure, and interaction between them. However, there may be other ways to achieve that, which more directly reflect how learning and communication take place, in interaction between actors and their environment.

Science

Concerning cultural evolution more generally, and science in particular, the problems of evolutionary theory are worse. Concerning the first issue, of replicators and interactors, it seems reasonably clear that scientists, and on a higher level of aggregation perhaps also scholarly societies, may be seen as interactors. Like organizations in general, scientific societies may have a shared cognitive focus determining group identity, which may satisfy the condition that interactors must have some coherent, durable identity. However, replicators are even more problematic than in the analysis of organizations. Are they theories, or underlying ideas, or elements from scientific paradigms? In the latter case they would carry all the problems associated with the notion of paradigms. Whatever they are, precisely, here also they 'float around', disembodied from their carriers. It is not entirely clear what the success criterion of selection is. If it is lack of falsification, this entails all the problems that the notion of falsifiability entails, as exhibited in an extensive literature on the philosophy or methodology of science. Here also, replication in communication, in publications, meetings at conferences and seminars and PhD training is more a matter of cognitive reduction, amplification and reconstruction than a matter of replication. As in the case of organizations and their capabilities, the survival and replication of purported replicators is not entirely dependent on success of interactors under selection. Here, in some disciplines more than in others, (even) more opportunities exist to mould the selection environment than in the case of firms in markets, in opportunities to create a selection environment of dedicated scientific associations with their proprietary journals.

Thus, if evolution is problematic in organizations, it is problematic a fortiori in science.

In Sum

In sum, like Nelson (2006) I have problems with the notions of interactors and replicators, particularly with the notion of replicators being tied to interactors and shaping them, more than they are shaped by them. More than Nelson (2006) I also have problems with the basic notions of variety generation, selection and replication/transmission. While I appreciate their value in yielding a view of how agency and structure interact, while avoiding both an overly rational view of agents and environmental determinism, I have problems with them. Variety generation is not blind and is informed by experience from selection. Selection occurs both internally in the interactor (by mental experimentation) and in its interaction environment, and is subject to collective, political processes. Replication entails transformation and thereby is a form of variety generation. I am afraid that adherence to the terminology of replicators and interactors sidetracks attention from where it should go: to the investigation of learning, in the sense of invention and creation, and investigation of communication and language. Therefore, I would be more comfortable with a different theoretical framing of the processes of invention, selection, and communication. However, I am not sure that it is useful to assign this the label of 'evolutionary theory'. If we drop the conceptual tools of replicators and interactors, doesn't the notion of evolution become too general and loose to yield much theoretical grip? It still serves to indicate an approach that is characterized by attention to dynamics and emergence, rather than rational design and choice, as a result of selection (by markets and institutions) upon a variety of competencies/capabilities (of firms) whose successes are transferred (by growth, imitation, training, consultancy, training, institutionalization, spin-off and other forms of mobility of people). But is that enough? We need to add content to how these processes work, and I believe this is to be done in terms of cognition, learning and communication, which is what in earlier chapters I set out to do.

Answers

Answers to the research questions posed in the introduction to this book are as follows:

Question 15: How can we avoid both excessive managerial rationalism and external determinism?
Answer: Here lies a great advantage of evolutionary theory: idea generation (variety creation) plus selection and transmission explain the emergence of new forms. While firms can learn and can to a greater or lesser extent affect their survival conditions, they cannot without mistake manage them completely, and some force of selection remains. While trials are informed, much error remains.

Question 16: Why are inter-industry differences larger than intra-industry ones?
Answer: Within industries, sharing technologies and markets to a larger extent than between industries, cognitive distance between firms is smaller, particularly concerning the competence dimension.

Question 17: To what extent are dynamic capabilities informed by demands from selection?
Answer: Selection pressures may indicate needs and opportunities to experiment with novel combinations, they may trigger an escape to novel selection conditions, and stagnation due to lack of growth or lack of selection may stimulate a shift to novel selection conditions to acquire new insights into limits and opportunities. Such exit may be guided by a search for optimal cognitive distance on the basis of experience in markets. Selection may give useful information about obstacles and opportunities in networks. In other words, 'allopatric speciation' is not necessarily blind.

Question 18: To what extent is there 'inheritance' of acquired characteristics?
Answer: Firms set exemplars to be imitated or avoided on the basis of how they fare in selection and on the basis of what they have learned in the selection process.

Question 19: To what extent can firms mould their selection environment?
Answer: Collectively, participants in successful breakthrough and

consolidation of an innovation (producers, users, intermediaries, labour, government) develop institutions (technical, organizational, behavioural, safety-related, educational, reporting and other) standards, market structures (for example distribution channels, financial markets), habits (for example of consumption) that fit the innovation and improve its efficient exploitation. After consolidation, such established institutions and powerful incumbents can to a greater or lesser extent actively block entry of challengers.

Question 20: To what extent is transmission a source of variety generation?
Answer: In perception and communication meanings are not simply transmitted but transformed in assimilation, yielding novel combinations of old and new perceptions, insights etc. Hence transmission entails variety generation.

NOTES

1. A recent example reported in the press is the finding that while children do not have an inborn fear of snakes, they have an inborn proclivity to notice snakes, more than most other animals, allowing them to rapidly develop a fear of them when appropriate.
2. In terms of N/K spaces, with N dimensions and with 'fitness' a function of a systemic whole of N features each of which on average depends on K other features, the landscape is 'rugged', with sharp peaks of fitness at different locations in the space (Levinthal, 2000).

Conclusions

The conclusions of this book, in the form of answers to the questions posed in the introductory chapter, are collected below.

CHAPTER 3

Question 1: Why do firms exist? What is the basis for organizational capability?
Answer: Organizations in general and firms in particular exist to limit cognitive distance, with a cognitive focus for coordination between complementary capabilities, with sufficient mutual understanding and motivation to collaborate.

Question 2: What is the (dis)advantage of firms relative to markets?
Answer: Firms exist to provide more cohesion (focus) for the sake of exploitation, while markets provide more variety for the sake of exploration. Organizational focus yields a constraint of myopia that can be compensated by outside collaboration. The duality of market and firm yields a solution, on the level of an economic system, to the problem of combining exploitation and exploration.

Question 3: What, if any, are limits to size of the firm?
Answers: Apart from familiar arguments of scale or scope, are the following. The general argument is that there is a trade-off between coordination for efficiency and variety for innovation. As firm size increases by expansion of the portfolio of activities or capabilities, one can maintain coordination at the expense of room for variety, or one can maintain room for variety at the expense of coordination. In the first case there will be a decrease of innovation, and in the second case a decrease of the rationale for combining activities in one firm. In more detail, the argument is as follows. To the extent that increase of size yields increasing systemic complexity, in a portfolio of activities or capabilities, local change of only one component increasingly requires wholesale systemic restructuring, which yields a systemic obstacle to change. This yields an incentive for break-up into more autonomous components, for the sake

of dynamic efficiency, even if it yields a decrease of static efficiency. As capabilities are added and become increasingly dissimilar and less complementary, the extent and complexity of cognitive coordination needed to exploit their combinations increases non-linearly and increasingly reduces variety within each capability. This reduces the potential and speed of innovation. This yields a need to limit internal expansion and, instead, to maintain cognitive variety in outside relationships. If capabilities yield little complementarity they also yield little mutual dependence as an incentive for collaboration.

Question 4: What, if any, are limits to growth of the firm?
Answer: Apart from limits to size, the speed of growth is limited by the speed at which new staff can adapt to organizational focus. This comes close to Penrose's argument. Also, it takes time to build up absorptive capacity and ability to collaborate, as a basis for further expansion by combination with new capabilities.

Question 5: What are problems of coordination?
Answer: One problem may lie in complex coherence of complementary capabilities. A second lies in problems of mutual understanding and willingness to collaborate between complementary capabilities. Related to both, a problem lies in the combination of exploitation and exploration, which is difficult in complex systems and difficult to combine in a single organizational focus.

Question 6: What are capabilities to solve them?
Answer: Ability to achieve sufficient stability, mutual understanding and willingness to collaborate, for the sake of exploitation, while allowing for variety of knowledge and autonomy and spirit of competition, for the sake of exploration, within the firm or in collaboration between firms. This point is elaborated in Chapter 4, in the analysis of inter-organizational relationships, and in Chapter 5, in the analysis of dynamic capabilities.

Question 7: What is the basis for organization-specific capabilities?
Answer: Mostly organizational cognitive focus, starting from the imprint of a founding entrepreneur, rooted in deep level cognitive categories, implemented and communicated by means of symbolic pictures, objects, stories, slogans, events and behaviours, including role models.

Question 8: What causes stability of organizations?
Answer: First, elimination by competitive pressures of dysfunctional or unsuccessful deviations from established activities/capabilities. This

applies in particular under systemic complexity, where even local deviation rapidly becomes dysfunctional. Second, the fact that incoming personnel self-select or are selected and socialized according to the culture associated with cognitive focus. Third, the fact that further cognition is constructed under shared organizational conditions.

CHAPTERS 4, 5 AND 6

Question 9: What are dynamic capabilities?

Answer: A first dynamic capability is to design and implement an organizational focus that provides sufficient alignment for exploitation, where needed, and yet is only limitedly cohesive, allowing for exploration, for example with a focus either on the deep level of fundamental categories, or with a focus only on the governance side.

A second dynamic capability is a high intellectual capability (absorptive capacity) and behavioural capability to collaborate across cognitive distance, based on learning from earlier collaboration, in order to achieve higher optimal cognitive distance, that is to operate efficiently at a higher cognitive distance. Related to that: governance capabilities, particularly the ability to identify and solve possible problems of spillover, mutual dependence, reputation and psychological safety, and the art to wisely employ trust. A third dynamic capability is the ability to employ a heuristic of invention for developing exploitation into exploration, by shifting activity to appropriate novel contexts that offer an opportunity of ongoing exploitation but also novel challenges to survival, insights into limitations of current practice, opportunities for experimenting with novel local elements, and the ability to shift to more radical architectural reconfigurations of old and new elements to realize the potential of emerging success of novelty. This requires great governance capabilities to deal with internal variety and to integrate it into a new organizational focus. A fourth dynamic capability is the capability to design networks of optimal density, if such design lies within the power of an organization, or to select such a network, and to select or develop an optimal position of centrality, carefully traded off with the effects of cognitive distance and density. Optimal network features, and one's position in a network, depend on stages of development. Thus, a related dynamic capability is to understand network dynamics and use that in the selection of networks and positioning in them, depending on one's strategy (for example focus on exploitation or exploration) and one's other capabilities (for example absorptive capacity, capability in collaboration).

CHAPTER 4

Question 9: See above.

Question 10: What determines the boundaries of organizations?
Answer: For a firm as a legal entity boundaries are determined by legal regulation of property, liability and authority. For a firm as an organization, that is as a form for coordinating activities, and for 'making knowledge work' (Schumpeter, Marshall), the boundary is determined by organizational cognitive focus: the activities and capabilities that fall within the reach of organization-specific meanings, understandings and culture.

Question 11: Why do organizations collaborate with others?
Answer: To compensate for organizational myopia caused by organizational focus, by means of complementary cognition, at a cognitive distance too large to realize efficiently within the firm.

Question 12: How is inter-organizational collaboration governed?
Answer: By some appropriate mix, given certain goals and external conditions of the firm, of instruments that yield reliability (control and/or trust). There are instruments of control in contractual limitation of opportunities for opportunism, material incentives to refrain from opportunism, the use of reputation mechanisms, hostages, and balance of mutual dependence. There are also factors of trust, beyond control, in shared values and norms of conduct, and in relation-specific routinized behaviour, empathy and identification.

Question 13: What are the effects of network features on the conditions and results of collaboration between firms?
Answer: On the competence side, novelty value of relationships is reduced by density of the network and long term exclusive ties, and is enhanced by cognitive distance and betweenness centrality. Absorptive capacity is reduced by cognitive distance, betweenness centrality, and short term, infrequent interaction and lack in investment in mutual understanding. Governance is enhanced by network density, centrality of a firm in its ego-network, and long-term, high trust ties.

CHAPTER 5

Question 9: See above.

Question 14: How to explain cluster dynamics?

Answer: Network dynamics can be explained in terms of changes in features of structure and strength of ties along the cycle of discovery, and a change of network focus. In the early stage of exploration, in novel combinations, ties tend to be volatile and dense, with frequent interaction, large cognitive distance, limited duration, limited specific investments, large scope (multi-plexity) of ties, governance to a large extent by reputation and personal bonding, complemented by more sparse and weak linkages to distant communities, and advantages for players with high betweenness centrality. Network focus is cohesive relative to other stages, though still less so than within organizations. Towards consolidation density decreases, frequency of knowledge exchange decreases, scope of ties decreases, ties last longer, specific investments increase, governance shifts from trust to contracts, ties become more impersonal, and advantage arises for players with high degree centrality. Peripheral players are at a disadvantage and new entry becomes increasingly difficult. Network focus breaks up or becomes more cohesive around a hub. In the following stages of generalization, differentiation and reciprocation, new outside ties arise, set up by some, especially peripheral players who may subsequently spin off from the network and start to develop their own network. This may lead on to the situation described at the start.

CHAPTER 6

Question 15: How can we avoid both excessive managerial rationalism and external determinism?

Answer: Here lies a great advantage of evolutionary theory: idea generation (variety creation) plus selection and transmission explain the emergence of new forms. While firms can learn and can to a greater or lesser extent affect their survival conditions, they cannot without mistake manage them completely, and some force of selection remains. While trials are informed, much error remains.

Question 16: Why are inter-industry differences larger than intra-industry ones?

Answer: Within industries, sharing technologies and markets, to a larger extent than between industries, cognitive distance between firms is smaller, particularly concerning the competence dimension.

Question 17: To what extent are dynamic capabilities informed by demands from selection?

Answer: Selection pressures may indicate needs and opportunities to experiment with novel combinations, they may trigger an escape to novel selection conditions, and stagnation due to lack of growth or lack of selection may stimulate a shift to novel selection conditions to acquire new insights into limits and opportunities. Such exit may be guided by a search for optimal cognitive distance on the basis of experience in markets. Selection may give useful information about obstacles and opportunities in networks. In other words, 'allopatric speciation' is not necessarily blind.

Question 18: To what extent is there 'inheritance' of acquired characteristics?
Answer: Firms set exemplars to be imitated or avoided on the basis of how they fare in selection and on the basis of what they have learned in the selection process.

Question 19: To what extent can firms mould their selection environment?
Answer: Collectively, participants in successful breakthrough and consolidation of an innovation (producers, users, intermediaries, labour, government) develop institutions (technical, organizational, behavioural, safety-related, educational, reporting and other) standards, market structures (for example distribution channels, financial markets), habits (for example of consumption) that fit the innovation and improve its efficient exploitation. After consolidation, powerful incumbents can to a greater or lesser extent actively block entry of challengers.

Question 20: To what extent is transmission a source of variety generation?
Answer: In perception and communication meanings are not simply transmitted but transformed in assimilation, yielding novel combinations of old and new perceptions, insights etc. Hence transmission entails variety generation.

References

Abelson, R.P. (1976), 'Script processing in attitude formation and decision making', in J.S. Carroll and J.W. Payne (eds), *Cognition and Social Behavior*, Hillsdale, NJ: Erlbaum, pp. 33–45.

Abernathy, W.J. (1978), *The Productivity Dilemma: Roadblock to Innovation in the Automobile Industry*, Baltimore, MD: Johns Hopkins University Press.

Abernathy, W.J. and J.M. Utterback (1978), 'Patterns of industrial innovation', *Technology Review*, **81**, 41–7.

Abernathy, W.J. and K.B. Clark (1985), 'Innovation: mapping the winds of creative destruction', *Research Policy*, **14**, 3–22.

Acs, Z. and D. Audretsch (1990), *Innovation and Small Firms*, Cambridge, MA: The MIT Press.

Ahuja, G. (2000), 'Collaboration networks, structural holes and innovation: a longitudinal study', *Administrative Science Quarterly*, **45**, 425–55.

Ahuja, G. and R. Katila (2004), 'Where do resources come from? The role of idiosyncratic situations', *Strategic Management Journal*, **25**(8–9), 887–907.

Aldrich, H. (1999), *Organizations Evolving*, London: Sage.

Almeida, P. and B. Kogut (1999), 'Localization of knowledge and the mobility of engineers in regional networks', *Management Science*, **45**(7), 905–17.

Amin, A. and P. Cohendet (2003), *Architectures of Knowledge: Firms, Capabilities and Communities*, Oxford: Oxford University Press.

Anderson, P. and M. Tushman (1990), 'Technological discontinuities and dominant designs: a cyclical model of technological change', *Administrative Science Quarterly*, **35**(4), 604–33.

Appleyard, M.M., N.W. Hatch and D.C. Mowery (2002), 'Managing the development and transfer of process technologies in the semiconductor manufacturing industry', in: G. Dosi, R.R. Nelson and S.G. Winter, (eds), *The Nature and Dynamics of Organizational Capabilities*, Oxford: Oxford University Press, pp. 183–207.

Argyris, C. and D. Schön (1974), *Theory in Practice: Increasing Professional Effectiveness*, San Francisco, CA: Jossey-Bass.

Argyris, C. and D. Schön (1978), *Organizational Learning*, Reading, MA: Addison-Wesley.

Arrow, K.J. (1974), *The Limits of Organization*, New York: Norton.

Arthur, B. (1989), 'Competing technologies, increasing returns, and lock-in by historical events', *Economic Journal*, **99** (March), 116–31.

Austin, J.L. (1955), 'How to do things with words', in J.O. Urmson (ed.), *The William James Lectures Delivered at Harvard University in 1955*, Oxford: Clarendon Press, 1962.

Bachelard, G. (1980), *La formation de l'esprit scientifique*, 11th edn, Paris: J. Vrin.

Bae, J. and M. Gargiulo (2003), Local action and efficient alliance strategies in the telecommunications industry, INSEAD working paper, report 2003/20/OB, Fontainebleau, France.

Barkema, H.G., O. Shenkar, F. Vermeulen and J.H.J. Bell (1997), 'Working abroad, working with others: how firms learn to operate international joint ventures', *Academy of Management Journal*, **40**, 426–42.

Barkow, J., L. Cosmides and J. Tooby (1992), *The Adapted Mind: Evolutionary Psychology and the Generation of Culture*, Oxford: Oxford University Press.

Bartlett, C.A. and S. Goshal (1989), *Managing Across Borders – Transnational Solution*, Boston, MA: Harvard Business School Press.

Barley, S.R. (1986), 'Technology as an occasion for structuring: evidence from observation of CT scanners and the social order of radiology departments', *Administrative Science Quarterly*, **31**, 78–108.

Bateson, G. (2000), *Steps to an Ecology of Mind*, Chicago, IL: University of Chicago Press.

Baum, J.A.C. and J.V. Singh (1994), 'Organizational hierarchies and evolutionary processes: some reflections on a theory of organizational evolution', in J.A.C. Baum and J.V. Singh (eds), *Evolutionary Dynamics of Organizations*, Oxford: Oxford University Press: pp. 3–20.

Bazerman, M.H. (1998), *Judgement in Managerial Decision Making*, New York: Wiley.

Beerkens, B.E. (2004), *External Acquisition of Technology, Exploration and Exploitation in International Innovation Networks*, PhD thesis, Eindhoven: ECIS. University Press.

Bennis, W.G. (1969), *Organizational Development: Its Nature, Origins and Prospects*, Reading, MA: Addison Wesley.

Berger, P. and T. Luckmann (1966), *The Social Construction of Reality*, New York: Doubleday.

Best, M.H. (2002), 'Regional growth dynamics: a capabilities perspective', in C. Pitelis (ed.), *The Growth of the Firm; The Legacy of Edith Penrose*, Oxford: Oxford University Press, pp. 179–95.

Bettis, R.A. and C.K. Prahalad (1995), 'The dominant logic: retrospective and extension', *Strategic Management Journal*, **16**(1), 5–14.

Birley, S., S. Cromie and A. Myers (1991), 'Entrepreneurial networks: their emergence in Ireland and overseas', *International Small Business Journal*, **4**, 56–74.

Blackler, F. (1995), 'Knowledge, knowledge work and organizations: an overview and interpretation', *Organization Studies*, **16**(6), 1021–46.

Blair, J.M. (1972), *Economic Concentration*, New York: Harcourt, Brace, Jovanovich.

Blau, P.M. (1970), 'A formal theory of differentiation in organizations', *American Sociological Review*, **35**(2), 201–18.

Blaug, M. (1997), *Economic Theory in Retrospect*, Cambridge: Cambridge University Press.

Bleeke, J. and D. Ernst (1991), 'The way to win in cross-border alliances', *Harvard Business Review*, (November/December), 127–35.

Bogenrieder, I. and B. Nooteboom (2004), 'Learning groups: what types are there?', *Organization Studies*, **25**(2), 287–314.

Bonacich, P. (1987), 'Power centrality: a family of measures', *American Journal of Sociology*, **92**, 1170–82.

Boulding, K.E. (1961), *The Image*, Ann Arbor, MI: University of Michigan Press.

Boyd, R. and P.J. Richerson (1985), *Culture and the Evolutionary Process*, Chicago, IL: University of Chicago Press.

Bradach, J.L. and R.G. Eccles (1989), 'Markets versus hierarchies: from ideal types to plural forms', *Annual Review of Sociology*, **15**, 97–118.

Bromiley, P. and L.L. Cummings (1992), Transaction Costs in Organizations with Trust, Carlson School of Management working paper, University of Minnesota, Minneapolis.

Brown, J.S. and P. Duguid (1991), 'Organizational learning and communities of practice: toward a unified view of working, learning, and innovation', *Organization Science*, **2**(1), 40–57.

Brown, J.S. and P. Duguid (1996), 'Organizational learning and communities of practice', in M.D. Cohen and L.S. Sproull (eds), *Organizational Learning*, London: Sage, pp. 58–82.

Brown, J.S. and P. Duguid (2001), 'Knowledge and organization: a social-practice perspective', *Organization Science*, **12**(2), 198–213.

Brusoni, S. (2006), 'The limits to specialization: problem solving and coordination in modular networks', *Organization Studies*, **12**(12), 1885–908.

Burgelman, R.A. (1983), 'A model of the interaction of strategic behavior, corporate context, and the concept of strategy', *Academy of Management Review*, **8**, 61–70.

Burns, T. and G.M. Stalker (1961), *The Management of Innovation*, London: Tavistock.

Burrell, G. and G. Morgan (1961), *Sociological Paradigms and Organizational Analysis*. London: Heinemann.

Burt, R.S. (1992), *Structural Holes: The Social Structure of Competition*, Cambridge, MA: Harvard University Press.

Burt, R.S. (2000), 'The network structure of social capital', in R.I. Sutton and B.M. Staw (eds), *Research in Organizational Behavior*, New York: Elsevier, pp. 345–423.

Campbell, D.T. (1974), 'Evolutionary epistemology', in D.T. Campbell, *Methodology and Epistemology for Social Science*, Oxford: Oxford University Press, pp. 393–434.

Campbell, D.T. (1987), 'Blind variation and selective retention as in other knowledge processes', in G. Radnitzky and W.W. Bartley III (eds), *Evolutionary Epistemology, Theory of Rationality, and the Sociology of Knowledge*, La Salle, PA: Open Court, pp. 91–114.

Campbell, D.T. (1994), 'How individual and face-to-face group selection undermine firm selection in organizational evolution', in J.A.C. Baum and J.V. Singh (eds), *Evolutionary Dynamics of Organizations*, Oxford: Oxford University Press, pp. 23–38.

Cantwell, J. (1990), 'A survey of the theories of international production', in C. Pitelis and R. Sugden (eds), *The Nature of the Transnational Firm*, London: Routledge, pp. 16–63.

Cantwell, J. (1995), 'The globalisation of technology: what remains of the product life cycle model?', *Cambridge Journal of Economics*, **19**(1), 155–74.

Cantwell, J. (2002), 'Innovation, profits and growth: Penrose and Schumpeter', in C. Pitelis (ed.), *The Growth of the Firm; The Legacy of Edith Penrose*, Oxford: Oxford University Press, pp. 215–48.

Casson, M. (1982), *The Entrepreneur: An Economic Theory*, Oxford: Martin Robertson.

Chandler, P. Hagström and Ö. Sölvell (eds), *The Dynamic Firm. The Role of Technology, Strategy, Organization and Regions*. Oxford: Oxford University Press.

Cheah, P.L. and P.L. Robertson (1992), 'The entrepreneurial process and innovation in the product life cycle', presentation to the international conference Joseph A. Schumpeter Society, Kyoto, August.

Chell, E. (1985), 'The entrepreneurial personality: a few ghosts laid to rest', *International Small Business Journal*, **3**(3), 43–4.

Chell, E., J. Haworth and S. Brearley (1991), *The Entrepreneurial Personality*, London: Routledge.

Chesbrough, H.W. (2003), *Open Innovation: The New Imperative for*

Creating and Profiting from Technology, Boston, MA: Harvard Business School Press.

Child, J. (2002), 'A configurational analysis of international joint ventures', *Organisation Studies*, **23**(5), 781–816.

Chiles, T.H. and J.F. McMackin (1996), 'Integrating variable risk preferences, trust transaction cost economics', *Academy of Management Review*, **21**(7), 73–99.

Choo, C.W. (1998), *The Knowing Organization*, Oxford: Oxford University Press.

Cohen, M.D. and P. Bacdayan (1996), 'Organizational routines are stored as procedural memory', in M.D. Cohen and L.S. Sproull (eds), *Organizational Learning*, London: Sage, pp. 403–30; first printed in *Organization Science*, **5**(4), 554–68 in 1994.

Cohen, M.D. and D.A. Levinthal (1990), 'Absorptive capacity: a new perspective on learning innovation', *Administrative Science Quarterly*, **35**, 128–52.

Cohen, M.D. and L.S. Sproull (eds) (1996), *Organizational Learning*, London: Sage, pp. 58–82, first printed in 1991 *Organization Science*, **2**(1) special issue.

Coleman, J.S. (1974), *Power and the Structure of Society*, New York: W.W. Norton and Co.

Coleman J.S. (1988), 'Social capital in the creation of human capital', *American Journal of Sociology*, **94** (special supplement), 95–120.

Colombo, M.G. and P. Garrone (1998), 'Common carriers entry into multimedia services', *Information Economics and Policy*, **10**, 77–105.

Cook, S.D.D. and D. Yanow (1996), 'Culture and organizational learning', in M.D. Cohen and L.S. Sproull (eds), *Organizational Learning*, London: Sage, pp. 430–5; first printed in *Journal of Management Enquiry*, **2**(4), 373–90, 1993.

Coriat, B. (2002), 'The abominable Ohno production system. Competences, monitoring, and routines in Japanese production systems', in G. Dosi, R.R. Nelson and S.G. Winter (eds), *The Nature and Dynamics of Organizational Capabilities*, Oxford: Oxford University Press, pp. 213–43.

Coriat, B. and G. Dosi (1998), 'Learning how to govern and learning how to solve problems: on the co-evolution of competences, conflicts and organizational routines', in A.D. Chandler, P. Hagström and Ö. Sölvell (eds), *The Dynamic Firm. The Role of Technology, Strategy, Organization and Regions*, Oxford: Oxford University Press, pp. 103–33.

Cowan, R., P.A. David and D. Foray (2000), 'The explicit economics of knowledge codification and tacitness', *Industrial and Corporate Change*, **9**(2), 211–53.

Craver, C.F. (2007), *Explaining the Brain: Mechanisms and the Mosaic Unity of Neuroscience*, Oxford: Oxford University Press.

Cyert, R.M. and J.G. March (1963), *A Behavioral Theory of the Firm*, Englewood Cliffs, NJ: Prentice-Hall.

Damasio, A.R. (1995), *Descartes Error: Emotion, Reason and the Human Brain*, London: Picador.

Damasio, A.R.(2003), *Looking for Spinoza*, Orlando, FL: Harcourt.

Das, T.K. and B.S. Teng (1998), 'Between trust and control: developing confidence in partner cooperation in alliances', *Academy of Management Review*, **23**(3), 491–512.

Das, T.K. and B.S. Teng (2001), 'Trust, control and risk in strategic alliances: an integrated framework', *Organization Studies*, **22**(2), 251–84.

David, P.A. (1985), 'Clio and the economics of QWERTY', *American Economic Review*, **75** (May), 332–7.

Davis, C.D., G.E. Hills and W. Laforge (1985), 'The marketing/small enterprise paradox, a research agenda', *International Small Business Journal*, **3**(3), 31–42.

Dawkins, R. (1983), 'Universal Darwinism', in D.S. Bendall (ed.), *Evolution from Molecules to Man*, Cambridge: Cambridge University Press, pp. 403–25.

Dellarosa, D. (1988), 'The psychological appeal of connectionism', *Behavioral and Brain Sciences*, **11**(1), 28–9.

Deutsch, M. (1973), *The Resolution of Conflict: Constructive and Destructive Processes*, New Haven, CT: Yale University Press.

DiMaggio, P.J. (1997), 'Culture and cognition', *Annual Review of Sociology*, **23**, 263–87.

DiMaggio, P.J. and W.W. Powell (1983), 'The iron cage revisited: institutional isomorphism and collective rationality in organizational fields', *American Sociological Review*, **48**(2), 147–60.

Dosi, G (1984), *Technical Change and Industrial Transformation*, London: Macmillan.

Dosi, G., R.R. Nelson and S.G. Winter (eds) (2000), *The Nature and Dynamics of Organizational Capabilities*, Oxford: Oxford University Press.

Doz, Y. (1986), *Strategic Management in Multinational Companies*, Oxford: Pergamon Press.

Dulbecco P. and V. Dutraive (2007), 'The meaning of the market: comparing Austrian and institutional economics', in G.M. Hodgson (ed.), *The Evolution of Economic Institutions*, Cheltenham, UK and Northampton, MA, USA: Edward Elgar, pp. 160–82.

Duncan, R. (1976), 'The ambidextrous organization: designing dual structures for innovation', in R. Kilmann, L. Pondy and D. Slevin (eds), *The Management of Organization*, vol. 1, New York: North Holland.

Dunning, J. (1996), 'The geographical sources of the competitiveness of firms: some results of a new survey', *Transnational Corporations*, **5**(3), 1–29.

Duysters, G., A.P. de Man (2003), 'Transitory alliances: an instrument for surviving turbulent industries', *R&D Management*, **33**(1), 49–58.

Dyer, J.H. and W.G. Ouchi (1993), 'Japanese-style partnerships: giving companies a competitive edge', *Sloan Management Review*, **35**, 51–63.

Edelman, G.M. (1987), *Neural Darwinism; the Theory of Neuronal Group Selection*, New York: Basic Books.

Edelman, G.M. (1992), *Bright Air, Brilliant Fire; On the Matter of Mind*, London: Penguin.

Edmonson, A. (1999), 'Psychological safety and learning behaviour in work teams', *Administrative Science Quarterly*, **44**, 350–83.

Eijck, J. van and H. Kamp (1997), 'Representing discourse in context', in J. van Benthem and A. ter Meulen (eds), *Handbook of Logic and Language*, Amsterdam: Elsevier, pp. 179–237.

Eldredge, N. and S.J. Gould (1972), 'Punctuated equilibria: an alternative to phyletic gradualism', in T.J.M. Schopf (ed.), *Models in Paleobiology*, San Franciso, CA: Freeman, Cooper and Co, pp. 82–115.

Esser, H. (2005), 'Rationality and bonding – the model of frame-selection and the explanation of normative conduct (in German)', in M. Held, G. Kubon-Gilke, R. Sturm (eds), *Normative und institutionelle Grundfragen der Okonomik*, Jahrbuch 4, Reputation und Vertrauen, Marburg: Metropolis, pp. 85–112.

Etzioni, A. (1988), *The Moral Dimension: Towards a New Economics*, New York: The Free Press.

Flaherty, M.T. (2000), 'Limited inquiry and intelligent adaptation in semi-conductor manufacturing', in G. Dosi, R.R. Nelson and S.G. Winter (eds), *The Nature and Dynamics of Organizational Capabilities*, Oxford: Oxford University Press, pp. 99–123.

Fleming, L. (2001), 'Recombinant uncertainty in technological search', *Management Science*, **471**: 117–32.

Fodor, J.A. (1975), *The Language of Thought*, New York: Thomas Y. Crowell.

Forsgren, M., U. Holm and J. Johanson (2005), *Managing the Embedded Multinational*, Cheltenham, UK and Northampton, MA, USA: Edward Elgar.

Foss, N.J. (1994), *The Austrian School and Modern Economics*, Copenhagen: Handelshojskolen Forlag.

Foss, N.J. (2002), 'Edith Penrose: economics and strategic management', in C. Pitelis (ed.), *The Growth of the Firm; The Legacy of Edith Penrose*, Oxford: Oxford University Press, pp. 147–64.

Foster, J. and J.S. Metcalfe (eds) (2001), *Frontiers of Evolutionary Economics: Competition, Self-organization and Innovation Policy*, Cheltenham, UK and Northampton, MA, USA: Edward Elgar.

Freeman, C.J. and C. Perez (1989), 'Structural crises of adjustment, business cycles and investment behaviour', in G. Dosi (ed.), *Technical Change and Economic Theory*, London: Francis Pinter.

Frege, G. (1892), 'On sense and reference' (in German), *Zeitschrift fur Philosophie und philosophische Kritik*, **100**, 25–50.

Fukuyama, F. (1995), *Trust, the Social Virtues and the Creation of Prosperity*, New York: Free Press.

Gambetta, D. (1988), 'Can we trust trust?', in D. Gambetta (ed.), *Trust; Making Breaking of Cooperative Relations*, Oxford: Blackwell, pp. 213–37.

Garud, R. and M.A. Rappa (1996), 'A socio-cognitive model of technology evolution; the case of cochlear implants', in J.R. Meindl, C. Stubbart and J.F. Porac (eds), *Cognition Within and Between Organisations*, London: Sage, pp. 441–74; first published in 1994 in *Organization Science* **5**(3), 344–62.

Geach, P. and M. Black (1977), *Philosophical Writings of Gottlob Frege*, Oxford: Blackwell.

Gersick, C.J.G. (1988), 'Time and transition in work teams: toward a new model of group development', *Academy of Management Journal*, **31**, 9–41.

Gersick, C.J.G. (1991), 'Revolutionary change theories: 2 multi-level exploration of the punctuated equilibrium paradigm', *Academy of Management Journal*, **16**(1), 10–36.

Ghoshal, S. and N. Nohria (1997), *The Differentiated MNC: Organizing Multinational Corporation for Value Creation*, San Francisco, CA: Jossey-Bass.

Ghoshal, S. and C.A. Bartlett (1990), 'The multinational corporation as an interorganisational network', *Academy of Management Review*, **15**(4), 603–25.

Ghoshal, S., M. Hahn and P. Moran (2002), 'Management competence, firm growth and economic progress', in C. Pitelis, *The Growth of the Firm; The Legacy of Edith Penrose*, Oxford: Oxford University Press. pp. 279–309.

Gibson, C. and J. Birkinshaw (2004), 'The antecedents, consequences and mediating role of organizational ambidexterity', *Academy of Management Journal*, **47**, 207–26.

Gilsing, V.A. and B. Nooteboom (2005), 'Density and strength of ties in innovation networks: an analysis of multi-media and biotechnology', *European Management Review*, **2**, 179–97.

Gilsing, V.A. and B. Nooteboom (2006), 'Exploration and exploitation in biotechnology', *Research Policy*, **35**(1), 1–23.

Gilsing, V.A., B. Nooteboom, W.P.M. van Haverbeke, G.M. Duijsters and A.V. d. Oord (2008), 'Network embeddedness and the exploration of novel technologies: technological distance, betweenness centrality and density', *Research Policy*, **37**, 1717–31.

Gioia, D.A. and P.P. Poole (1984), 'Scripts in organizational behaviour', *Academy of Management Review*, **9**(3), 449–59.

Gould, S.J. (1989), 'Punctuated equilibrium in fact and theory', *Journal of Social Biological Structure*, **12**, 117–36.

Granovetter, M.S. (1973), 'The strength of weak ties', *American Journal of Sociology*, **78**(6), 1360–81.

Granstrand, O., P. Patel and K. Pavitt (1997), 'Multi-technology corporations: why they have distributed rather than distinctive core competencies', *California Management Review*, **39**(4), 8–25.

Greiner, L.E. (1972), 'Evolution and revolution as organizations grow', *Harvard Business Review*, **50** (July–August), 37–46.

Grey, C. and C. Garsten (2001), 'Trust, control, post-bureaucracy', *Organization Studies*, **22**(2), 229–50.

Groot, A.D. de (1969), *Methodology: Foundations of Inference and Research in the Social Sciences*, The Hague: Mouton.

Gulati, R. (1995), 'Familiarity breeds trust? The implications of repeated ties on contractual choice in alliances', *Academy of Management Journal*, **38**, 85–112.

Habermas, J. (1982), *Theorie des kommunikativen Handelns* [*Theory of Communicative Action*], Teil 1 und 2, Frankfurt: Suhrkamp.

Habermas, J. (1984), *Vorstudien und Ergänzungen zur Theorie des kommunikatieven Handelns* [*Preliminary Studies and Elaborations to the Theory of Communicative Action*], Frankfurt: Suhrkamp.

Hagedoorn, J. (1993), 'Understanding the rationale of strategic technology partnering: interorganizational modes of cooperation and sectoral differences', *Strategic Management Journal*, **14**, 371–85.

Hagedoorn, J. and J. Schakenraad (1994), 'The effect of strategic technology alliances on company performance', *Strategic Management Journal*, **15**, 291–309.

Hagedoorn, J. and G.M. Duysters (2002), 'Satisficing strategies in dynamic inter-firm networks, the efficacy of quasi-redundant contacts', *Organization Studies*, **23**, 525–48.

Hagerty, M.R. (1999), 'Testing Maslow's hierarchy of needs: national quality of life across time', *Social Indicators Research*, **46**(3), 249–71.

Hamel, G. (1991), 'Competition for competence and inter-partner learning within international strategic alliance', *Strategic Management Journal*, **12**, special issue, 83–103.

Hannan, M.T. and J. Freeman (1977), 'The population ecology of organizations', *American Journal of Sociology*, **88**, 929–64.

Hannan, M.T. and J. Freeman (1984), 'Structural inertia and organizational change', *American Sociological Review*, **49**, 149–64.

Hannan, M.T. and J. Freeman (1989), *Organizational Ecology*, Cambridge, MA: Harvard University Press.

Hansen, M.T. (1999), 'The search-transfer problem: the role of weak ties in sharing knowledge across organization subunits', *Administrative Science Quarterly*, **44**, 82–111.

Hardin, R. (2002), *Trust and Trustworthiness*, New York: Russell Sage Foundation.

Hayek, F.A. (1945), 'The use of knowledge in society', *American Economic Review*, **35**, September, 519–30.

Hayek, F.A. (1976), *The Sensory Order*, Chicago, IL: University of Chicago Press.

He, Z. and P. Wong (2004), 'Exploration vs. exploitation: an empirical test of the ambidexterity hypothesis', *Organization Science*, **15**, 481–94.

Hébert, R.M. and A.N. Link (1982), *The Entrepreneur*, New York: Praeger.

Hedberg, B.L.T. (1981), 'How organizations learn and unlearn', in P.C. Nystrom and W.H. Starbuck (eds), *Handbook of Organizational Design*, Vol. 3–27, New York: Oxford University Press.

Helper, S. (1987), 'Supplier relations innovation: theory application to the US auto industry', PhD thesis, Harvard University.

Helper, S. (1990), 'Comparative supplier relations in the US Japanese auto industries: an exit/voice approach', *Business Economic History*, **19**, 1–10.

Henderson, R.M. and K.B. Clark (1990), 'Architectural innovation: the reconstruction of existing product technologies and the failure of established firms', *Administrative Science Quarterly*, **35**, 9–30.

Hendriks-Jansen, H. (1996), *Catching Ourselves in the Act: Situated Activity, Interactive Emergence, Evolution and Human Thought*, Cambridge, MA: MIT Press.

Hill, C.W. L. (1990), 'Cooperation, opportunism and the invisible hand: implications for transaction cost theory', *Academy of Management Review*, **15**(3), 500–13.

Hippel, E. von (1988), *The Sources of Invention*, Oxford: Oxford University Press.

Hippel, E. von (1999), '"Sticky information" and the locus of problem solving: implications for innovation', in A.D. Chandler, P. Hagström and Ö. Sölvell (eds), *The Dynamic Firm. The Role of Technology, Strategy, Organization and Regions*, Oxford: Oxford University Press, pp. 60–77.

Hippel, E. von (2005), *Democratizing Innovation*, Cambridge, MA and London: MIT.

Hirschman, A.O. (1970), *Exit, Voice and Loyalty: Responses to Decline in Firms, Organisations and States*, Cambridge, MA: Harvard University Press.

Hodgson, G.M. (1993), *Economics and Evolution: Bringing Life Back into Economics*, Cambridge: Polity Press.

Hodgson, G.M. (2002a), 'The legal nature of the firm and the myth of the firm-market hybrid', *International Journal of the Economics of Business*, **9**(1), 37–60.

Hodgson, G.M. (2002b), 'Darwinism in economics: from analogy to ontology', *Journal of Evolutionary Economics*, **12**, 259–81.

Hodgson, G.M. (2006), 'What are institutions?', *Journal of Economic Issues*, **60**(1), 1–25.

Hodgson, G.M. and T. Knudsen (2004), 'The firm as interactor', *Journal of Evolutionary Economics*, **14**, 281–307.

Hodgson, G.M. and T. Knudsen (2006), 'Why we need a generalized Darwinism, and why generalized Darwinism is not enough', *Journal of Economic Behavior and Organization*, **61**, 1–19.

Holland, J.H. (1975), *Adaptation in Natural and Artificial Systems*, Ann Arbor, MI: University of Michigan Press.

Holland, J.H. (1996), *Hidden Order; How Adaptation Builds Complexity*, Cambridge, MA: Perseus Books.

Holland, J.H., K.J. Holyoak, R.E. Nisbett and P.R. Thagard (1989), *Induction; Processes of Inference, Learning and Discovery*, Cambridge MA: MIT Press.

House, R.J., P.J. Hanges, M. Javidan and P.J. Dorfman (2004), *Leadership, Culture and Organizations: The Globe Study of 62 Societies*, Newbury Park, CA: Sage.

Hull, D.L. (1988), *Science as Process; An Evolutionary Account of the Social and Conceptual Development of Science*, Chicago, IL: University of Chicago Press.

Hurford, J.R. (2007), *The Origins of Meaning*, Oxford: Oxford University Press.

Janssen, Th. M.V. (1997), 'Compositionality', in J. van Benthem and A. ter Meulen (eds), *Handbook of Logic and Language*, Amsterdam: Elsevier, 417–73.

Johannisson, B. (1986), 'Network strategies: management technology for entrepreneurship and change', *International Small Business Journal*, **5**, 19–30.

Johanson, J. and J. Vahlne (1977), 'The internationalization process of the firm – a model of knowledge development and increasing foreign market commitment', *Journal of International Business Studies*, **8** (Spring/Summer), 23–32.

Johanson, J. and J. Vahlne (1990), 'The mechanism of internationalization', *International Marketing Review*, **7**(4), 11–24.

Johnson-Laird, P.N. (1983), *Mental Models*, Cambridge: Cambridge University Press.

Jorna, R. (1990), *Knowledge Representations and Symbols in the Mind*, Tübingen: Stauffenburg Verlag.

Kahneman, D. and A. Tversky (1979), 'Prospect theory: an analysis of decision making under risk', *Econometrica*, **47**, 263–91.

Kahneman, D., P. Slovic and A. Tversky (eds) (1982), *Judgment under Uncertainty: Heuristics and Biases*, Cambridge: Cambridge University Press.

Katz, J.J. (1986), 'Common sense in semantics', *Notre Dame Journal of Formal Logic*, **23**(2), 174–218.

Kay, N. (2002), 'Hercules and Penrose', in C. Pitelis (ed.), *The Growth of the Firm: The Legacy of Edith Penrose*, Oxford: Oxford University Press, pp. 81–100.

Kets de Vries, M.F.R. (1977), 'The entrepreneurial personality, a person at the cross roads', *Journal of Management Studies*, **14** (1), 34–57.

Kirzner, I.M. (1973), *Competition and Entrepreneurship*, Chicago, IL: University of Chicago Press.

Kirzner, I.M. (1985), *Discovery and the Capitalist Process*, Chicago, IL: University of Chicago Press.

Klein Woolthuis, R., B. Hillebrand and B. Nooteboom (2005), 'Trust, contract and relationship development', *Organization Studies*, **26**(6), 813–40.

Knoke, D. and K. Chermack (2005), 'All bonds do tie me every day: confirmed ties and social network status', paper for the EGOS conference.

Kogut, B. and U. Zander (1992), 'Knowledge of the firm, combinative capabilities, and the replication of technology', *Organization Science*, **3**, 383–97.

Kolb, D. (1984), *Experiential Learning: Experience as the Source of Learning and Development*, Englewood Cliffs, NJ: Prentice-Hall.

Krackhardt, D. (1999), 'The ties that torture: Simmelian tie analysis in organizations', *Research in the Sociology of Organizations*, **16**, 183–210.

Kuhn, T.S. (1970), *The Structure of Scientific Revolutions*, 2nd edn, Chicago, IL: University of Chicago Press.

Von Krogh, G. (1998), 'Care in knowledge creation', *California Management Review* **40**(3), 133–53.

Lakatos, I. (1970), 'Falsification and the methodology of scientific research programmes', in I. Lakatos and A. Musgrave (eds), *Criticism and the Growth of Knowledge*, Cambridge: Cambridge University Press.

Lakatos, I. (1978), *The Methodology of Scientific Research Programmes; Philosophical Papers*, vols. 1 and 2, edited by J. Worrall and G. Curry, Cambridge: Cambridge University Press.

Lakoff, G. and M. Johnson (1980), *Metaphors We Live By*, Chicago, IL: University of Chicago Press.

Lakoff, G. and M. Johnson (1999), *Philosophy in the Flesh*, New York: Basic Books.

Lancaster, K. (1966), 'A new approach to consumer theory', *Journal of Political Economy*, **74**, April: 132–57.

Langlois, R.N. (1998), 'Personal capitalism as charismatic authority: the organizational economics of a Weberian concept', *Industrial and Corporate Change*, **7**(1), 195–214.

Langlois, R.N. and P.L. Robertson (1995), *Firms, Markets and Economic Change*, London: Routledge.

Lave, J. and E. Wenger (1991), *Situated Learning; Legitimate Peripheral Participation*, Cambridge: Cambridge University Press.

Lazaric, N. and E. Lorenz (eds) (2003), *Knowledge, Learning and Routines*, Cheltenham, UK and Northampton, MA, USA: Edward Elgar.

Lazonick, W. (2002), 'The US industrial corporation and the theory of the growth of the firm', in C. Pitelis (ed.), *The Growth of the Firm: The Legacy of Edith Penrose*, Oxford: Oxford University Press, pp. 249–78.

Levinthal, D.A. (2000), 'Organizational capabilities in complex worlds', in G. Dosi, R.R. Nelson and S.G. Winter (eds), *The Nature and Dynamics of Organizational Capabilities*, Oxford: Oxford University Press, pp. 363–79.

Lewicki, R.J. and B.B. Bunker (1996), 'Developing and maintaining trust in work relationships', in R.M. Kramer and T.R. Tyler (eds), *Trust in Organizations: Frontiers of Theory Research*, Thousand Oaks, CA: Sage Publications, pp. 114–39.

Lewontin, R. (1983), 'The organism as the subject and object of evolution', *Scientia*, **118**, 63–82.

Lindenberg, S. (2000), 'It takes both trust and lack of mistrust: the workings of cooperation and relational signalling in contractual relationships', *Journal of Management and Governance*, **4**, 11–33.

Lindenberg, S. (2003), 'Governance seen from a framing point of view: the employment relationship and relational signalling', in B. Nooteboom and F.E. Six (eds), *The Trust Process; Empirical Studies of the Determinants and the Process of Trust Development*, Cheltenham, UK and Northampton, MA, USA: Edward Elgar, pp. 37–57.

Linsky, L. (1971), *Reference and Modality*, Oxford: Oxford University Press.

Lippman, S. and R.P. Rumelt (1982), 'Uncertain imitability: an analysis of interfirm differences in efficiency under competition', *Bell Journal of Economics*, **13**, 418–38.

Loasby, B. (2002), 'The significance of Penrose's theory for the development of economics', in C. Pitelis (ed.), *The Growth of the Firm; The Legacy of Edith Penrose*, Oxford: Oxford University Press, pp. 45–60.

Lorange, P. and J. Roos (1992), *Strategic Alliances*, Cambridge: Blackwell.

Los, B. (1999), 'The empirical performance of a new interindustry technology spillover measure', in P.P. Saviotti and B. Nooteboom (eds), *Technology and Knowledge; From the Firm to Innovation Systems*, Cheltenham, UK and Northampton, MA, USA: Edward Elgar, pp. 118–51.

Lotman, Y.M. (1990), *Universe of the Mind; A Semiotic Theory of Culture*, London: I.B. Tauris.

Lounamaa, P.H. and J.G. March (1987), 'Adaptive coordination of a learning team', *Management Science*, **33**, 107–23.

Lundvall, B.A. (1988), 'Innovation as an interactive process: from user-producer interaction to national systems of innovation', in G. Dosi, C. Freeman, R. Nelson, G. Silverberg and L. Soete (eds), *Technical Change and Economic Theory*, London: Pinter, pp. 349–69.

Macaulay, S. (1963), 'Non-contractual relations in business: a preliminary study', *American Sociological Review*, **28**, 55–67.

Maccarini, M.E., P. Scabini and A. Zucchella (2003), 'Internationalisation strategies in Italian district-based firms: theoretical modeling and empirical evidence', presentation to Conference on Clusters, Industrial Districts and Firms: The Challenge of Globalization, Modena, 12-13 September.

Madhavan, R., D.R. Gnyavali and J. He (2004), 'Two's company, three's a crowd? Triads in cooperative-competitive networks', *Academy of Management Journal*, **47**(6), 918–27.

Maguire, S., N. Philips and C. Hardy (2001), 'When "silence=death", keep talking: trust, control and the discursive construction of identity in the Canadian HIV/AIDS treatment domain', *Organization Studies*, **22**(2), 285–310.

March, J.G. (1991), 'Exploration and exploitation in organizational learning', *Organization Science*, **2**(1), 101–23.

March, J.G. and H.A. Simon (1958), *Organizations*, New York: Wiley.

Maslow, A. (1954), *Motivation and Personality*, New York: Harper.

McAllister, D.J. (1995), 'Affect- and cognition based trust as foundations for interpersonal cooperation in organizations', *Academy of Management Journal*, **38**(1), 24–59.

McClelland, J.L., D.E. Rumelhart and G.E. Hinton (1987), 'The appeal of parallel distributed processing', in D.E. Rumelhart, J.L. McClelland and the PDP research group (eds), *Parallel Distributed Processing; Explorations in the Microstructure of Cognition, Vol. 1: Foundations*, Cambridge, MA: MIT Press, pp. 3–44.

McEvily, B. and A. Zaheer (1999), 'Bridging ties: a source of firm heterogeneity in competitive capabilities', *Strategic Management Journal*, **20**(12), 1133–56.

McKelvey, W. (1982), *Organizational Systematics: Taxonomy, Evolution, Classification*, Berkeley, CA: University of California Press.

Mead, G.H. (1934), *Mind, Self and Society; From the Standpoint of a Social Behaviorist*, Chicago, IL: Chicago University Press.

Meindl, J.R., C. Stubbart and J.F. Porac (eds) (1998), *Cognition Within and Between Organisations*, London: Sage.

Merleau-Ponty, M. (1942), *La structure du comportement*, Paris: Presses Universitaires de France.

Merleau-Ponty, M. (1964), *Le visible et l'invisible*, Paris: Gallimard.

Metcalfe, J.S. (1998), *Evolutionary Economics and Creative Destruction*, London: Routledge.

Miner, A.S. (1991), 'Organizational evolution and the social ecology of jobs', *American Sociological Review*, **56**, 772–85.

Minsky, M. (1975), 'A framework for representing knowledge', in P.H. Winston (ed.), *The Psychology of Computer Vision*, New York: McGraw-Hill, pp. 211–80.

Mintzberg, H. (1979), *The Structure of Organizations*, Englewood Cliffs, NJ: Prentice-Hall.

Mintzberg, H. (1983), *Structure in Fives: Designing Effective Organizations*, Englewood Cliffs, NJ: Prentice-Hall.

Mintzberg, H. (1989), *Mintzberg on Management*, New York: The Free Press.

Mokyr, J. (1990), *The Lever of Riches: Technological Creativity and Economic Progress*, Oxford: Oxford University Press.

Murakami, Y. and T.P. Rohlen (1992), 'Social-exchange aspects of the Japanese political economy: culture, efficiency and change', in S. Kumon and H. Rosorsky (eds), *The Political Economy of Japan, Vol. 3, Cultural and Social Dynamics*, Stanford, CA: Stanford University Press, pp 63–105.

Narduzzo, A., E. Rocco and M. Warglien (2000), 'Talking about routines in the field', in G. Dosi, R.R. Nelson and S.G. Winter (eds), *The Nature and Dynamics of Organizational Capabilities*, Oxford: Oxford University Press, pp. 27–50.

Nelson, R.R. (ed) (1993), *National Innovation Systems: A Comparative Analysis*, New York: Oxford University Press.

Nelson, R.R. (2006), 'Economic development from the perspective of economic theory', The Other Canon Foundation and Tallin University of Technology working papers in technology governance and economic dynamics 02, TTU Institute of Humanities and Social Science.

Nelson R.R. and S. Winter (1982), *An Evolutionary Theory of Economic Change*, Cambridge: Cambridge University Press.

Nietzsche, F. (1885), *Jenseits von Gut und Böse*, 1988 edn, Stuttgart: Reclam.

Nonaka, I. and H. Takeuchi (1995), *The Knowledge Creating Company*, Oxford: Oxford University Press.

Noorderhaven, N.G. (1996), 'Opportunism and trust in transaction cost economics', in J. Groenewegen (ed.), *Transaction Cost Economics and Beyond*, Boston, MA: Kluwer, pp 105–28.

Nooteboom, B. (1982), 'A new theory of retailing costs', *European Economic Review*, **17**, 163–86.

Nooteboom, B. (1984), 'Innovation, life cycle and the share of independents: cases from retailing', *International Small Business Journal*, **3**(1), 21–33.

Nooteboom, B. (1986), 'Plausibility in economics', *Economics and Philosophy*, **2**, 197–224.

Nooteboom, B. (1992), 'Towards a dynamic theory of transactions', *Journal of Evolutionary Economics*, **2**, 281–99.

Nooteboom, B. (1993), 'Firm size effects on transaction costs', *Small Business Economics*, **5**, 283–95.

Nooteboom, B. (1994), 'Innovation and diffusion in small business: theory and empirical evidence', *Small Business Economics*, **6**, 327–47, reprinted in N. Krueger (ed.), *Entrepreneurship: Critical Perspectives on Business and Management*, London: Routledge, vol. III, pp. 327–47 (2002).

Nooteboom, B. (1997), 'Path dependence of knowledge: implications for the theory of the firm', in L. Magnusson and J. Ottoson (eds), *Evolutionary Economics and Path Dependence*, Cheltenham, UK and Lyme, USA: Edward Elgar, pp. 57–78.

Nooteboom, B. (1999a), *Inter-firm Alliances: Analysis and Design*, London: Routledge.

Nooteboom, B. (1999b), 'Innovation and inter-firm linkages: new implications for policy', *Research Policy*, **28**, 793–805.

Nooteboom, B. (2000), *Learning and Innovation in Organizations and Economies*, Oxford: Oxford University Press.

Nooteboom, B. (2001), 'From evolution to language and learning', in J. Foster and S. Metcalfe (eds), *Frontiers of Evolutionary Economics: Competition, Self-organisation and Innovation Policy*, Northampton, MA and Cheltenham, UK: Edward Elgar, pp. 41–69.

Nooteboom, B. (2002), *Trust: Forms, Foundations, Functions, Failures and Figures*, Cheltenham, UK and Northampton, MA, USA: Edward Elgar.

Nooteboom, B. (2003), 'Problems and solutions in knowledge transfer', in D. Fornahl and T. Brenner (eds), *Cooperation, Networks and Institutions in Regional Innovation Systems*, Cheltenham, UK and Northampton, MA, USA: Edward Elgar, pp. 105–25.

Nooteboom, B. (2004a), 'Governance and competence, how can they be combined?', *Cambridge Journal of Economics*, **28**(4), 505–26.

Nooteboom, B. (2004b), *Inter-organizational Collaboration, Learning and Networks; An Integrated Approach*, London: Routledge.

Nooteboom, B. (2005), The industrial and social dynamics of retailing, and effects of opening hours, unpublished paper accessed at www.bartnooteboom.nl.

Nooteboom, B. (ed.) (2006), *Knowledge and Learning, Vol. I: Fundamentals of Embodied Cognition, Vol II, Knowledge and Learning in Organizations*, Cheltenham, UK and Northampton, MA, USA: Edward Elgar.

Nooteboom, B. (2007), 'Service value chains and effects of scale', *Service Business*, **1**, 119–39.

Nooteboom B., and R. Klein Woolthuis (2005), 'Cluster dynamics', in R.A. Boschma and R. Kloosterman (eds), *Learning from Clusters: A Critical Assessment*, Dordrecht: Springer, pp. 51–68.

Nooteboom, B. and F.E. Six (eds) (2003), *The Trust Process; Empirical Studies of the Determinants and the Process of Trust Development*, Cheltenham, UK and Northampton, MA, USA: Edward Elgar.

Nooteboom, B. and R. Went (2008), 'Innovation and organization', in B. Nooteboom and E. Stam (eds), *Micro-Foundations for Innovation Policy*, Amsterdam: Amsterdam/Chicago University Press, pp. 219–48.

Nooteboom, B., J. Berger and N.G. Noorderhaven (1997), 'Effects of trust and governance on relational risk', *Academy of Management Journal*, **40**(2), 308–38.

Nooteboom, B., W.P.M. Van Haverbeke, G.M. Duijsters, V.A. Gilsing and A.V. d. Oord (2007), 'Optimal cognitive distance and absorptive capacity', *Research Policy*, **36**, 1016–34.

Nussbaum, M.C. (1990), *Love's Knowledge. Essays on Philosophy and Literature*, Oxford: Oxford University Press.

Nussbaum, M.C. (2001), *Upheavals of Thought, The Intelligence of Emotions*, Cambridge: Cambridge University Press.

Orsenigo, L., F. Pammolli, M. Riccaboni, A. Bonaccorsi and G. Turchetti (1998), 'The evolution of knowledge and the dynamics of an industry network', *Journal of Management and Governance*, **1**, 147–75.

Ouchi, W.G. (1980), 'Markets, bureaucracies, clans', *Administrative Science Quarterly*, **25**(1), 129–43.

Pascal, B. (2005 [1670]), *Pensées*, Indianapolis, IN: Hackett.

Patel, P. and K. Pavitt (1999), 'The wide (and increasing) spread of technological competencies in the worlds largest firms: a challenge to conventional wisdom', in A.D. Chandler, P. Hagström and Ö. Sölvell (eds), *The Dynamic Firm; The Role of Technology, Strategy, Organizations, and Regions*, Oxford: Oxford University Press, pp. 192–213.

Patel, P. and K. Pavitt (2000), 'How technological competences help define the core not the boundaries of the firm', in G. Dosi, R.R. Nelson and S.G. Winter (eds), *The Nature and Dynamics of Organizational Capabilities*, Oxford: Oxford University Press, pp. 313–33.

Peirce, C.S. (1957), *Essays in the Philosophy of Science*, Indianapolis, IN: Bobbs-Merrill.

Péli, G. and B. Nooteboom (1999), 'Market partitioning and the geometry of the resource space', *American Journal of Sociology*, **104**(4), 1132–53.

Penner-Hahn, J. and J. Myles Shaver (2005), 'Does international research and development increase patent output?, An analysis of Japanese pharmaceutical firms', *Strategic Management Journal*, **26**, 121–40.

Penrose, E. (1959), *The Theory of the Growth of the Firm*, New York: Wiley.

Pettit, P. (1995), 'The virtual reality of homo economicus', *The Monist*, **78**(3), 308–29.

Pfeffer J. and G.R. Salancik (1978), *The External Control of Organizations: A Resource Dependence Perspective*, New York: Harper and Row.

Piaget, J. (1970), *Psychologie et epistémologie*, Paris: Denoël.

Piaget, J. (1972), *Insights and Illusions in Philosophy*, London: Routledge and Kegan Paul, first published in French 1965.

Piaget, J. (1974), *Introduction a l'épistémologie génétique*, Paris: Presses Universitaires de France.

Pisano, G. (2000), 'In search of dynamic capabilities: the origins of R&D competence in biopharmaceuticals', in G. Dosi, R.R. Nelson and S.G. Winter (eds), *The Nature and Dynamics of Organizational Capabilities*, Oxford: Oxford University Press, pp. 129–54.

Pitelis, C. (ed.) (2002), *The Growth of the Firm; The Legacy of Edith Penrose*, Oxford: Oxford University Press.

Podolny, J. (2001), 'Networks as the pipes and prisms of the market', *American Journal of Sociology*, **107**, 33–60.

Podolny, J. and J. Baron (1997), 'Resources and relationships: social networks and mobility in the workplace', *American Sociological Review*, **62**, 673–93.

Polanyi, M. (1962), *Personal Knowledge*, London: Routledge.

Polanyi, M. (1969), *Knowing and Being*, Edited by Marjorie Grene, Chicago, IL: University of Chicago Press.

Pompe, J.H., M.H. Bruyn and J.V. Koek (1986), *Entrepreneurship in International Comparative Perspective* (in Dutch), University of Groningen.

Popper, K.R. (1959), *The Logic of Scientific Discovery*, London: Hutchison.

Popper, K.R. (1970), 'Normal science and its dangers', in I. Lakatos and A. Musgrave (eds), *Criticism and the Growth of Knowledge*, Cambridge: Cambridge University Press, pp. 51–8.

Popper, K.R. (1973), *The Open Society and its Enemies*, vol. 2, London: Routledge and Kegan Paul.

Porter, M.E. (1980), *Competitive Strategy*, New York: The Free Press.

Porter, M.E. (1985), *Competitive Advantage*, New York: The Free Press.

Porter, M.E. (1990), *The Competitive Advantage of Nations*, New York: Free Press.

Postrel, S. (2002), 'Islands of shared knowledge: specialization and mutual understanding in problem-solving teams', *Organization Science*, **13**(3), 303–20.

van Praag, C.M. (1996), *Determinants of Successful Entrepreneurship*, Tinbergen Institute Research Series, Amsterdan: Thesis publishers.

Prahalad, C. and G. Hamel (1990), 'The core competences of the corporation', *Harvard Business Review*, May–June, 79–91.

Putnam, H. (1975), *Mind, Language and Reality: Philosophical Papers*, vol. 2, Cambridge: Cambridge University Press.

Quine, W.V. and J.S. Ullian (1970), *The Web of Belief*, New York: Random House.

Quinn, J.B. (1982), *Strategies for Change*, Homewood, IL: Irwin.

Quinn, J.B. (1992), *Intelligent Enterprise*, New York: The Free Press.

Reagans, R. and B. McEvily (2003), 'Network structure and knowledge transfer: the effects of cohesion and range', *Administrative Science Quarterly*, **48**, 240–67.

Realu, A. (2005), 'Reconsidering individualism and collectivism', *NIAS Newsletter*, **53**, accessed at www.nias.knaw.nl.

Richardson, G.B. (1972), 'The organization of industry', *Economic Journal*, **82**, 883–96.

Richardson, G.B. (2002), 'Mrs. Penrose and neoclassical theory', in C.

Pitelis (ed.), *The Growth of the Firm; The Legacy of Edith Penrose*, Oxford: Oxford University Press, pp. 37–44.

Ring, P. and A. van de Ven (1992), 'Structuring cooperative relationships between organizations', *Strategic Management Journal*, **13**, 483–98.

Ring, P. and A. van de Ven (1994), 'Developmental processes of cooperative interorganizational relationships', *Academy of Management Review*, **19**(1), 90–118.

Romanelli, E. and M.Y. Tushman (1994), 'Organizational transformation as punctuated equilibrium: an empirical test', *Academy of Management Journal*, **37**(5), 1141–66.

Rosch, E. (1977), 'Human categorization', in N. Warren (ed.), *Advances in Cross-cultural Psychology*, vol.1, New York: Academic Press.

Rosch, E. (1978), 'Principles of categorization', in E. Rosch and B.B. Lloyd (eds), *Cognition and Categorization*, Hillsdale, NJ: Lawrence Erlbaum.

Rose, S. (1992), *The Making of Memory*, New York: Doubleday.

Rosenkopf, L. and P. Almeida (2003), 'Overcoming local search through alliances and mobility, *Management Science*, **49**, 751–66.

Rosenkopf, L. and A. Nerkar (2001), 'Beyond local search: Boundary-spanning, exploration, and impact in the optical disc industry', *Strategic Management Journal*, **22**, 287–306.

Rothwell, R. (1985), 'Innovation and the smaller firm', presentation to the First International Technical Innovation and Entrepreneurship Symposium, Utah Innovation Foundation, Salt Lake City, 11-13 September.

Rothwell, R. (1986), 'The role of small firms in technological innovation', in J. Curran (ed.), *The Survival of the Small Firm*, Aldershot: Gower.

Rothwell, R. (1989), 'Small firms, innovation and industrial change', *Small Business Economics*, **1**, 51–64.

Rothwell, R. and W. Zegveld (1985), *Innovation and the Small and Medium Sized Firm*, London: Francis Pinter.

Rowley, T., D. Behrens and D. Krackhardt (2000), 'Redundant governance structures: an analysis of structural and relational embeddedness in the steel and semiconductor industries', *Strategic Management Journal*, **21**, 369–86.

Rumelhart, D.E., J.L. McClelland and the PDP research group (1987), *Parallel Distributed Processing; Explorations in the Microstructure of Cognition, Vol. 1: Foundations*, Cambridge, MA: MIT Press.

Rumelhart, D.E, G.E. Hinton and J.L. McClelland (1987), 'A general framework for PDP', in D.E. Rumelhart, J.L. McClelland and the PDP research group (eds), *Parallel Distributed Processing; Explorations in the Microstructure of Cognition, Vol. 1: Foundations*, Cambridge, MA: MIT Press, pp. 45–76.

de Saussure, F. (1979), *Cours de linguistique generale*, Paris: Payot.

Schein, E.H. (1985), *Organizational Culture and Leadership*, San Francisco, CA: Jossey-Bass.

Schumpeter, J.A. (1909), *Theorie der wirtschaftlichen Entwicklung*, Leipzig: Duncker und Humblot.

Schumpeter, J.A. (1939), *Business Cycles: A Theoretical, Historical and Statistical Analysis of the Capitalist Process*, New York and London: McGraw Hill.

Schumpeter, J.A. (1942), *Capitalism, Socialism and Democracy*, New York: Harper and Row.

Scase, R. and R. Goffee (1980), *The Real World of the Small Business Owner*, London: Croom Helm.

Scott, W.R. (1992), *Organizations; Rational, Natural, and Open Systems*, 3rd edn, Englewood Cliffs, NJ: Prentice-Hall.

Searle, J.R. (1969), *Speech Acts*, Cambridge: Cambridge University Press.

Searle, J.R. (1992), *The Rediscovery of the Mind*, Cambridge, MA: MIT Press.

Seeman, M. (1959), 'On the meaning of alienation', *American Sociological Review*, **24**, 783–91.

Shackle, G. (1961), *Decision, Order and Time in Human Affairs*, Cambridge: Cambridge University Press.

Shank, R.C. and R.P. Abelson (1977), *Scripts, Plans, Goals and Understanding*, Hillsdale, NJ: Lawrence Erlbaum.

Shanon, B. (1988), 'Semantic representation of meaning: a critique', *Psychological Bulletin*, **104**(1), 70–83.

Shanon, B. (1990), 'What is context?', *Journal for the Theory of Social Behaviour*, **20**(2), 157–66.

Shanon, B. (1993), *The Representational and the Presentational*, New York: Harvester/Wheatsheaf.

Shapiro, S.P. (1987), 'The social control of impersonal trust', *American Journal of Sociology*, **93**, 623–58.

Simmel, G. (1950 [1917]), *The Sociology of Georg Simmel*, translation by Kurt Wolff, Glencoe, IL: The Free Press.

Simon, H.A. (1976), *Administrative Behavior*, 3rd edn, New York: Free Press.

Simon, H.A. (1983), *Reason in Human Affairs*, Oxford: Basil Blackwell.

Six, F.E. (2005), *The Trouble with Trust, the Dynamics of Interpersonal Trust Building*, Cheltenham, UK and Northampton, MA, USA: Edward Elgar.

Six, F. and B. Nooteboom (2010), 'Actions that build interpersonal trust: a relational signaling approach', *Review of Social Economy*, **68**, forthcoming.

Smircich, L. (1983), 'Organization as shared meaning', in L.R. Pondy, P.J. Frost, G. Morgan and T.C. Dandridge (eds), *Organizational Symbolism*, Greenwich, CN: JAI Press, pp. 55–65.

Smith, A. (1998), *An Inquiry into the Nature and Causes of the Wealth of Nations*, originally published 1776, Oxford: Oxford University Press.

Smolensky P. (1988), 'On the proper treatment of connectionism', *Behavioral and Brain Sciences*, **11**, 1–74.

Spender, J.C. (1989), *Industry Recipe*, Oxford: Basil Blackwell.

Spender, J.C. (1999), 'The geographies of strategic competence: borrowing from social and educational psychology to sketch an activity and knowledge based theory of the firm', in: A.D. Chandler, P. Hagström and Ö. Sölvell (eds), *The Dynamic Firm. The Role of Technology, Strategy, Organization and Regions*, Oxford: Oxford University Press, pp. 417–39.

Spinoza, B. (1996 [1677]), *Ethics*, London: Penguin Books.

Stanworth, J. and Curran, J. (1973), *Management Motivation in the Smaller Business*, Aldershot: Gower.

Stanworth, M.J.K. and J. Curran (1976), 'Growth and the small firm – an alternative view', *Journal of Management Studies*, **13**(2), 95–110.

Stinchcombe, A.L. (1965), 'Social structure and organizations', in J.G. March (ed.), *Handbook of Organizations*, Chicago, IL: Rand McNally, pp. 142–93.

Stuart, T. (1998), 'Network positions and propensities to collaborate: an investigation of strategic alliance formation in a high-technology industry', *Administrative Science Quarterly*, **43**, 637–68.

Stuart, T. and Podolny J. (1996), 'Local search and the evolution of technological capabilities', *Strategic Management Journal*, **17** (Summer special issue), 21–38.

Sydow, J. (2000), 'Understanding the constitution of interorganizational trust', in C. Lane and R. Bachmann (eds), *Trust In and Between Organizations*, Oxford: Oxford University Press, pp. 31–63.

Tanriverdi, H. and N. Venkatraman (2005), 'Knowledge relatedness and the performance of multibusiness firms', *Strategic Management Journal*, **26**, 97–119

Taylor, C. (1989), *Sources of the Self: The Making of the Modern Identity*, Cambridge: Cambridge University Press.

Teece, D.J. (1986), 'Profiting from technological innovation: implications for integration, collaboration, licensing and public policy', *Research Policy*, **15**, 285–305.

Teece, D.J. (1988), 'Technological change and the nature of the firm', in G. Dosi, C. Freeman, R. Nelson, G. Silverberg and L. Soete (eds), *Technical Change and Economic Theory*, London: Pinter, pp. 256–81.

Teece, D., G. Pisano and A. Shven (1997), 'Dynamic capabilities and strategic management', *Strategic Management Journal*, **18**(7), 509–33.

Teece, D., G. Pisano and A. Shuen (2000), 'Dynamic capabilities and strategic management', in G. Dosi, R.R. Nelson and S.G. Winter (eds), *The Nature and Dynamics of Organizational Capabilities*, Oxford: Oxford University Press, pp. 334–62.

Thiel, C. (1965), *Sinn und Bedeutung in der Logik Gottlob Freges*, Meisenheim am Glan: Anton Hain.

Thompson, J.D. (1967), *Organizations in Action*, New York: McGraw-Hill.

Thurik, A.R. (1996), 'Small firms, entrepreneurship and economic growth', in P.H. Admiraal (ed.), *Small Business in the Modern Economy*, Oxford: Basil Blackwell, pp. 126–52.

Tillaart, H.J.M. van den, H.C. van der Hoeven and F.W. van Uxem (1981), *Independent Entrepreneurship* (in Dutch), Zoetermeer: ITS/EIM.

Turvani, M. (2007), 'The relevance today of Edith Penrose's theory of the growth of the firm', in G.M. Hodgson (ed.), *The Evolution of Economic Institutions*, Cheltenham, UK and Northampton, MA, USA: Edward Elgar, pp. 211–32.

Tushman, M.L. and P. Anderson (1986), 'Technological discontinuities and organizational environments', *Administrative Science Quarterly*, **31**, 439–65.

Tushman, M.L. and E. Romanelli (1985), 'Organizational evolution: a metamorphosis model of convergence and reorientation', in B.A. Staw and L.L. Cummings (eds), *Research in Organizational Behavior*, Greenwich, CN: JAI Press, pp. 171–222.

Tversky, A. and D. Kahneman (1983), 'Probability, representativeness, and the conjunction fallacy', *Psychological Review*, **90**(4), 293–315.

Uzzi, B. (1996), 'The sources and consequences of embeddedness for the economic performance of organizations: the network effect', *American Sociological Review*, **61**, 674–98.

Uzzi, B. (1997), 'Social structure and competition in interfirm networks: the paradox of embeddedness', *Administrative Science Quarterly*, **42**, 35–67.

Veblen, T.B. (1919), *The Place of Science in Modern Civilization and Other Essays*, New York: Huebsch.

Vossen, R.W. and B. Nooteboom (1996), 'Firm size and participation in R&D', in A. Kleinknecht (ed.), *Determinants of Innovation: The Message from New Indicators*, London: Macmillan, pp. 155–68.

Vygotsky, L.S. (1962), *Thought and Language*, edited and translated by E. Hanfmann and G. Varkar, Cambridge MA: MIT Press.

Walker, G., B. Kogut and W. Shan (1997), 'Social capital, structural holes, and the formation of an industry network', *Organization Science*, **8**, 109–12.

Watts, D.J. (1999), 'Networks, dynamics, and the small world phenomenon', *American Journal of Sociology*, **105**, 493–527.

Werner, H. and B. Kaplan (1963), *Symbol Formation*, New York: Wiley.

Weick, K.F. (1979), *The Social Psychology of Organizing*, Reading, MA: Addison-Wesley.

Weick, K.F. (1995), *Sensemaking in Organisations*, Thousand Oaks, CA: Sage.

Weick, K.F. and K.H. Roberts (1993), 'Collective mind in organizations: heedful interrelating on flight decks', *Administrative Science Quartery*, **38**, reprinted 1996 in Michael D. Cohen and L.S. Sproull (eds), *Organizational Learning*, London: Sage, pp. 330–58.

Weick, K.E. and R.E. Quinn (1999), 'Organizational change and development', *Annual Review of Psychology*, **50**, 361–86.

Wijnberg, N.M. (1990), *Innovation, competition and small business*, PhD dissertation, Erasmus University Rotterdam, Alblasserdam, Netherlands: Haveka.

Weintraub, E.R. (1988), 'The neo-Walrasian program is progressive', in N. de Marchi (ed.), *The Popperian Legacy in Economics*, Cambridge: Cambridge University Press, pp. 213–30.

Wenger, E. and W.M. Snyder (2000), 'Communities of practice: the organizational frontier', *Harvard Business Review*, January-February, 139–45.

Whitehead, A.N. (1929), *The Function of Reason*, Princeton, NJ: Princeton University Press.

Williams, B. (1988), 'Formal structures and social reality', in: D. Gambetta (ed.), *Trust; Making and Breaking of Cooperative Relations*, Oxford: Blackwell, pp. 3–13.

Williams, A.J. (1977), 'The independent entrepreneur', in A. Bardow (ed.), *The Worker in Australia – Contributions from Research*, St Lucia: University of Queensland Press, pp. 113–47.

Williamson. O.E. (1975), *Markets and Hierarchies: Analysis and Anti-trust Implications*, New York: The Free Press.

Williamson, O.E. (1985), *The Economic Institutions of Capitalism; Firms, Markets, Relational Contracting*, New York: The Free Press.

Williamson, O.E. (1993), 'Calculativeness, trust and economic organization', *Journal of Law and Economics*, **36**, 453–86.

Williamson, O.E. (1999), 'Strategy research: governance and competence perspectives', *Strategic Management Journal*, **20**, 1087–108.

Winograd, T. (1980), 'What does it mean to understand language?', *Cognitive Science*, **4**, 209–41.

Witt, U. (ed.) (1993), *Evolutionary Economics*, Aldershot: Edward Elgar.

Witt, U. (2004), 'On the proper interpretation of "evolution" in economics and its implications for production theory', *Journal of Economic Methodology*, **11**, 125–46.

Witt, U. (2005), 'The evolutionary perspective on organizational change and the theory of the firm', in K. Dopfer (ed.), *The Evolutionary Foundations of Economics*, Cambridge: Cambridge University Press, pp. 339–64.

Wittgenstein, L. (1976), *Philosophical Investigations*, Oxford: Basil Blackwell.

Wuyts, S., M.G. Colombo, S. Dutta and B. Nooteboom (2005), 'Empirical tests of optimal cognitive distance', *Journal of Economic Behavior and Organization*, **58**(2), 277–302.

Wyatt, S. (1985), 'The role of small firms in innovative activity', *Economia and Politica Industriale*.

Yelle, L.E. (1979), 'The learning curve: historical review and comprehensive survey', *Decision Sciences*, **10**, 302–28.

Yli – Renko, H., E. Autio and H.J. Sapienza (2001), 'Social capital, knowledge acquisition, and knowledge exploitation in young technology-based firms', *Strategic Management Journal*, **22**, 587–613.

Zaheer, A., B. McEvily and V. Perrone (1998), 'Does trust matter? Exploring the effects of interorganizational and interpersonal trust on performance', *Organization Science*, **9**(2), 141–59.

Zand, D.E. (1972), 'Trust and managerial problem solving', *Administrative Science Quarterly*, **17**(2), 229–39.

Zollo, M. and S.G. Winter (2002), 'Deliberate learning and the evolution of dynamic capabilities', *Organization Science*, **13**(3), 339–51.

Zucchella, A. (2006), 'Local cluster dynamics: trajectories of mature industrial districts between decline and multiple embeddedness', *Journal of Institutional Economics*, **2**(1), 21–44.

Zucker, L.G. (1986). 'Production of trust: institutional sources of economic structure', in Barry, Staw and Cummings (eds), *Research in Organizational Behavior*, vol. 8, New York: Elsevier, pp. 53–111.

Index

Printed by Printforce, United Kingdom